FATAL NEGLECT

For Rosie Celyn Hurst

FATAL NEGLECT
WHO KILLED DYLAN THOMAS?

David N. Thomas

seren

Seren is the book imprint of
Poetry Wales Press Ltd
57 Nolton Street, Bridgend, CF31 3AE, Wales
www.seren-books.com

© David N. Thomas, 2008

ISBN 978-1-85411-480-8

The publisher works with the financial assistance
of the Welsh Books Council.

Printed in Plantin by CPD Ltd, Blaenau Gwent

Contents

Photographs

1. A Case of Cold Feet

Movie stars and mobsters, pimps, plumbers and politicians – you name it. He had autopsied them all. But this bloated corpse on the mortuary table was a double-first: a Welshman and a famous poet to boot. Over the top of his half-glasses, Milton Helpern peered at the clock on the far side of the room: 2.40 on a cold November afternoon, with more snow forecast. He nodded to the stenographer, put on surgical gloves and started the external inspection. This was the moment when an autopsy could bring a man to life:

> Adult white male appearing to be about 40 years of age; 5'5" tall; estimated weight 180lb; obese trunk; puffy face; wavy brown hair on head; moderate frontal baldness; brown eyes; unshaven face; several days growth of brown hair; teeth in upper jaw irregular in alignment, rather widely spaced – in the lower jaw also some irregularity – all teeth show discoloration...

The detailed inspection continued for several minutes, ending with a comment on the small scars above the man's eyebrows, though those on his wrists went unnoticed. Then Helpern made an incision down the length of the body to the pelvis, cutting through the rib cage to expose the upper organs. He lifted out the lungs and passed them along for weighing. The mortuary assistant called out the weight and placed them on the dissecting bench.

Helpern was already there, waiting impatiently – death wasn't just an ending for him. It was also an entrance into another person's past. And for this dead poet, there could have been no better entry than through his chest. The man had emphysema and bronchitis. And the bronchi – the two main airways – were coated with a membrane of pus. As he explored further, Helpern could see that the infection had spread to nearly every part of the lungs. He turned to the stenographer and said "Bronchopneumonia very evident."

After the autopsy was completed, Helpern went to his office and thought about the death certificate. The immediate cause of death was pressure on the brain. But what had caused the brain to get congested and swell? He decided that the primary cause of Dylan Thomas' death was pneumonia, which had impaired the supply of oxygen to the brain.

But what kind of pneumonia? The hospital's Medical Summary sent with the body made no mention of pneumonia before or at admission, so Helpern concluded it had started in hospital. But, through no fault of his own, he was wrong about this, and eleven years would pass before the error was discovered.

In December 1964, William Murphy, a doctor and psychoanalyst with an interest in Dylan's death, set off from his home in Maryland to travel to St Vincent's hospital in New York. When he arrived, he was led to a waiting room and given Dylan's medical file. He is still the only person known to have had access to the poet's hospital records.

The file revealed that Dylan had pneumonia and extensive bronchitis when he was admitted to hospital. In the preceding twelve hours, he had been so ill that his doctor had been called out on three occasions to see him. If he had diagnosed the chest disease, Dylan could have been treated with penicillin or one of the other available drugs. He had died a needless death.

At first, William Murphy wanted the facts to be known. He sent a three-page memorandum summarising the hospital notes to Constantine FitzGibbon, one of Dylan's early biographers. But as Murphy got cold feet, he persuaded FitzGibbon not to publish anything that would harm the doctor or the hospital. The memorandum ended up in a university archive where, for over three decades, it went unnoticed by a succession of writers and researchers. As a result, the full story of the poet's death has never been told.

2. Dylan's Bucking Broncho

Dylan Marlais Thomas died in the early afternoon of November 9 1953. The first rumours were of a brain haemorrhage, followed by reports that he had been mugged. Then came the stories about booze, that he had drunk himself to death, eighteen double whiskies in a New York bar. Later, there was talk of a drugs overdose, and even that he had been poisoned by a rose thorn. Later still, there were revelations about morphine, red herrings about diabetes, and speculations about Dylan wanting to die, that he was tired of writing and of life. Some even suggested the death was self-inflicted, suicide by drinking.

Many blamed American hospitality, and others asked whether Dylan would have lived if America had provided a free health service. There were questions about the quality of his care. Why hadn't his New York doctor diagnosed his chest disease? Why was there a two hour delay in taking the unconscious Dylan to hospital? And how was it possible for a relatively young man – he had just turned thirty-nine – to die in a city which boasted some of its country's finest hospitals?

There was also the matter of the cover-up, in which some of Dylan's friends and doctors had concealed the truth about his death. I was interested in the whereabouts of a missing "intimate record", written by Dylan's New York lover, that described his last hours. Liz Reitell was the principal witness to his collapse – perhaps the most extraordinary aspect of the death is that she was never thoroughly questioned about what happened.

Then there was a ragbag of disparate issues that puzzled me. Did New York's polluted air have any bearing on the death? What was wrong with Dylan's voice on the morning of his collapse that he sounded, said a friend, like Louis Armstrong? Dylan's American tour agent, John Brinnin, had serious financial problems. Was there anything to suggest that he had put his extravagant lifestyle before Dylan's well-being?

I was also intrigued by the way Dylan's dying was inextricably bound up with the birth of his most famous work, *Under Milk*

Wood. I wondered if the effort of finishing the play, and of taking the lead role in four New York productions, had pushed him over the edge. Had he himself not said, just eleven days before he collapsed, that the play's third performance had taken the life out of him?

Whilst there are still many questions about Dylan's death, the answers are not to be found simply by looking at his health during his last three weeks in New York. His decline had begun well before then. My starting point in his medical biography is sixteen years earlier, in 1937, when he made his first radio broadcast, launching the reading voice that would eventually take him to America. It was also the year in which Liz Reitell and John Brinnin began their college careers and thus the trajectories that would bring them all together in New York in 1953.

Dylan never made it to college but in 1937 he started on his own journey of exploration when he married Caitlin Macnamara. She soon got to know about his chest. In an early letter, he described a bout of bronchitis and laryngitis that left him weak and without a voice, feeling hot at one moment and cold the next. These would have been an unremarkable set of symptoms but for the fact that he would experience them again in the days before his collapse.

Within a month of writing to Caitlin they were on honeymoon, and within a year they were living in Laugharne, kept going with generous advances from James Laughlin, an American publisher. Dylan was also doing his best to bring in money, trying to raise a grant for his writing on the grounds that he had weak lungs. Then, out of the blue, opera entered his professional life and, as it turned out, booked a place at his dying as well. Samuel Barber wrote to suggest that they collaborate on a chamber opera. There was even money available to bring Dylan to America but the idea was shelved when Barber was drafted into military service in late 1942.

Dylan had been very worried about his own conscription. He had considered a number of ruses to avoid it, but he was eventually rejected as unfit because, he explained, he had an unreliable lung. Thereafter, he coughed and spluttered his way through the war, complaining of ailments as various as itching feet, mumps, gout and coughs that confined him to bed. By now, he also had a

1. Dylan, slim and healthy in Laugharne, 1940

history of bringing up blood and mucus.

He served the war effort by writing documentary films. One of these was *Conquest of a Germ*, which sang the praises of the early antibiotics in fighting pneumonia and TB. Whilst writing the script in London, he fell ill once again, going down with an infection that made his chest feel like raw steak. It was, he said, either laryngitis, bronchitis or asthma; it impaired his breathing and produced a food-losing cough.

Dylan had collaborated with a team of doctors to make the film, and undoubtedly gained some understanding of the dynamics of infections and their prevention. In his case, the remedy for avoiding a lifetime of bronchial complaints was straightforward:

2. Majoda, New Quay, as it was in 1945

give up smoking, don't inhale other people's smoke, stay away from polluted air and find accommodation that was dry, warm and free from damp.

His London flat during the war was hardly suitable, awash with mice, falling plaster and rainwater from a leaking roof. Caitlin wisely spent as much time as she could at a secluded mansion in west Wales, living with Vera Phillips and her family, who had escaped there from the bombing of Swansea. She had been a friend of Dylan's since childhood and, in August 1943, he was best man when Vera married William Killick, a commando in the SOE.

Killick went off to war, whilst Vera moved to New Quay, renting a bungalow overlooking the sea. In the autumn of 1944, she encouraged Dylan and Caitlin to move to Majoda, a flimsy asbestos chalet a few fields away on the edge of the cliffs. They lived there through one of the coldest winters on record. But Dylan was settled and happy, and it showed in his writing – he wrote several poems and began work on a couple of film scripts. He also made a start on a play that seven years later would become known as *Under Milk Wood*. As Dylan beavered away, Vera and Caitlin kept each other company, whiling the days away dancing, sketching and getting to know the town's many pubs. It was, by all accounts, the best time of their lives.

But in February 1945, things took a turn for the worse. William Killick returned to New Quay on leave, having spent eighteen months behind enemy lines in Greece. He was nervous, weary and tense, aggrieved that Vera had wasted so much of his money and unsettled by her friendship with both Caitlin and Dylan. The two women were by now the closest of friends but they stood, not so much at the edge of love, but of madness, looking on helplessly as Killick tried to come to terms with the trauma of battle.

Within a few weeks of his return, he finally cracked. On the afternoon of March 6, he went on a pub crawl, eventually landing up in the Black Lion. Dylan was there, and an argument about the merits of the war ended in a brawl. The two men were pulled apart and Dylan made his way back to Majoda. Killick also returned home, intent on revenge. He retrieved a sub-machine gun and, under cover of darkness, approached Majoda. He let off several rounds in the air, before firing another four into the living room. As Caitlin and Dylan cowered on the floor, Killick burst

3. William and Vera Killick, New Quay, 1945

inside, firing more bullets in the ceiling and threatening to set off a grenade.

The shooting was a profound shock, and Dylan was deeply distressed by the incident. Letters to his friends petered out, and those that he did send reflected his unhappiness. He was, he wrote, limp and exhausted but hopeful of being fit, and able to work on his writing. But he would never again have such a productive spell, and the shooting would come back to haunt him in the days before his death. He gave evidence at Killick's trial and soon after left New Quay, its magic broken. That summer, he found himself at a party in London, where he recited verses from *Under Milk Wood*, probably the first public airing of the play.

Dylan was now desperate for accommodation, but his next two lodging places were hardly conducive to good health, and what they had in common was dampness. He moved first to Welsh Carmarthenshire, where his parents lived. Two cottages lay side by side in a wet hollow, next to a little stream that flowed past. Dylan and family stayed in the larger cottage which, warned a housing survey, had extensive rising and penetrating damp. He commuted back and forth to London, but even the rain-soaked weekends got him down. Escape was on his mind, and at the end of July he wrote at length about settling permanently in America.

Then, a few months later, he moved to Oxford, to a tiny summer hut on the banks of the Cherwell. It was, said a visitor, a rather swampy place, and even in the hottest months of the year the cold vapours from the river could be keenly felt after dusk. Yet it wasn't summer when they moved in but December, and the start of another inhospitable winter. But at least they could now afford some comforts. *Deaths and Entrances* was published in February, and immediately sold out; three thousand more copies were quickly printed.

Radio would also bring a regular income. Dylan made twice as many broadcasts in 1946 as in the whole of the previous nine years, and he would continue to make some twenty a year until he moved to Laugharne in 1949. Whilst the BBC work produced money, and turned Dylan into a public figure, the programmes and their rehearsals would mean a good deal more of his time being spent in foggy, smoggy London.

Not surprisingly, Dylan felt he still needed a flat there, and by now it was a dingy, damp basement in Chelsea. On March 10 1946, some friends came to visit and found him "laid out with a haemorrhage." They rushed him to St Stephen's hospital, where he was admitted as a case of haematemesis i.e. vomiting blood. But the doctors also found something quite different. His notes record recurrent bouts of depression. He was also in a state of apprehension, with raised blood pressure, tremor and shaking hands. His pulse was rapid, his pupils dilated and his central nervous system overactive. This collection of signs led the doctors to diagnose 'anxiety'. It was, almost to the day, the first anniversary of the Majoda shooting.

Further examination showed that Dylan's liver was tender and enlarged, the first real suggestion of the effect of alcohol and poor diet on his body. On the good side, three liver tests revealed no damage. He also tested negative for diabetes, and the doctors could find nothing wrong with his chest – there was no indication at this stage of the serious chest disease that would later strike him down.

Dylan was discharged with a prescription for phenobarbitone, a highly addictive sedative. He was also given a follow-up appointment which he failed to keep, complaining that the doctor had joked with him about being a poet. He returned to his watery shack on the Cherwell. Two months later, he was ill again, this time writing to a friend that he'd had a bad bout of gastric flu. But the real problem, wrote Dylan harking back to his days in St Stephen's, was nothing more than the occupational complaints of nervousness and high blood-pressure.

His letters hint at continuing ailments throughout the year, as well as anxiety about his young son's asthma. He shamelessly exploited Llewelyn's chest problems to extract £1,000 from James Laughlin, making up a story that Llewelyn had TB and needed to enter an expensive sanatorium. Laughlin also agreed to help Dylan visit America; Dylan spelled out nine conditions, including having a house in the hills, preferably in the Adirondacks, a better place for his chest than an Oxford meadow.

Dylan was still living beside the river the following year, 1947. Opera was again in the air; Elisabeth Lutyens had asked him to write the libretto for *The Pit*, a chamber opera about coal miners trapped underground, but he failed to deliver. Two weeks into the new year, he became very excited about the chance of working with William Walton on an opera about London's bombed slums. It would be, he boasted, the biggest English operatic event of the century.

But for the moment, bad weather was providing all the drama. It started in January, and continued to worsen thereafter. February was the coldest month for a hundred and thirty years. Oxford had continuous frost for sixteen days, along with heavy falls of snow that also covered most of England. Then on March 7, torrential rain accompanied a thaw, putting much of the country under water. A week later, the Cherwell hut was damaged in a storm, and the meadow flooded again. Dylan became so ill with flu that he had "icicles hanging from his cough."

The little wooden hut was neither a safe nor a healthy place to be living in. But Edith Sitwell had already come to the rescue. Convinced that he needed an overseas holiday, she had arranged a travel scholarship to Italy for him.

The whole family set off in April from a soggy England, eventually renting a bullet-pocked villa in the hills above Florence that had once been the headquarters of Field Marshall Kesselring. From the terrace, Dylan could see the Villa Mirenda where Lawrence had written *Lady Chatterley's Lover*. Just beyond, lay Osbert Sitwell's Italian home, Castello di Montegufoni where, three years before, Wynford Vaughan Thomas, Dylan's lifelong Swansea friend, had chanced upon Botticelli's *Primavera*, hidden there for safety during the war.

Dylan had little interest in Italian art or culture but his health, spirits and appetite improved in the sunshine, and sometimes his energy was too much for his Italian companions. He ended the holiday on the island of Elba, where he drank with the mayor, had stone-throwing competitions with the local miners and tinkered with his early draft of *Under Milk Wood*. Another writer staying in the same hotel saw the death that was soon to come: "The strange impression that I had was that he was a passenger... someone who was passing through this world... but not to stay until he was old."

They returned in September to yet another damp cottage that in winter was often stranded in a lake of flooded fields; the countryside, said Dylan, was low, sodden and rheumatic. This was South Leigh, a small village west of Oxford. There was a pub and a post office, and Dylan got hold of a caravan, in which he continued to work on *Under Milk Wood* and other scripts, including his film operetta, *Me and My Bike*.

One of his neighbours thought he was 'nervy', whilst another felt that his health 'wasn't all that good.' He went to see a local doctor, who gave him pills and advised him to give up drinking. A year after moving in, autumn brought a renewal of earlier problems. The weather in November 1948, with its damp and foggy conditions, was not the best for those with respiratory difficulties. In the middle of the month, he went to London to read 'Extraordinary Little Cough' on the radio. A few days later, he was cycling round South Leigh in the fog, which was enveloping the country with a vengeance – deaths from bronchitis more than doubled, reported *The Lancet*. Whilst the South Leigh station master was worried about Dylan's bouts of coughing, the poet himself saw his chest problems as an opportunity for musical whimsy: he was so cold in the fog that he felt he could sing an opera, all the parts, and "do the orchestra with my asthma."

In March 1949, Dylan flew to Prague for a writers' conference. On a tour of the freezing city, his guide noticed that he was wheezing and out of breath, and an interpreter that he was coughing a good deal. He was invited to a party, where he narrated parts of *Under Milk Wood*. He returned to South Leigh for a few more months. Since he was now showing increasing signs of chest problems, his next move was not the wisest he could have made.

An even more extraordinary cough

At the beginning of May, the family moved to the bronchial heronry, as Dylan called it, the Boat House, standing at the edge of the estuary at Laugharne. Life there began with flu and injections but things soon began to pick up.

A letter arrived from John Brinnin, who had recently been appointed director of the Poetry Center in New York. He invited Dylan to America, undertaking to pay his fare out, as well as $150 for each of three poetry readings at the Center. Brinnin also offered to arrange other engagements, for all of which he would take an agent's fee of fifteen percent. Dylan wanted to take Caitlin with him. She was ill, and he thought a trip to America would do her good, though he recognised, prophetically, that it would be a "queer place for a rest-cure."

Brinnin's proposal raised Dylan's spirits, but he soon sank back into an estuarine gloom, plagued by debts, stomach trouble and "a sort of breakdown", all in a baby-packed, freezing house, as he described it in a July letter. According to an official survey, the Boat House was in reasonably good condition, with no structural dampness. Its problem was its location, facing the full force of the moisture-laden winds of the estuary. It needed a good deal of heating, but this would have been difficult – money was short, and coal was still rationed. Supplies of gas and paraffin were also restricted, and the heaters they fuelled produced an unhealthy amount of water vapour.

Soon after moving in, Dylan's chest problems began in earnest, and a local doctor prescribed several medicines, as well as a paint for his throat. But usually, he preferred to stay clear of the doctor, and to buy his medicine from the chemist. As his chest got worse, he bought linctus and other items including, like Mr Pritchard in *Under Milk Wood*, Friar's Balsam. Mr Pritchard also smoked asthma mixture, a popular herbal remedy for chest problems, some brands of which were said to have contained cannabis. Perhaps Dylan had also discovered its therapeutic qualities.

By the autumn of 1949, he was complaining of gout, gastritis, influenza and cracked ribs. His letters also record his bronchial woes: phlegm on his lungs, pleurisy, bronchitis and pneumonia. Some of this should be taken with a pinch of salt because he had long perfected the art of turning a sneeze into a seizure, in order to fend off those to whom he owed money or scripts. But even so, it is clear that from late 1950 onwards his health continued to deteriorate.

Both Dylan and Caitlin – who herself became seriously ill with pneumonia – blamed their respiratory problems on the rain and damp mists of the estuary. Whatever the causes, others noticed the consequences – his daughter, Aeronwy, recalls him huffing and puffing up the steep path to the Boat House, like a stranded turtle. His neighbours remember him stumbling breathless around Laugharne on his walking stick, as he came back from Brown's Hotel, where his drinking would not have helped – the alcohol would have depressed his breathing.

Dylan's mother, Florence, lived in a house opposite Brown's. She was worried that when he walked down from the Boat House to see her, he was so exhausted that he couldn't speak. After his death, she remarked that "I don't wish him to come back, because he was suffering a lot the last few years, with his chest…".

According to Florence, he had always been "very weak" in the chest, and as a boy had suffered from asthma very badly. As soon as he was old enough, he was sent on long holidays to his various aunts in the Welsh countryside. There were endless, nagging fears about TB, though the closest Dylan ever came to it was visiting one of his New Quay friends in a sanatorium.

There was more to this than the worries of an over-protective mother. Florence knew better than most how many of Dylan's relatives had suffered from chest complaints: his grandfathers had died of pneumonia and bronchitis, and two of his aunts, while still in their thirties, from pulmonary TB. One of her uncles was so afflicted with chest problems that his doctor advised him to take up smoking as a cure.

This would not have been a remedy that Florence would have wanted for her son. His first cigarette had been at grammar school, perhaps even earlier, and he was a chain-smoker thereafter. It is hardly surprising that Milton Helpern found some emphysema when he examined Dylan's lungs at the post-mortem.

Then there is the question of diet. From the time he left home for London in 1934, Dylan showed very little interest in food. For much of his adult life, he ate little, and what he did eat was of poor nutritional value. One of his London friends remembers that the only breakfast Dylan cared for was ice-cream dropped in a glass of beer. Another recalls breakfasts of beer with an apple or a piece of cake. Later, in America, it was often two raw eggs in a glass of beer or sherry.

Dylan's money usually went on drink and cigarettes. Eventually, beer became a substitute for food. At South Leigh, said his friends, he seemed indifferent to eating. Down in Laugharne, he kept to his childish diet of sweets and biscuits, relieved only by Caitlin's dark green stews, risottos and sometimes fish and cockles from the estuary. Even in the best restaurants, he usually ate little; he was once taken to the Etoile but failed to eat anything of what he had ordered.

The effects on Dylan's health of his drinking, smoking and poor diet were exacerbated by his sleep deficit. Many of his friends have described his inability to sleep, or his lack of interest in doing so. His medical notes from St Stephen's record that he could find sleep only with the aid of alcohol. Caitlin has related his sleeping problem to the anxiety condition that the doctors at St Stephen's had diagnosed, noting that after sleeping for a few hours, he would wake up and start worrying – "he would just lie there, tormenting himself."

Besides alcohol, he may have found other solutions for his sleeping problems. There were sedatives at the Boat House; just a few weeks after moving in, Caitlin was prescribed night and day doses of phenobarbitone. In 1951, Dylan used a barbiturate called Seconal in a suicide attempt.

His way of life in Laugharne did nothing to halt his physical decline, for his time there was hardly restful. There were four trips to America, a visit to Iran, many journeys to London for radio broadcasts, and commitments around Britain to take part in poetry readings and other events. His first American tour took place in 1950. He left in late February, swapping a wet Laugharne for a zero cold New York, escaping into an American dream armed with little more than a few letters of introduction and the address of Samuel Barber whose music, he said, he loved.

The tour was particularly gruelling. He criss-crossed America in every direction, giving poetry readings virtually every other day and attending innumerable receptions and dinners given in his honour. This would have been an exhausting schedule even for a fit and healthy person, but Dylan was far from that. Just seven days into his tour, a student in his audience at Mount Holyoke thought he looked liked someone "who had been cooked too long and who expects to fall away from the bones of all resolve."

The following day, March 3, he was at Amherst; his host warned Brinnin that Dylan was a very sick man, who was being put at risk by a long lecture tour. The next reading was at Bryn Mawr, the day after the fifth anniversary of the Majoda shooting. Auden was also about the campus; a young student, Jane Augustine, interviewed both poets. Auden, she wrote, was articulate, logical and expansive. Dylan was moody, subjective and hesitant, but she had been advised he was unwell. Augustine noted that "his eyes, with their hidden appeal for me to be brief, showed the effort he was making to suppress his discomfort." She later recalled that he "looked terribly ill."

Six readings later, on March 20, he was in Urbana, Illinois, to take part in the university's Festival of Contemporary Arts. Little is known about his reading, except that Vera Stravinsky was in the audience. Favourably impressed, she reported back to her husband, who was appearing in the Festival the following evening.

Dylan ploughed on, coughing his way across the continent, with graphic descriptions provided by John Brinnin: "Several times already that morning he had fitfully broken into spells of coughing that racked the whole length of his body, brought tears to his eyes, and left him momentarily speechless…". Brinnin also observed Dylan vomiting blood. He does not implicate alcohol or drunkenness in these attacks.

America also brought an exacerbation of Dylan's sleeping difficulties. His busy schedule often forced him to travel overnight, sleeping as best he could on trains and planes. On his first trip to New York, and probably on all his others, he took sleeping pills because of the noise from the city: "without some drug, I couldn't sleep at all."

The drugs seemed to come too easily. On just his third night in America, Brinnin gave him a sedative to help him sleep, and the next night called a doctor whose prescription had Dylan asleep in minutes. A few weeks later, he was seen cramming a handful of sleeping pills in his mouth. In New York, one of his girlfriends gave him pills and capsules for everything that was or might be wrong with him. Then in Iowa, his host saw him taking pills which Dylan claimed were for morning sickness. He was there for almost two weeks, but ate virtually nothing. It was milk and a pill at breakfast, usually followed by vomiting, and that was it for the rest of the day. He was advised to see a doctor about the vomiting but he replied that they had only one cure for anything that ailed him – stop drinking.

As Dylan struggled through the arduous tour, Brinnin was also feeling the strain. His visitor was wonderful but impossible, bringing Brinnin close to exhaustion and, he wrote, the edge of madness. He acknowledged that this was not so much because of the poet's behaviour but his own inability to comprehend or deal

4. John Brinnin, on tour with Cartier-Bresson, 1947

with it. Dylan was a child waiting to be taken care of, "scared of everything except his mother."

Some of Brinnin's friends complained he was neglecting them and many others wondered why he was spending so much time and energy on Dylan: "I don't envy you the care of the man, yet there must be rewards I am not myself able to perceive." One of these was financial: Brinnin's fee from the tour would be $810, money he badly needed to shore up his income. Instead, he eased his mind by buying a new Studebaker convertible, even though he knew it was something he could not afford.

Part of Brinnin's emotional turbulence had come from falling in love with Dylan, who had done very little to discourage him. During a bawdy and drunken conversation, Dylan, who had dabbled in gay sex in his younger days, was asked what he wanted from life. He playfully prodded Brinnin with his finger and replied "I want him."

At the end of the visit, Brinnin was part of the large party that saw Dylan off. As the ship's horn blew its warning sound for departure, Brinnin kissed him full on the lips, and held the kiss in front of the assembled friends. When the gang-plank was drawn up, Brinnin felt an overwhelming wave of desolation and stood on the quayside in a flood of tears. But he was soon to realise that his love had an unspoken corollary, an impulse to get rid of Dylan, as he put it with chilling ambiguity. It was an impulse that grew into an obsession that Brinnin said he was never able to curb.

Dylan arrived home in June; he was, said Caitlin, dead to the world. The trip had lasted three months, with net earnings of $1,918 at best. This was £685, about £17,000 in today's terms, some £200 per day. But not everyone had been paid off, and the taxman would soon be knocking on the door for his share.

A quiet month in Laugharne had Dylan feeling better again. He travelled to London in August to meet up with an excited Brinnin, in Europe for the first time since the end of the war. They went on a round of pubs, clubs and parties, at one of which Dylan made a pass at Lena Horne. The partying did him little good and Brinnin found himself back in a familiar role: "Dylan has been as kind as he can be, but half the time *he* has to be taken care of, so I am partly the visitor and partly the attendant."

Dylan returned to Laugharne, whilst Brinnin went to Paris, travelling on borrowed money, wondering if he should swim the Channel to stay solvent. Instead, he boarded Air France's *Epicurean Special*, settling down to martinis, champagne, a five course meal and cognac. To save money, he stayed for a while with the thirty-two year old poet Myron O'Higgins ("the negro boy I first met at Yaddo"). Brinnin also thought up a few more wheezes for squeezing money out of friends, acknowledging that he was just holding on by "the most silken thread of a shoelace."

He held on long enough to go to Florence, to a villa in the hills, complete with Roman terraces, gardens, colonnades, swimming pool and tennis court – it was the Villa del Beccaro where Dylan and family had stayed in 1947. Then it was the train to Venice, and a gondola along the moon-lit Grand Canal to sip champagne with Peggy Guggenheim and Venetian royalty.

He also met up again with a young photographer with whom he had danced the nights away on the passage across the Atlantic.

He and Rollie McKenna had been instantly drawn to each other; the only issue, they later said, was who was going to be the first to get the other on the dance floor. After that, it was clear sailing. She was on the rebound from a failed marriage to a naval officer; Brinnin was enchanted with her air of bemused authority, and enthralled with her easy mastery of art and its history. But most of all, he confided, she gave him a tingling masculine glow.

Brinnin limped home penniless to America, sneaking into First Class in the hope of catching a glimpse of Josephine Baker. His money problems had been no temporary inconvenience. He was generally inept at managing his finances. Part of his difficulties was not having a tenured university post. Just like Dylan, he led a hand-to-mouth existence, eking out a living through teaching contracts and speaking engagements. He earned money where he could, describing it as street-walking on Grubb Street. Making ends meet was difficult, and he relied on loans and gifts from an old friend, John Thompson, a fellow English academic. Brinnin's begging letters to his "much-abused miracle" were every bit as ingenious, and devious, as Dylan's were to his benefactors.

To make matters worse, Brinnin had expensive tastes – not just showy cars, but also winter holidays in the sun and early summers on the New England coast. His annual jaunts to Europe, where he hobnobbed as much with the well-bred as the well-read, became money-sapping excursions that were usually subsidised by Thompson. Brinnin's deepest joy was the liners that took him across the sea. He travelled in luxury in Cabin Class staterooms, enjoying the company of the really rich, as he put it, soaking up a lifestyle that he admitted was beyond his means.

As Brinnin recovered from his European adventures, Dylan travelled up and down to London. His New York girlfriend, Pearl Kazin, arrived in October but she saw nothing of him. He was ill for several weeks, she reported, first with pleurisy, and then with pneumonia. He went to see a doctor, who told him to give up drinking. That same month, he sent thirty-nine pages of *Under Milk Wood* to the BBC.

Both Brinnin and Dylan saw out the year dealing with their money problems. Brinnin pleaded chronic poverty to Thompson, whilst Dylan implored his benefactor, Margaret Taylor, to help him pay for coal. But it was an oil company that came to his rescue. He spent January and February of the new year in Iran, earning money by making a public relations film for British Petroleum.

Brinnin spent his first few months of 1951 in some anguish. A creditor was taking him to court, he was behind on his car repayments and in trouble over his income tax. Bill Read, his long-term partner, had decided to find a woman to marry and, worst of all, Brinnin's hair was falling out in great chunks, a problem that would cost him (and Thompson) dear in medical treatment.

But Brinnin had his comforts. The Poetry Center was now firmly established as a major cultural institution, his fourth collection of poetry was due out and late one afternoon he struck lucky in a downtown bar, picking up a Yale student called Sandy, who invited him up to see his "tinted pix of bulldogs in sweaters." The next day, February 3, Brinnin went to visit McKenna, still uncertain of the direction of their friendship, but knowing that he was about to be introduced to her family.

Come the summer, he returned to Europe, again with help from Thompson. After Paris and Venice, he travelled down to Laugharne. He met Caitlin for the first time, who vowed that Dylan would never set foot in America again. But soon she was persuaded to go with him, attracted by the prospect of a winter away from the Boat House. Brinnin also wanted the sun, and headed off to Capri and Cannes. On his return home, he found a letter waiting for him from James Laughlin, urging him to take care of Dylan if he returned to America: "I don't see how he can survive long at the present pace."

That autumn, Dylan was ill as usual; he was afflicted, he claimed, with gout, a strained back, bronchitis, fits, and a sense of disaster. As he sat in the Boat House listening to the broadcast from Venice of Stravinsky's *The Rake's Progress*, he might also have sensed a new opportunity. If he did, it was not long in coming. In early January 1952, he met the film director, Michael Powell, who suggested a collaboration with the composer. Dylan agreed and so did Stravinsky but no money could be found.

A few weeks later, Dylan and Caitlin sailed for America for a four-month visit. Brinnin left Boston at dawn and drove to New York to meet them. As they came off the *Queen Mary*, he handed them a small square of red carpet and a box of gardenias. He drove them out of the city to spend two days with McKenna at her imposing country house, its fifteen rooms done up in the style of the Museum of Modern Art. Just up the road was Thornedale, her family's eight hundred acre estate, to where a shy and nervous Brinnin had been taken to meet the grand matriarch.

After photo-shoots in the snow, burgers at Howard Johnson and dinner parties at which Caitlin insulted McKenna's friends, it was back to New York, where the Thomases spent most of their first month. Brinnin was already so fed up with their behaviour that he had decided to give up "being the good uncle in charge of a couple of brawling Katzenjammer Kids." But the money was good. Delighted with the packed houses for Dylan's two readings at the Poetry Center, Brinnin put on a third and his reservations about "the whole entrepreneurial enterprise I'd sidled into all but vanished." He also kept up his professional responsibility for his visitor, making a point of seeing him at least once a week when Dylan was in New York.

The critic, Anatole Broyard, met Dylan at a party in February, and thought that he looked swollen, like an inflatable toy that had been over-inflated. He was soon confined to bed, and taking sleeping pills once more. At a reading in Vermont, he looked strained and tired, with alternating chills and fever; after breakfast the next morning, he and Francis Colburn, a well-known humorist and painter, swallowed phenobarbitone and atropine together.

With Caitlin in tow, Dylan then set off across the continent on a reading tour that was as gruelling as the first. They both became ill, swinging between exhaustion, exhilaration and *ennui*. Caitlin's presence did little to change his habits – one of his hosts noted that in four days at his house, Dylan ate only once and that was just a single rasher of bacon.

On returning to Laugharne in May, he was sick with what he thought was sunstroke from having sat in the sun watching cricket at Lord's. It turned out to be pleurisy, though it wasn't serious, he said, but it had stopped him writing.

By now, Dylan had started sliding down the slippery bronchial slope to his collapse in November 1953. His chronic lack of sleep, together with his smoking, drinking, poor diet and overwork, combined to produce a general debilitation that was gradually making his body more and more vulnerable to illness. His death

26

5. Cordial in Vermont, February 1952

was certainly not inevitable but he would soon reach a point where just one incident, night of excess, accident or person – perhaps even a doctor – would make it so.

Caitlin recognised the damage that was being done to his health – as the *Nieuw Amsterdam* had sailed away from America, she had written to Brinnin, pleading with him not to invite Dylan to America again. She warned him, presciently, that he would be doing her husband a fatal disservice if he encouraged him to undertake another tour.

3. A Fatal Disservice Done

By the time Brinnin received Caitlin's letter, he was already drawing up a programme of speakers for the next season at the Poetry Center. But he had long become tired of his work there. It was poorly paid and blighted by the drudgery of commuting regularly from Boston to New York. He had to hire the speakers, entertain them in New York, and be the compère at their readings.

Brinnin was a prize asset the Center had no wish to lose, so in July 1952 it appointed an administrative assistant to help him. Having drifted aimlessly through the art world and marriage, it was Elizabeth Reitell's first real job, outside the army, since graduating as a student some ten years earlier. But Brinnin soon realised she was very competent, and promoted her to assistant director.

Confident in Reitell's abilities, he set off in August on another grand tour of Europe. He had planned to go with his new love, the writer Bill Goyen, but in the end he invited an old flame, Howard Moss, the poetry editor of the *New Yorker*. Reitell was there to say farewell, together with Moss' mother and Brinnin's too, partying in a stateroom filled with bouquets, champagne and greeting cards that wished them everything from "Bum Voyage" to "Oo La La in Gay Paree." Lining the rails off the coast of France, Brinnin nudged Moss' elbow to let him know he was standing next to Bob Hope.

They made three visits to London, during which Brinnin had tea with T.S. Eliot, got drunk with Edith Sitwell and enjoyed a twelve hour drinking session with Louis MacNeice, signing him up for a reading tour the following year. Moss and Brinnin also discovered a gay club much to their liking where, they noted approvingly, the clientele was above reproach in deportment and dress.

Brinnin finished off his visit in early September, meeting up with Dylan in a north London pub. They drank beer, played table football and talked about another trip to America. They agreed on two performances of Dylan's half-written play, which was given the name of *Under Milk Wood* in the taxi taking Brinnin to catch his train. At the station, they met up with Moss, who was being bid goodbye by an adoring young man, dismissed by Dylan as "an adolescent boil with simper and spindles attached."

For Brinnin, October arrived with its usual financial crisis, caused this time by both the extravagance of his European tour, and by his incautious handling of two of his teaching contracts. He was forced to borrow $300 from John Thompson to see him through to the new year.

For Dylan, autumn brought its familiar crop of respiratory problems, variously described in his letters as pneumonia, bronchitis and colds. With rain and gales sweeping the country, he felt trapped and depressed as heavy drizzle settled over Laugharne, creeping "chalky and crippling" into his bones. Revealing just a touch of self-pity, he complained he was croaking and snuffling about the Boat House like an old, slippered crow.

An early visitor after Brinnin had been another American, a young student who was destined to become the country's Poet Laureate. Donald Hall was in his final year at Oxford, where he was President of the Poetry Society. He had travelled to Laugharne to take Dylan back to give a reading; he looked, said Hall, as bloated as ever, resembling one of those little fish that blow themselves up with air to frighten their predators. When Dylan said he wanted to die, Hall asked why. "Just for the change," he replied. As for poetry, Dylan described it as a dark river flowing within him. All he had to do was send down a bucket and pull up the words – easy work but slow.

The Oxford visit was a great success, though the rest of the year bumped to an end with the usual worries about bills, as well as the threat of bailiffs being sent in by the taxman. And, just before Christmas, Dylan's father died of pneumonia. The new year – 1953 – started as badly as the old one had finished. In the first few months, Dylan's sister died of liver cancer, one of his patrons took an overdose of sleeping pills, three friends died at an early age and Caitlin had another abortion.

The weather and events were also against him. In January, Laugharne was steeped in fog and mired in a bloody murder that shocked the whole town. Dylan escaped to London to perform in a play, and was there for most of the month. This was not what the doctor would have ordered for a chesty man. Fog lay about the city for several days. There were also higher than normal levels of air pollution following the Great Smog of early December, which had already produced a large increase in deaths from bronchitis and pneumonia.

Dylan returned to Laugharne at the beginning of February, laid low with bronchitis and flu. He had also lost his voice, forcing him to pull out of a recording for the BBC. All he was able to do, he said, was grieve and sneeze. He went up to London again at the end of February, only to find himself caught in another severe bout of smog. There were other problems, too, and they did not escape the notice of his friends:

> *Billy, it happened in Brown's, didn't it?*
> I was with him one afternoon... Dylan had his elbow on the mantelpiece. All of a sudden, he dropped, like a log.
> *How long was he out?*
> About a minute and a half.
> *You knew nothing of the blackouts, Mably, but you could see something was wrong.*
> I could see he wasn't well. He drank steadily, but not terribly excessively, and I believe that he drank less towards the end of his life because he really couldn't drink very much without suffering.
> *Suffering in which way?*
> Well, he very quickly got ill. He was just sick very easily... I think towards the last that his health really began to fail.

By mid-March, Dylan was preparing to return to America. Brinnin was already planning his return to Europe, relieved that he had just got rid of MacNeice, whom he described as a first-class noodle after he turned up twelve hours late for his opening reading at the Poetry Center.

Dylan had promised Brinnin that he would embark from his liner with *Under Milk Wood* complete. He arrived in New York on April 21 1953. He was clear-eyed, hale and sober, said Brinnin, who described this third visit as one of modest drinking, general sobriety and abstinence for whole days at a time. That evening at the Algonquin hotel, Brinnin introduced him to Liz Reitell, who had been given the job of producing the play. But they took an instant dislike to each other - she just wasn't Dylan's type, or so it seemed at first: "*He* thought, she's one of those cold American girls. *I* thought, why all the fuss over this fool?"

Dylan was restrained and evasive, even apprehensive. Reitell towered over him, a striking woman with an air of authority and a booming voice. A friend, whom Reitell helped get into politics, praised her "fierce brazenness", calling her smart, aggressive and articulate. She was a gutsy New Yorker, not afraid to do battle. The word most used to describe her during her later wildlife campaigns was "warrior". In 1983, a visiting film maker thought Reitell had the look and poise of a Sioux chief.

But there was a downside. She was, said another friend, highly emotional and opinionated, sometimes belligerent, with little restraint in her devotion to a cause. Her determination and single-mindedness could often make her inflexible and, once she had decided on a course of action or idea, nothing and nobody could change her mind. This would prove to be a valuable asset in getting *Milk Wood* staged but it would not serve Dylan well during his illness and last days.

As events developed, Reitell also took on the role of Dylan's literary secretary, though she had no qualifications and little experience, whether as producer or secretary. But what she brought to both roles was a logical mind and an excellent vocabulary, which helped make her "a brilliant wordsmith." She later worked for the playwright Arthur Miller, claiming that she helped him with his writing. He found her an intelligent, efficient and hearty woman.

Reitell and Dylan soon found they had much in common: word play, storytelling, a generous disposition and a freewheeling sense of humour. And, for most of the time, she liked his roaring behaviour. She, too, was a drinker and talker and, as far as bad behaviour was concerned, she acknowledged that she was very good at it herself. She liked legendary figures, she once said, always preferring to meet a Dylan Thomas over an Edith Sitwell. And, as the relationship developed, they also shared a fantasy:

> we were going to live in Montana...in a ranch by the mountains. He loved the feel of pony's noses. He said: "Have you really ever felt a pony's nose? Pony noses are so soft and velvety, they smell so wonderful."

But now, at their first meeting in the Algonquin, Reitell was shocked and angry when Dylan revealed that *Milk Wood* was still only half-written, with the premiere just three weeks away, and all seats sold. She wanted to set him to work immediately but he left the city to tour the east coast on another tough schedule of poetry readings.

Between April 24 and May 13, Dylan did fourteen readings, almost one a day. He started off in Haverford College in the suburbs of Philadelphia with a packed evening, some of whose sessions were dry; his host, John Lester Jr., had warned that the college was a den of Quakerism. Dry or wet, cricket-mad Dylan and Lester would have had much to talk about. He was the son of John Ashby Lester, one of the great figures in American cricket, who had once scored a century at Lord's.

Three days later, Dylan was at Bennington college, where Brinnin and Reitell had first met and where Martha Graham had put together her ballet, *Deaths and Entrances*. The students were all women, and they were warned in advance that 'Dylan' was pronounced like penicillin. After the reading, he seems to have met up with the writer Shirley Jackson and her husband, Stanley Hyman, with whom he had enjoyed a riotous supper on his 1950 tour. Not long after Dylan's death, Jackson wrote *Weep for Adonais*, a critical portrait of the self-serving academics who had hovered around him during his last American visits.

The next morning, he set off for Syracuse university to face a programme that was typical of the demands being made of him. The main event was at 4pm, an odd hour to be reading poetry, remarked Dylan in his introduction. It was followed by a cocktail party, a dinner with some of the faculty and, at 8pm, a discussion with students and staff that finished with drinks.

The following day, April 29, he travelled to Williamstown, Massachusetts. At his reading there, he declared that he liked none of his own poems, save 'And death shall have no dominion'. Afterwards, there was a session in the Alumni Hall, where he sat in the centre of "a glittering throng ringed about him on the floor." It was celebrity exposure with all of the attendant strains and stresses.

The rest of the tour followed a similar pattern, taking in three more readings in Massachusetts, where Reitell harried him by phone to finish *Milk Wood*. Other engagements followed across the east coast until, on May 12, he went south to Duke university in North Carolina. Here he read "like the best of Dickens in spots, very savoury." Then it was a flight back the next day to the university of Connecticut, where supper with the dean was interrupted by a phone call from Reitell. Dylan promised he would stay up all night to finish the play. After supper, came the reading and yet another reception.

Early next morning, an exhausted Dylan caught the train to New York, to take part in an afternoon rehearsal for the premiere that evening of *Under Milk Wood*, with the second half of the play still not complete. Threatening to cancel the performance, Reitell locked him in a room in Rollie McKenna's apartment and squeezed the final part out of him, whilst he protested that he was too ill and weary to write: "I can't, I simply can't do this." But she made him, and he did, and the last lines of the script were handed to the actors as they were putting on their make-up. Within hours of the play ending, Dylan and Reitell were lovers.

Enter Dr Feel Good

Whilst Reitell had grown closer to Dylan, Brinnin was moving away from him. He had decided to stop being his minder because love for Dylan, he wrote, could only lead to a devastating denial of oneself. Brinnin described his new attitude as self-protective, declaring that he had come to pay little attention to Dylan's habits or movements. This was a critical moment in a chain of neglect that would prove fatal.

But at least other people were looking after him. For much of this trip, he was ill with gastritis, and needed an inhaler to help his breathing. Reitell took him to see her own family doctor, Milton Feltenstein, who gave him injections of ACTH, a cortisone secretant which acted as a general tonic but also helped with his breathing. But Dylan's most painful malaise was gout, and Feltenstein seems to have injected morphine to relieve the pain. Oscar Williams, his unofficial American agent, had an altogether different worry, one that lay at the heart of Dylan's growing debilitation:

He wasn't really eating. The stomach probably tried to live on the beer… on top of that he didn't sleep.

Why was that?

He was living not eight hours a day, he was living twenty-four hours a day. He was too busy to sleep, and almost too busy to eat.

He wore himself out…

He was living fast, but it wasn't fast in the sense of loose, it was fast in the sense he was crowding three lives into one.

For the next week, Dylan was in New York, providing the opportunity for his romance with Reitell to blossom. Then, on May 20, he was off to Amherst for a reading; the college paper recalled the vibrant behaviour of his 1950 visit, and quoted a condescending Louis MacNeice who thought him "a most picturesque personality."

Dylan spent the next day touring the New England country-side with Brinnin, who found him at his happiest and most relaxed, showing little inclination for a drink. The following morning Stravinsky phoned Brinnin's apartment. He invited Dylan to his suite in Boston's Sheraton Plaza hotel. Stravinsky noticed that he looked swollen; Dylan was more concerned about his gout, though he said he preferred it to Feltenstein's injections. They drank whisky and talked about opera. Composer and poet got on well, a friendship sealed by Dylan with an impromptu rendering of Yeats' 'The Wild Old Wicked Man.' They agreed to work together on an opera about the destruction of the planet by the atom bomb. Stravinsky invited him to stay at his home in Hollywood and, on his return there from Boston, he started on the building of a new guest room. The die was now cast.

When Brinnin returned from teaching in the late afternoon, he found Dylan in a state of giddy excitement. They toasted the Stravinsky project with a bottle of wine and went out on the town to celebrate, not at the opera, the theatre or even the burlesque but at a Johnnie Ray concert.

Singing snatches of *Madame Butterfly* and *Aida*, Dylan returned to New York the next day for yet another poetry reading, and a reunion with Liz Reitell. Their lovemaking soon became a little more challenging when he fell down some stairs and broke an arm. Feltenstein arranged for him to be put in plaster and gave him something to ease the pain, probably morphine. With his arm in a sling, Dylan took part in the second reading of *Under Milk Wood* on May 28.

Afterwards, there were drinks with Gladys LaFlamme and Francis Colburn, his hosts in Vermont the previous year. They had been in the audience, and saw that Dylan was unwell during the performance. When they left him at midnight, he was looking very ill, they said, standing forlornly on an emptying street, closely watched over by Brinnin and Reitell, who took him back to his hotel. As they put him to bed, he was too ill for even the briefest exchange of words. This was to be Brinnin's last act of guardianship.

The next day Feltenstein was called to see Dylan. He lectured him on his health and then gave him "absolute deliverance" from his pain, a phrase which suggests he was given morphine again. He needed to rest but the next few days were frantic; he flew to Washington to complete his Departing Alien form, made recordings of his poems and, drawn moth-like once more to the operatic light, had lunch with Samuel Barber. As Dylan's health deteriorated, Reitell rang Brinnin in Boston, worried that he might not make it to London. Brinnin told her "he always gets where he's going", and went back to watching television.

One of Dylan's last engagements had been with Cyrilly Abels, the editor of *Mademoiselle*. She brought with her the magazine's guest fiction editor, a young intern called Candy Bolster. Dylan was not feeling at his best, and he later apologised for feeling like "an old pudding with feet."

Back at the office, the "Dylan Thomas episode" was about to erupt. One of the other guest editors was furious she had not been at the meeting. For the next two days, a dejected Sylvia Plath hung around the White Horse and the Chelsea, hoping for another chance to meet the writer whom she loved, said one of her boyfriends, almost more than life itself. But Dylan was already on his way home to Laugharne, thanks largely to Feltenstein's injections. A few weeks later, Plath slashed her legs to see if she had the courage for suicide.

Brinnin and Reitell were now indebted to Feltenstein. He had managed to get Dylan back on his feet, thus ensuring the success of the first two performances of *Milk Wood*. He might have thought his work was done but in just a few months time he would play a central role in the sequence of events that led to Dylan's death. Yet more than fifty years on, and as many books about Dylan, we have been left with little more than the doctor's name and address. This suggests a puzzling lack of curiosity about the person who did more than most to send the poet to an early grave.

Milton Darwin Feltenstein had had a tough start in life. His father, the son of Polish-speaking Russians, had emigrated to New York from Germany in 1884 and worked as a millinery sales-man. His mother, whose parents were from Poland, had been born in English-speaking Canada. He was their first child, born in 1901, and his names were probably a symbol of aspiration.

The young Feltenstein grew up amongst the poverty of the over-crowded tenements of the Bronx and Queens. Nothing is known of his time at school, but he later enrolled at City College, which had a reputation for both academic excellence and student radicalism. Dubbed the proletarian Harvard, it was especially popular with Jewish students because they were at the time largely denied access to the established universities.

Feltenstein took an arts degree but he had already decided to become a doctor, a challenging option during a period when the profession was deeply infected with anti-semitism. Against all odds, he gained entry to Columbia University's elite medical school, qualifying as a doctor in 1931 and finishing in the first third of his class. He did his internship at Manhattan's Beth Israel Hospital, and worked there for the rest of his career.

He also built up a flourishing private practice in Gramercy Park, a fashionable area of the city. This he achieved partly through treating people, including many writers and artists, for alcoholism or psychiatric problems, giving them injections and pills that were supposed to help them cope better with daily life.

Feltenstein liked getting close to his celebrity patients and attending their private views and first nights. His circle of friends was wide, not least because he was married to Pat Liveright, who claimed to be a relation of the great American publisher, Horace Liveright. She was a painter and one of the foremost portrait photographers of her time – Albert Einstein was one of her subjects. It was a very interesting family altogether; a son-in-law

6. Dr Milton Feltenstein, 1931

spoke Mandarin and Liveright herself went to China in 1976. On her return, she rebuked a *Time* magazine correspondent for using the word 'Mandarin', dismissing it as a class-conscious word.

In politics, the Feltensteins were a left-leaning family. Approaching retirement, he bought a house in the self-governing community of Free Acres in New Jersey. It had been established in 1910 as a radical experiment in cooperative living. By the time the Feltensteins moved there fifty years later, it still enjoyed something of a reputation as a colony of liberal artists and writers; but the Feltensteins were the harbingers of change, amongst the first of a new wave of wealth and privilege.

Dylan and Feltenstein got on well. Dylan liked his wit and sense of fun, claiming that he hadn't yet found another doctor like him. He would also have responded well to Feltenstein because he had long felt a strong identification with Jews and Jewish suffering:

7. Feltenstein again, a self-portrait, 1960s

"You can call me a Welsh Zionist," he had once told a journalist. "I'm a Welshman who likes Jews."

Feltenstein also had a broad hinterland; he enjoyed painting and sculpting, and collected art. He was known as an entertaining raconteur. He was an outspoken and gregarious person who, in some respects, was just like Dylan – after a few drinks, he liked to swear and tell off-colour jokes in front of women, and delighted in provoking people:

> He used to say the right (wrong) thing in a wrong (right) place in order to shock... very open and transparent in his deeds. Obviously quite liberal in his thinking. One day he came with Pat for a dinner at Minnie's place. As soon as he got into the house, he said: "Minnie, let's go to bed!" Minnie, being used to hearing such outrageous things, answered: "OK Milton, let me finish the cooking first."

Whilst many friends enjoyed his stories and outspoken behaviour, others were able to see behind the façade of congeniality. There seem to have been difficulties in the marriage. A friend observed that Pat Liveright "had been through some hard times personally." Another Free Acres resident acknowledged that Feltenstein "could be a bastard" with an unforgiving nature. He was a wealthy man but he had deliberately excluded one of his daughters from his will.

In some quarters, Feltenstein enjoyed a reputation as a respected physician who was always up-to-date on medical matters. He was seen as a generous doctor who charged according to the means of his patients, making him popular in New York's Chinatown. But, unfortunately for Dylan, he was also a doctor who was known to take short cuts. Reitell would later describe him as a wild doctor who believed injections could cure anything.

He was known, too, as an arrogant and dogmatic man. Feltenstein, said a neighbour, was brash and overbearing, making waves wherever he went: "Do you know the saying, 'you can always tell so and so, but you cannot tell him much.' That's my memory of Feltenstein. Over-confident, or maybe just that he knew better than anybody. I can't imagine him doubting his own judgment."

Flight of no return

Dylan returned from this third visit to America exhausted. Caitlin noticed he was finding it much harder to recover, and she had no doubts about the reason: the trips to America were damaging his health. Brinnin had come to the same conclusion a few weeks earlier, that the reading tours were seriously debilitating physically, as well as insufficiently rewarding.

From his 1952 tour, Dylan's net gain had been $393 (£140) for four months' work, equivalent today to some £3,000. His latest six-week trip in the spring of 1953 had produced net earnings of $267. Brinnin was the major beneficiary of the two visits; he pocketed over $2,000, three times as much as Dylan himself. Brinnin had raised his agent's fee to a hefty twenty-five

Finale acc' Dylan Feb Jan - 1952
Total Fees   5572.00
Agents 25%   1393.00
              4179.00
Travel   1986.00
              2193.00
Living   1800.00
              (393.00)

April - June '53

TOTAL FEES   2555.00
Agents' 25%   638.75
              1916.25
Travel   855.50
              1060.75
Living   615.00
               445.75

8. Dylan's American tour earnings, final accounts 1952 and spring 1953. Brinnin has omitted Dylan's medical expenses of $178 from the 1953 figures; when these are added in, his net earnings fall from $445 to $267. See the note on p176 for details

percent. He was charging it on Dylan's gross earnings, and even taking a fee for the events at the Poetry Center, from which he was already receiving a salary.

Brinnin acted as Dylan's Chancellor of the Exchequer, as he put it. He received the cheques – usually made out in his name – for Dylan's fees and banked them. He paid Dylan's bills, and handed out cash as and when he needed it. On his first trip,

Brinnin naively gave him a book of signed blank cheques to pay his bills, and this might help to explain why Dylan got through so much money.

Brinnin kept detailed financial accounts and tried on several occasions to get Dylan to examine them but was rebuffed by a complete lack of interest. If Dylan had bothered to study them, or given them to his accountant, it would have been clear that Brinnin's records were not entirely beyond question. During the spring 1953 trip, he claimed from Dylan's earnings a plane fare that he knew had already been paid by Haverford College. And $764 of fees that Dylan had earned on the tour did not appear in Brinnin's final accounts. There is no way of knowing whether Dylan or his estate ever received this money.

Whilst Dylan was recovering in Laugharne, Brinnin was completing arrangements for his summer outing to Europe. His main problem, as always, was finding the money to pay for it. The Poetry Center had agreed to help but only with part of the cost, so he was relying on his fees as an agent to bridge the gap. Yet such were the state of his finances – he was hanging on, he said, by the nails – that he realised his plans for Europe that year could be seen as madness. But liners and the sea had become an addiction, and travel an escape from his problems. By 1953, Brinnin had become a scrounging, insolvent playboy with an expensive habit to fund.

Throughout the spring he had been laid low by a prolonged bout of nervous exhaustion, during which he suffered from insomnia, shakes and daytime torpor. Then in early summer he was overcome by depression, brought on by "a deep bladder infection." He was confined to bed, given day and night doses of penicillin and sulphur, and forced to wear what he called the most obscene little garment in the history of costume. And just as he was getting better, his doctor killed himself.

The infection and depression eventually cleared up and, in early August 1953, he sailed in the grip of a hurricane to Gibraltar, this time with Bill Read. Brinnin found Spain painful, Paris meaningless and Brussels dull.

After dallying in Italy with Truman Capote and Noel Coward, he made his way to London, from where he planned to travel to Wales. Capote had warned him that Dylan was intent on destroy-

9. Brinnin pushing out the boat, Italy 1953

ing himself, and had chided him for being nothing more than the poet's wet nurse. Brinnin had replied that he was going to Laugharne for one purpose only – to dissuade Dylan from another American trip. This was somewhat short of the truth because it had already been agreed some months earlier that he would come back to New York in October.

Dylan had spent the summer working on *Under Milk Wood*; his progress had been desultory, and he failed to write the new passages he had set himself to do. But he did go to a drama school at the beginning of August and read from the play. This was its first full British reading. The same month, he recorded 'The Outing' for television; the stills show that he was puffy and bloated. There is little in his letters about his health, but it seems that he went to see a doctor – this might have been on the occasion of the blood clot and blackout reported by his Swansea friend, the composer Daniel Jones.

Brinnin eventually swung into Laugharne at the beginning of September, accompanied by Rollie McKenna. He was soon being teased for keeping posh company on his European travels. He assured Dylan that he would rather be with him than with anyone else, though he might have had a few doubts when Caitlin served up a supper of under-cooked duck. Emerging unscathed from the meal, Brinnin, McKenna and Dylan walked hand-in-hand into town, nervous that the Laugharne murderer was still at large.

The next day, discussions about America began afresh.

10. Dylan, bloated on television, August 1953

Brinnin was deeply ambivalent about the matter. On the one hand, he was worried about the damage that Dylan would do to his health. He also felt the potential for harm to himself. He couldn't face the thought, he said, of putting together another Dylan visit, because the previous ones had "pretty well stopped my life and the work I had to do." Furthermore, he was bored with Dylan and now found his company tedious – his love's corollary, as he had put it, was now in the ascendant. He might also have been concerned that his own reputation, both social and literary, would be tarnished by yet more reports of Dylan's roaring behaviour.

On the other, Brinnin badly needed the money that would come to him from another tour; his agent's fees would help boost his income and clear up his debts. He was also writing an article on Dylan for *Mademoiselle*, for which another tour would provide excellent publicity and help boost sales of the magazine. And further performances of *Under Milk Wood* would enhance Brinnin's professional standing even further.

Such ambivalence on Brinnin's part would not provide a propitious platform from which to plan or oversee a further trip. Dylan himself seemed intent on going, largely, thought Brinnin, as an escape from himself and his problems. Eventually, they decided that a further visit could be justified only on financial grounds – the proposed collaboration with Stravinsky in Hollywood, as well as a plan for a contract with a lecture agent, would lead to a long-term improvement in Dylan's annual income.

Brinnin was pleased with the proposal for a lecture contract. It would mark the end of his interest in any further visits by Dylan to America – he would finally be off my hands, said Brinnin with a sense of relief. His feelings of release, together with the off-loading of his responsibilities on Reitell, were to be another link in the chain of neglect.

He agreed to arrange a short programme of work so that Dylan could earn enough money to support himself while he worked with Stravinsky. Dylan was now snared financially – the plan to increase his long-term earnings depended in part on the Stravinsky project, but to do this he was committed to putting on three performances of *Milk Wood*, as well as five other engagements between October 24 and November 13, before travelling to California. The snare would play a part in his death – it would be money, not drink, that would play the more decisive part in Dylan's demise.

Caitlin was unhappy about Dylan's proposed trip, but he wanted to come to America, thought Brinnin, against all hazards. Yet writing to Stravinsky a month before his departure, Dylan hinted at his anxiety about the money-making goals of the visit. He knew that once he was in New York, he was on his own. Money for California, he assured Stravinsky, would come somehow. Dylan's friends in Laugharne noticed his ambivalence about the visit. They were also concerned about his health. Phil Richards of the Cross House Inn was one of them:

> I think Dylan was a sick man then, you know. I don't think he was a very strong man. I don't think he wanted that last trip.
> *Ivy, you and Ebie ran Brown's Hotel. You were very close to Dylan...*
> I know he didn't want to go the last time.
> *Ebie?*
> He didn't want to go. And they wanted him to sign on for five years, the last time. He said "I wouldn't live five months out there."
> *Why was that?*
> Didn't like the food, didn't like the booze there. He didn't like their way of living, you know. Dylan liked a good old pint of beer – well, you couldn't get that out there. Only this old moonshine and damned dope! Poor old feller.
> *And Milk Wood, Ivy?*
> Really and truly, it could have been written about any village in any part of the world, couldn't it, whether it was China or anywhere. Of course, it wasn't really written in Laugharne at all. It was written in New Quay, most of it.

By late September 1953, Dylan began making preparations for the visit. He went to the dentist to have an artificial tooth screwed into his jaw bone, and had his hair cut by a neighbour. When he looked in the mirror he said "That's the best haircut I've ever had. It's gonna last me a lifetime." And so it did.

In true *Milk Wood* style, Dylan bought a new pair of trousers from a draper who was Caitlin's lover, and then he and Florence went for tea with a local minister. He also gave another reading of the play at a local arts club. There was, too, a farewell party. His hosts knew all about the blackouts, having witnessed a dozen or so in the last year.

Caitlin was so concerned about the blackouts, and Dylan's persistent headaches, that she consulted David Hughes, one of the Laugharne doctors. He offered an appointment but Dylan failed to turn up. Hughes was not surprised; Dylan was not just careless about his health, he said, but careless about himself in every way. As for the blackouts, Hughes thought they were probably fainting spells associated with stress.

On the morning of October 9, Dylan and Caitlin woke to the sound of a cold wind rattling the windows of the Boat House. Dylan put on his tweed suit and packed a small case of warm clothes. They called in to say goodbye to Florence, who was just as unhappy as Caitlin about the trip but had her own explanation for Dylan's wish to go: "He always felt that he had to get out from this country because of his chest being so bad."

Caitlin had decided to travel with Dylan as far as London. They stopped off in Swansea where he met up with Vernon Watkins, who saw that he was unwell. Dylan spoke to him about his reluctance to go to America, but he felt it as necessary, said Watkins, to raise money. He knew that he ought to see a doctor but feared that he would be pronounced unfit and the trip cancelled. Instead, Dylan had sent off for a *Sunday Pictorial* diet sheet, a curious resort for a man who ate next to nothing.

In London, he stayed with Harry Locke and his wife. One of Dylan's closest London friends, Locke was a comedian who later made a name for himself in the *Carry On* series of films. Dylan was with them for ten days, the first few of which were a frenzy of writing to finish *Milk Wood*. They noticed that he was having trouble with his chest, suffering "terrible" coughing fits that made him go purple in the face.

Dylan spent a good deal of time meeting up with friends. Many had the impression that he was saying goodbye to them, and that they would never see him again. Some thought he looked sick during those last few days in London. He was also, said one, very depressed and gloomy. The BBC producer, Philip Burton, invited him to his flat but the evening was interrupted by another of Dylan's blackouts. Burton was adamant that it had not been caused by too much alcohol.

Those that saw the most of him were the landlords of the various pubs that he visited, including Sean Treacy of the King's Arms and Gaston Berlemont of the French House. Both had known him for many years, and both were aware of the deterioration in his health:

> *Sean, what did he look like to you?*
> I thought he was really looking pretty shaken. And I wondered how the hell he could go on a lecture tour, and how he was going to do it... he didn't look very well then, before he went to the States the last time.
> *In what way?*
> The complexion was gone, and he was blown up. I think that's a good description. You know, puffy face... the only thing I can say is that I was very sorry when I'd heard he'd died but I wasn't surprised. Not at all. No, I thought that was well on the cards.
> *Gaston?*
> He got old very suddenly, and the shoulders were no longer square, and drooped. I remember his last night here. When he left to go to America – he really was looking old then, looking very old.

On his last evening in London, Dylan had another blackout. The next day, October 19, he went to see his doctor for a small-pox vaccination certificate. After an extended lunch party, Caitlin and the Lockes accompanied him to the airport bus station. He was still unhappy, and turned his thumbs down as the bus pulled away. He knew, said Harry Locke, that he wasn't coming back.

Down in Lampeter, the university town where William Killick had been put on trial, Mr Rowland was happy with his 1954 poetry programme. Dylan had written to him accepting an invitation to do a reading in March. He asked for his expenses and a five guineas fee, adding "...what a long time ahead you do plan! I hope we're not all dead by then."

4. The Final Weeks

Money drives, controls and defeats me – John Brinnin, 1952

Although Brinnin left Laugharne with mixed feelings about Dylan's autumn visit, he was soon able to put all his worries behind him. He sailed back in grand style on the *S.S. Atlantic*, celebrating his thirty-seventh birthday in mid-ocean with cake and champagne. He arrived home two days before the start of the university semester, and only four weeks before Dylan was due in New York on October 20.

Brinnin ran out of time. Just five days before Dylan's arrival, he was still "fearfully busy", putting the finishing touches to an extensive season at the Poetry Center and beginning what he described as a full-scale teaching year. His commitments around the east coast, and sometimes further afield, kept him "on the edge of departure continually." He was also at work on his biography of Gertrude Stein. As events developed, Brinnin's programme, together with his policy of self-protectiveness, would push Dylan even further to the margins of his interest and attention.

Within his crowded work schedule, Brinnin noted that he was "doing what I can" to make sure that Dylan found his forthcoming visit to New York profitable. It would hardly be that because eighty percent of everything he earned would go on expenses. Dylan's net earnings from the three performances of *Milk Wood* and his five other engagements would be only $257 at best. That would give him some $10 a day to live on for the proposed month in Hollywood. With Stravinsky providing the accommodation, it would be just enough if Dylan was very careful. But if there was any substantial fall in his net earnings, then the Stravinsky project would be in danger. And there was no Plan B in place – Brinnin had not arranged any readings in California for Dylan to raise extra money, nor had Stravinsky's efforts to do so come to anything.

The financial arrangements post-Stravinsky were even more

precarious. On his return to New York in December, Dylan would appear in two more productions of *Milk Wood*, followed by a poetry reading. This money – $600 – would not be sufficient to meet all his costs, let alone provide enough to take back to Laugharne.

Brinnin's last-minute efforts meant that the programme he put together for Dylan was not just unsound financially but was also badly planned. The first week in New York would be one of intense pressure but the second held no engagements at all. Dylan would be in the city with absolutely nothing to do. Brinnin's alarm bells should have been ringing.

Unfortunately, he had other things on his mind. As Dylan was setting out for America, Brinnin was negotiating a new contract with the Poetry Center. He was fed up with commuting to New York. He had also heard that December would undoubtedly bring confirmation of tenure at the University of Connecticut. So by October 15 he had already decided to resign as the Center's Director and, from early 1954, to become its consultant, acting as a guide and mentor rather than a programme executive.

This change in role might have been another factor in fraying the thread of responsibility that joined him to Dylan. Did Brinnin now become just a little demob happy? It is a familiar story – a new job in prospect, the security of tenure just around the corner, the mind drifting away from the responsibilities of the present to the opportunities of the future. He was even, in October 1953, planning his next summer's trip to Europe.

But the one thing he was not planning to do was to go to New York to meet Dylan on his arrival in America. It was the first time he had not done so. Of course, Reitell would have been desperate to go herself, but perhaps it was also a sign of Brinnin's newly-relaxed attitude to his visitor. So as Dylan was flying into Idlewild, Brinnin was at his desk, busy with his writing. Later, he joined Bill Read for an early dinner and an outing to The Old Howard, Boston's famous burlesque house.

Brinnin's love of the theatre, as well as his passion for the sea, were both rooted deeply in his childhood. His father was a theatre scenery painter, working in Halifax, Nova Scotia, where Brinnin was born in 1916. His mother was from the town, and they lived in a modest clapboard house owned by one of her uncles, a retired sea captain. Her family was shot through with sailors and marine engineers, and Brinnin dreamed of the sea in his little room high over the harbour, a room from which he could see the place where Samuel Cunard had been born. At the corner of the street was a cemetery, where his mother would take him to wonder at the headstones of people who had drowned in the *Titanic*.

In 1920, the family moved to Detroit. They ended up renting an apartment in a crowded property that had thirty-four other residents, many of them English Canadians. It was a poor but aspirational lower middle-class neighbourhood of clerks and carpenters, auditors and book-keepers, production managers and master plumbers.

Brinnin's paternal grandfather had already died, burned to death after knocking over an oil lamp during a drunken binge. When Brinnin was twelve, his sister also died. He grew up as an only child, living in a building that mostly housed young couples, with just two children of his own age living there. He was, he later said, ill at ease on the macadamed streets of treeless outer Detroit. His early days were made bearable only by the prospect of long summer vacations back in Nova Scotia, where he watched hungrily the comings and goings of the luxury liners. When he was just nine years old, he asked his mother to take him to one of the shipping offices. He collected up dozens of brochures and told the puzzled clerk: "I want to go to Europe."

After the brochures and their glossy photos, came the paintings of Europe, courtesy of many adolescent hours spent in the Detroit Museum of Art. A Catholic schooling led to college, which Brinnin abandoned as quickly as his religion, immersing himself completely in Detroit's left-wing arts scene. He joined the Young Communist League and the city's John Reed Club, a literary group aligned with the American Communist Party. He set up a couple of progressive magazines, and contributed poems to revolutionary publications under the name Isaac Gerneth. He also worked with Walter Reuther in the fledgling United Auto Workers union, doing office work and distributing flyers.

In 1936, Brinnin's father died, followed by the deaths of close friends in Spain and in the war against Japan. Mother and son became even closer, and as an adult he continued to live with her for many years. Although his father's death brought financial difficulties, Brinnin decided to return to college, this time to the University of Michigan. He supported himself by running a shop, the Book Room, which became a focus for those interested in poetry and avant-garde literature. It was also a place where you could buy the *Daily Worker*, albeit from under the counter, and get advice on where to go in Europe – Brinnin had made his first visit in 1935, a six-week tour that took in the Soviet Union.

He had a brilliant career at college, winning the prestigious Hopwood Award three times. He boasted he was already on first name terms with Auden, though in reality he had only recently met him and had been too shy to talk. He graduated in 1942, an idiosyncratic young man who, said a college magazine, liked to write in a warm room and change his collars whenever they got dirty. His poem, 'The Desperate Heart', a story of lost love and the anguish of not being able to forget, provided a moment of fame. It inspired, and gave the text for, Valerie Bettis' solo dance of the same name. First performed in 1943, it made a major impact on audiences and critics alike.

Afterwards came a brief period of graduate study at Harvard, teaching at Vassar and, in 1947, an assignment to travel across America with Henri Cartier-Bresson; the two men quickly fell out, and the trip was not a happy one for Brinnin. In 1949, he was appointed director of the Poetry Center at the YM/YW Hebrew Association in New York. It was only a part-time job, and he made it a success, but he hankered after a secure post in a prestigious university.

By now, he was known as a critic, anthologist and poet, and he aspired to be recognised as a man of letters. He was also known as a cultivated, reserved and fastidious person. To some, he came across as condescending, certain that his place in the literary pecking order would be assured. He was an exemplar of the cocooned academic, absorbed in his work and career, name-droppingly determined to be a literary and social success.

Caitlin thought he lived in a rarefied stratosphere of his own, out of touch with the real world. One of his close friends agreed, remarking that real life was something in which Brinnin remained uninterested until his later years. He himself was more poetic in referring to his lack of anchorage, admitting to "a mind that swims without ever coming to land." And in this cerebral pond, stuff happened. Events got the better of him. He dubbed himself the Fiasco Kid, the guy who always got the hot soup spilled over him by the waiter.

Brinnin later acknowledged that he had once cared little about other people and their problems. This indifference was exacerbated by his own ill-health. Blunted by various ailments and hypochondria, he could be insensitive to the needs of those around him. He suffered from migraine and rheumatoid arthritis. Obsessed with illness, he carried a large case of medicines wherever he went. One of his pills was phenobarbitone, upon which he was dependent to ease his physical aches and mental pains.

Some of Brinnin's need for drugs came from his unsettled, and often anguished, romantic life. He lived in an open relationship with Bill Read, and enjoyed many liaisons, both home and abroad. He denied that he and Dylan were ever lovers, but a letter written closer to the time of Dylan's death suggests otherwise: "He knew me well," wrote Brinnin, "and, without blinking, joined me easily in any concern that seemed important, whether it had to do with poetry, or every day, or destiny, or money, or sex."

Brinnin's words are not without some ambiguity – did they have sex or just talk about it? In any event, Dylan's triangular relationship with Brinnin and Reitell was colourful – the director of the much-respected Poetry Center was in love with him, and they might have had sex, as was the assistant director, who certainly had, and both were responsible for his care and well-being. Within this triangle, Brinnin and Reitell were also good friends, having known each other since her student days. There was a prospect in all this for scandal in the prim-and-proper America of the early 1950s, particularly if Brinnin and Reitell's love for Dylan, and its attendant self-absorption, had played a part in the events that led to his death.

Reitell and Brinnin had other things in common besides Dylan. They both enjoyed dance and the theatre, and each was passionate about art. Like Brinnin, Reitell grew up an only child, and she, too, had parents who wanted her to achieve. She was born in 1920 into a household with a strong religious background. Her father, Charles, came from a family of German Dunkards, a deeply conservative Baptist sect. Her mother, Jane,

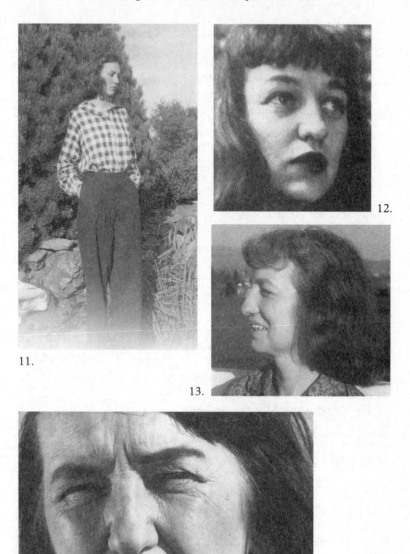

11. Liz Reitell, moody and pensive, Bennington, 1937   12. Reitell, a little older.   13.And older still   14. From tiger mother to eco-warrior, 1983

was a devout Presbyterian. At college, she was keen on missionary work, wanting to emulate her great-aunt, who had been one
of the earliest and most zealous Presbyterians to go to Africa. The
young Jane was also active as a street-corner speaker in the suffra-
gette movement. Saving lost souls and fighting for the cause
would be in her daughter's blood.

Both parents passed on an early love of the arts; Jane was an
accomplished pianist and her husband a talented painter. Their
home was both scholarly and literary – Jane had a Master's in
English, and published short stories in *The Saturday Evening Post*
and poetry in *The New Yorker*. She was a skilled editor, a gift
handed down to her daughter, who used it to good effect in
helping Dylan revise and finish *Under Milk Wood*.

Charles Reitell was an economics professor and a manage-
ment consultant, a role that made him a wealthy man. But he was
a writer, too. He published a number of academic books, as well
as *Let's Go Fishing*, a lyrical and popular guide to catching fish
that still nets good prices in antiquarian book shops today.
Impressed by his knowledge, the state governor made him a Fish
Commissioner. This was probably his most satisfying, if not his
most illustrious, appointment and Reitell worked hard on
environmental issues that affected fish and fishing, as did his
daughter many years later.

Liz Reitell's early life was unsettled. As her father moved from
job to job, she was sent to a number of private schools, including
an innovative high school patronised by New York's elite families.
Afterwards, she went to Bennington, at that time an exclusive
liberal arts college for women. She graduated in 1941 with a
degree in theatre design, dance and drama literature. One of her
teachers, the renowned Martha Hill who founded Bennington's
dance school, said of her "One can work with Elizabeth as one
does a colleague – rather than a student - with perfect faith that
she will discharge mature responsibilities if humanly possible…"

On leaving college, Reitell mooched around the fringes of
showbiz, marrying the songwriter Adolph Green and getting to
know Leonard Bernstein. Then she joined the army, serving as a
first lieutenant and marrying again, this time to a soldier. In 1946,
she went back to art school, but it was hardly a period of quiet and
consolidation. Over the next few years, she studied in five different

places. The last of these was in France, where she went with her close friends, the painter Zubel Kachadoorian and the author and illustrator, Ashley Bryan.

This was not the kind of career that her parents had expected of her. Her father was a man who judged people on how financially successful they were, and he disapproved of the choices she had made in both her work and personal life. And Reitell was herself unhappy; she had come through two broken marriages, and had failed to make her mark as a painter and set designer. She became depressed and took to drink.

Reitell is the most important witness in understanding what happened to Dylan. She was with him most of the time, day and night, during the first two weeks of the fatal fourth trip. Brinnin, on the other hand, spent just a dozen hours or so with Dylan. She later made notes for Brinnin, which he used in his account of the death given in *Dylan Thomas in America*. He was happy to acknowledge their existence in 1964, writing of Reitell's "intimate record." But ten years later, when the biographer Paul Ferris was in pursuit of the record, Brinnin declared that he neither had a copy nor any memory of it.

In fact, Brinnin had met or conferred with Reitell on three occasions in 1955 to help him write about the last weeks of Dylan's life. Brinnin took notes as she talked but she also told Ferris she had her own "written-out enormously long notes." These notes, both Brinnin's and Reitell's, would have been of great value in understanding Dylan's last days, but they have disappeared - they are not to be found even in Brinnin's extensive collection of papers in the University of Delaware. Fortunately, we can listen to Liz Reitell directly because, in 1983, she gave a series of interviews in which she talked about Dylan, including observations on his last days.

Having provided him with information about Dylan's collapse, Brinnin then asked Reitell to read a final draft of his book. She took the opportunity to make a good number of comments and revisions. In truth, it would be more accurate to describe Brinnin's account of Dylan's death as the Brinnin-Reitell account. She herself saw it that way, referring to it as "my book" because of the part she played in writing it.

Brinnin's role in the neglect leading to the death makes him a key player in events, and not merely a recorder of them. His reliance on Reitell means that his story of Dylan's death must be treated with caution because it covers up for her and contains a number of evasions and falsehoods about why Dylan died. His book, said one critic, has a scent of fraudulence. Calling Brinnin untruthful, Dorothy van Ghent, the widely-respected professor of English at Vermont, noted several errors in the text that "seem significant of the probability of more important and damaging falsifications."

Van Ghent also suggested that Brinnin was a second-rate poet, who had exploited his friendship with Dylan for financial gain and academic status. Written just one year after his book came out, this was strong stuff. It invited a response, either academic or legal, but none came. Over time, Brinnin's book became further discredited as others came forward to point to yet more mistakes, exaggerations and omissions.

My account begins with Reitell and her close friend, the architect Herb Hannum, who later became her third, but not last, husband. My focus will be on Dylan's health, rather than on the daily pantomime of his life in New York. I shall show that he was ill on arrival, and that within days he was to experience problems with his breathing that would gradually worsen.

It is a tale of Dylan's deterioration through two long and ineptly planned weeks that culminated in his collapse at midnight on November 4/5. Dylan's fate would now rest in the hands of a rather unholy trinity: a neurotic, self-absorbed academic with a chaotic lifestyle, a failed artist struggling to find meaning in her life and an arrogant doctor with a reputation for being a needle and pill merchant.

Worked to death: Tuesday October 20 – Wednesday October 28

With Brinnin relaxing at home, Liz Reitell went to Idlewild to meet Dylan. She arrived early at the airport, "simply swelling with joy" at the prospect of seeing him again for the first time since their three-week romance in the spring. But she was also aware that there was still a good deal of work to be done on *Milk Wood* and, within hours of stepping off the plane, Dylan would be rehearsing the play for two more performances on October 24 and 25.

But he was a sick man, arriving in New York with a history of blackouts and chest problems, and relying on an inhaler to aid his breathing. He was usually reluctant to admit to difficulties with his health, but all that had changed. He himself was now the first to recognise the extent of his sickness:

> ...really only a little booze on the plane but mostly frightened and sick at the thought of death. I felt as sick as death all the way over. I know I've had a lot of things wrong with my body lately, especially the past year or so. I've been warned by doctors about me, but I could never really believe them...

Reitell was shocked at his appearance. He looked pale, delicate and shaky, not his usual robust self. She realised immediately that Dylan had changed since his last trip in May, when he was, she said, basically a healthy man: "in the Fall, that had totally changed... he was very ill when he got here." Autumn, of course, had always been a bad time of the year for Dylan's health, and particularly for his chest.

Within minutes of landing, he complained of the heat. For most of his stay, afternoon temperatures were above 65°F, and often reached 70°, until the evening of November 4, when it turned much colder. Dylan also suffered, as he had done from the time of his very first trip, from the city's super-hot, steam-heated hotel rooms and apartments, most of which would have had their heating on, despite the weather.

Perhaps the most significant environmental factor that affected Dylan's chest problems was air quality – New York was one of the most polluted of American cities, and the effects of pollution would have been aggravated by the warm weather. In the four days before Dylan collapsed on November 4, air quality worsened appreciably, especially on November 2. It continued to deteriorate, and by the middle of the month the city experienced an exceptionally severe bout of air pollution that killed some two hundred people.

None of these factors on their own may have been important. But together, and especially in combination with Dylan's drinking, smoking and use of barbiturates, they could well have exacerbated his breathing difficulties. We do know that the search for fresh air was to prove a "constant theme" of his stay in New York.

Reitell took Dylan back to the Hotel Chelsea, to a small, dark and stuffy room, where he remained for a few days before being moved – "it was very important to him to have the air and the light." That evening, with no chance to rest from the rigours of a seventeen-hour plane journey, Dylan took the first rehearsal of *Under Milk Wood*.

Afterwards, he went to the White Horse, a dingy but atmospheric Celtic bar in an ethnically mixed, though mainly Irish, neighbourhood of longshoremen and truck drivers. George Reavey, a writer who had known Dylan in London since the 1930s, was there, and he noted that he was subdued and worried.

On his first full day in the city, Dylan and Reitell went sightseeing but he was unwell. They went back to the hotel, where she gave him half a grain of phenobarbitone to help him sleep. From then on, says Reitell, the role of nurse became her most important function. She soon became nervous about leaving him alone, fearing that he might fall and fatally injure himself – "this dreadful illness that was coming, he would feel wretched… he'd vomit and be torn apart by coughing."

The following day, October 22, Dylan took another rehearsal. The cast had already noticed he was ill, with bad breath and a sweating, blotchy face. One recalled that Dylan was not well for much of the time, and that his illness quickly became the most important factor in their work with him. After the rehearsal, Dylan went out to dinner at Herdt's – this was to be his last proper meal. Thereafter, Reitell found it a struggle to persuade him to eat anything.

Brinnin arrived in New York the next evening and checked into the Midston House Hotel. He went out on the town with friends, hanging around the bars of Greenwich Village. Dylan was at the Poetry Center for the play's third rehearsal. But he was too ill to take part. He was both shivering and burning with fever, one minute too hot, the next freezing cold. He managed to get on the stage, but then collapsed on the floor. Herb Hannum picked him up and Dylan, gasping for breath, said "I'm too tired to do anything. I can't fuck, I can't eat, I can't drink… I'm even too tired to sleep...I 've seen the gates of hell tonight... I'm too sick too much of the time." He was taken back to the hotel where he fell into bed, exhausted.

The incident, serious though it was, hardly seems to merit Dylan's description of having seen hell's gates. The phrase might have been one of his exaggerations but it's also possible that what happened was even worse than the account that Brinnin passed on in his book. In one of its drafts, he refers to Dylan having an 'attack' at the rehearsal, and mentions the possibility of a stroke. Brinnin suggests that Dylan had a blackout, or something comparable. Thirty years later, he described it as Dylan going "into a physical spasm."

The next morning, October 24, Dylan met up with Hannum for breakfast and told him: "My health is totally gone... It's something I don't know about. I never felt this way before and it scares me." Reitell took him to see Milton Feltenstein, a decision she regretted for the rest of her life. The good doctor injected Dylan with ACTH, and then lectured him on agreeing to a programme of medical care, pointing out that the injection would provide nothing more than a short-term prop. It has been claimed that Feltenstein also prescribed benzedrine, but Reitell has disputed this.

They went off to the fourth rehearsal of *Milk Wood*, with Dylan complaining of a "terrible pressure", as if there were an iron band around his skull. Brinnin arrived at the Center and was so shocked by Dylan's appearance that he could barely stop himself from gasping aloud. Dylan's face "was lime-white, his lips loose and twisted, his eyes dulled, gelid, and sunk in his head."

Brinnin questioned Reitell about it. She left him in no doubt that it was serious, telling him it was "something new and dreadful... I don't know what it means." He later recalled that his instinct had told him that something was radically wrong with Dylan. This should have been Brinnin's wake-up call, the moment to give his full attention to Dylan's health. He was, after all, his tour agent. He was also a senior staff member of the organisation which had invited Dylan to America – on both counts, Brinnin had a duty of care.

But he has acknowledged that, after the rehearsal, he talked only briefly with Reitell about Dylan's illness. There were other things to take care of, and Dylan's health took second place. Brinnin had a 2.30pm meeting with William Kolodney, his boss at the Poetry Center. Over a convivial session drinking whisky sours, they discussed Brinnin's plans for his new role as a consultant.

He then went off to meet Dylan and Reitell for drinks, but they did not turn up, and this proved to be a critical point in Dylan's demise. Instead of devoting his energies to dealing with the poet's ill-health, Brinnin turned in on himself, absorbed by his own feelings for Dylan, and "downcast" by his failure to keep the drinks date. At the evening performance of *Milk Wood*, Dylan was still sick and Brinnin felt alarm over the illness that he could read in his face. He failed again, both as friend and tour manager, to take any action.

The poet and critic, Reinhard Paul Becker, who had just published a German translation of *Deaths and Entrances*, was also in the audience. Afterwards, he went backstage, and found Dylan close to collapse, standing in his dressing room with his hands clinging to the back of a chair. Almost stammering, Dylan said: "I suppose I should be saying how glad I am to see you, but this circus out there has taken the life out of me for now." Becker stayed only briefly, but they arranged to meet again.

Dylan and Reitell came to see Brinnin the next morning, October 25, to talk about money. Brinnin's sense of having been "carelessly neglected" by Dylan now deepened. The "affectionate intimacy" of their relationship had disappeared. Brinnin was shocked with "disillusion...disappointment and anger... I was barely able to speak."

They drove together to the matinee performance of *Milk Wood* but Brinnin was in the grip of a "withering depression" and, instead of seeing the play, he spent the afternoon being comforted by Rollie McKenna. All thoughts of Dylan's health, and of his own professional responsibilities for Dylan's well-being, were now gone. Some of the actors, however, realised immediately that Dylan was very ill, including Roy Poole and Nancy Wickwire, who particularly noticed that he had lost his voice:

> He was desperately ill. As a matter of fact, we didn't think that
> we would be able to do the last performance because he was
> so ill... Dylan literally couldn't speak he was so ill...we really
> felt we're going to have to cancel it... still my greatest

memory of it is that he had no voice.
But the show went on.
The doctor gave him a shot of something and he seemed to recover... it was the most beautiful, inspiring, fantastic performance he ever gave of the play. After it was over he collapsed again... it was after this Sunday afternoon performance, it was the following Wednesday, that Dylan went into hospital and subsequently died. So it's even more important. *Roy?*
He was in bad physical condition... he drank quarts of ginger ale during that last performance, something I had never seen him do before.

The matinee was hailed as an outstanding performance and Reitell must have been pleased. But she had worked Dylan hard to achieve it. Within just five days, this sick man had been put through four rehearsals and two performances of *Milk Wood*, and there were at least two sessions of revising the script.

Brinnin and Reitell knew that Dylan's illness was not the usual gout or gastritis or the effects of drinking – both realised that it was something new and ominous. Brinnin was bewildered, upset and alarmed, as he put it, by what he recognised as serious signs of illness in Dylan. So why did they not cancel the New York performances of *Milk Wood* and his other engagements there?

Brinnin might not even have realised that cancellation was necessary. He later claimed he had got used to Dylan being ill but then recovering in time for his engagements. He probably also calculated that Feltenstein's injections could be relied upon to get Dylan through his commitments, as they had done a few months earlier during the May visit.

But self-interest really lay at the heart of the matter. Cancellation would have dented Brinnin's reputation and that of the Poetry Center. It would also have damaged his finances. They were in a worse mess than usual and he could not afford to have Dylan's engagements called off. He needed his agent's fee because his salary was due to be halved at the beginning of November.

And, as usual, Brinnin was up to his ears in debt. His long summer trip to Europe had been expensive. The income tax authorities were chasing him, threatening legal action. He had also paid Dylan's airfare to New York, as well as his expenses during his first days in the city. To do this, he had misappropriated money given to him by John Thompson for safekeeping. He told Thompson that to cope with his debts, he had been relying on claiming back from Dylan's earnings the money he was owed.

As for Reitell, there's little doubt that she was driven to get the play staged, and to make it succeed. Such unwavering determination was rooted in her character. She was, too, an only child who knew she had not lived up to her parents' expectations. She had a failed career and two broken marriages behind her – *Milk Wood* offered her a rare chance for a success in life.

Yet as Dylan gamely struggled on, a victim of Brinnin's financial embarrassment and Reitell's ambition, they stood feebly by, doing nothing effective about his deteriorating health. They were content to go along with Feltenstein's pills and injections, even though Reitell knew the doctor's medications were just a temporary boost to help Dylan get through the day. Why, then, did she not seek more appropriate medical care for him, even something as basic as a second or specialist opinion? Why was Dylan not taken to see Brinnin's New York doctor?

Again, it might have been a question of money. Feltenstein had a flexible pricing policy. On at least one occasion, he charged only a token fee when attending Dylan on the spring 1953 tour. It could have been very costly to have ditched him. Reitell also placed far too much faith in him, as she herself later acknowledged:

> I just took the doctor's word for it, assumed that he was being treated properly… boy, it's unbearable for me to think that because I'd had my family physician be Dylan's doctor… unbearable to think that if he'd had another doctor he might have lived. I can't bear that thought.

Reitell had probably become over-dependent on Feltenstein. He was the only doctor that she knew, and she had come to rely on him for help in her struggles with alcohol and periods of illness. Feltenstein could have unwittingly reinforced her dependence by the feelings of friendship that he easily cultivated with his patients. And both dependency and friendship can lead to misplaced loyalty – perhaps Reitell felt that going to another doctor, even for a second opinion, would have been a betrayal of a family friend.

Another factor was the fear of hospitalisation. Dylan came without medical insurance, and none was provided by the Poetry Center. When he needed to see Feltenstein in the spring of 1953, Reitell and Brinnin had paid the bills, and reclaimed the money from his earnings. But neither had the private means to fund specialist or hospital treatment. Free care was available in the municipal hospitals but Dylan might not have been eligible, and Reitell would probably have shied away from them – widely perceived as hospitals for the poor, they weren't quite the place to send a celebrity.

Here the snare that had been set in Laugharne just a month earlier snapped shut. Any hospital or specialist's bills would have eaten away at Dylan's earnings. They would also have been reduced if being in hospital had meant cancelled engagements. But Brinnin and Reitell knew very well that Dylan needed his earnings to fund his four weeks working with Stravinsky. Cancelling just one of his *Milk Wood* performances, or running up the medical fees of his previous trip, would have left him with an impossible $2 a day on which to live in California.

There was one other matter that kept Dylan away from better medical care. This was Reitell's saviour drive, her determination to rescue not only *Milk Wood* but its author as well, to save Dylan from himself and his drinking. Her missionary gene had kicked in and he had become her lost soul and good cause. She wanted, she said, not to reform Dylan but to save his life. She became, said a friend, his "militant guardian." The house manager at the Poetry Center said much the same, describing Reitell as Dylan's "tiger mother."

Such zealous protectiveness can lead to errors of judgement. Once she had fixed on the idea that she and Feltenstein could get him through, there was probably little that would have changed Reitell's mind. Perhaps she was so focused on her personal responsibility, as she saw it, to rescue Dylan that she was unable to see other options or to realise that she needed further help. This myopia was exacerbated both by Brinnin's indifference and by the difficulty she experienced in engaging Dylan in a serious discussion about his health.

Both Reitell's sense of guardianship and Brinnin's lack of real-world anchorage help to explain why they were unable to place Dylan's ill-health in a wider context of resources and networks that might have been able to help. Brinnin and Reitell were in a closed loop, seemingly unable or unwilling to reach outside, to talk to others about Dylan's developing illness.

They did not consult with Caitlin, perhaps understandably, even though Brinnin had the Boat House telephone number. Nor did they discuss matters with Dylan's London agent, David Higham, nor even with James Laughlin, who was well placed personally, and as Dylan's American publisher, to advance money to pay for appropriate medical treatment. Then there were the wealthy patrons of the arts, such as Ellen Borden Stevenson, with whom Dylan had stayed on his 1952 trip and who thereafter continued to keep him in funds – she was also organising his forthcoming visit to Chicago. She was known as someone who was always ready to offer financial help, as she did later when Dylan was in hospital.

Brinnin would have had to work through Oscar Williams to raise funds from Stevenson and, as it happened, he was at the party that followed the performance of *Under Milk Wood* on October 25. But yet again, the last thing on Brinnin's mind was Dylan's health. He and Reitell spent most of the time discussing the dangers of being in love with Dylan. They saw themselves as victims of an enchantment. Reitell said she was losing all sense of her own existence. Dylan had warned her on several occasions that he felt like a murderer, killing off through betrayal those that loved him the most. The briefest review of Dylan's emotional life, they concluded, would suggest that no man was more adept in killing what he loved.

As their discussion concluded, Reitell told Brinnin that she would tell Dylan that she could no longer be with him, or take care of him. Brinnin's alarm bells should really have been ringing now. Reitell's decision had serious implications for Dylan's well-being and thus for Brinnin's own duty of care, particularly with the second week approaching when Dylan would have no work engagements to keep him occupied.

That same night, Brinnin left for Boston; he did not see Dylan again until November 5, when he was lying in coma in hospital.

As his train pulled away from Grand Central, he would have been greatly relieved that Dylan had earned $400 from the two performances of *Under Milk Wood*. This was just enough to replace the money that he had misappropriated from John Thompson to pay for Dylan's airfare and other expenses.

Brinnin arrived back in the early morning and drove "very drunk & weary" to his university classes. Then he returned home for two days of socialising, shopping and teaching. He was also busy with arrangements for the next six speakers at the Center who were due in quick succession over the coming weeks. His job there was draining away his time and energy, with "packed houses all along [and] more subscribers than we know what to do with."

Brinnin buried his head deeply in the Boston sand. His actions were justified, he wrote later, because he believed that Reitell's own long bouts with ill health would make her sensitive to any worrisome change that Dylan might show. This was a fatuous judgement that Brinnin wisely removed from the published version of his book. It provides another insight into his lack of anchorage in the real world.

In New York meanwhile, Dylan was not feeling at his best; not surprisingly, the two *Milk Wood* performances had taken their toll. The day after the matinee, he was both ill and mentally confused. He got drunk in the Algonquin, and went into a raving fantasy about his family and war, talking of blood, mutilation and death in a way that seemed to recall William Killick's shooting at New Quay in 1945. At the White Horse in the evening, Dylan was too ill to stay for more than a few minutes so Reitell took him back to the hotel. She had relented and was still taking care of him.

The following day, October 27, was Dylan's thirty-ninth birthday. In the evening, he went to a party in his honour but was so unwell that he left after an hour. Yet again they returned to the hotel where Reitell put him to bed. That was the lowest that she had ever seen him; his birthday party, she recalled, marked the beginning of the end.

Brinnin phoned from Boston later in the evening to wish him happy birthday but Dylan barely responded. Brinnin "sensed that he was either ill or had had too much to drink." He could have talked to Reitell to find out which was the case, but he chose not to, even though it was barely three days since he had seen for himself the seriousness of Dylan's condition.

Here was the first opportunity lost for Brinnin to return to New York, take control of the situation and press for a second, or specialist, medical opinion. And he could so easily have returned; the next day, he went to Storrs, to the University of Connecticut. He finished his teaching at 2pm and could then have travelled to see Dylan, who was just some two hours drive away. Instead, Brinnin went back to Boston, spending the late afternoon and evening with Bill Read, before going to the cinema.

Dylan had now been in New York for a week, and for much of the time he had been a sick man, showing signs of fever and fatigue and, on at least one occasion, gasping for breath. He had also temporarily lost his voice. He was having vitamin injections from Milton Feltenstein, as well as ACTH and phenobarbitone, the last given by Reitell but presumably prescribed for her by Feltenstein. Nothing is known about how many times Dylan took this sedative on this last trip but he had grown used to taking it in New York to help with his chronic sleeping problems. If his liver was damaged, a regular intake of phenobarbitone would have accumulated in his body, and adversely affected his breathing.

Despite being unwell, Dylan took the subway to his two engagements on October 28 in order, he said, to save money. The Stravinsky project was imminent, and made even more real by a letter from the composer. The new guest room was ready and he wanted to know the date of his arrival in Hollywood. Dylan also needed to take money back to Laugharne; not only did Caitlin have to be placated but he now had to fund the school fees of their two older children. He was also worried about the debts he had left behind in the town though, unknown to him, they had already been paid in full.

After a reading at City College, he took part that evening in a symposium held at Cinema 16. George Reavey was there. There was no more keen observer of Dylan's health, and he was another to note Reitell's militant guardianship:

> *How did Dylan seem?*
> He was looking rather ill on the platform... very, very sad and sick looking.
> *How did you feel about this?*

> I was becoming worried... I said to myself I must talk to
> Dylan alone and warn him. But this finally proved impossible.
> *Why was that?*
> He was moving about in a sort of daze and was always
> surrounded. Reitell was doing all the planning for him.
> Messages to the Hotel Chelsea were not being delivered to
> him.

Afterwards, Dylan went to the White Horse, returning with Reitell to the Chelsea just after four in the morning. Brinnin was tucked up in bed in Boston, perhaps dreaming of the pleasant weekend ahead. He was off to Washington to do some research, and then back home for Halloween to entertain Rollie McKenna.

Romantic dreams aside, Brinnin also had the satisfaction of knowing that the money he would soon receive for Dylan's City College and Cinema 16 engagements would almost cover his agent's fee for the first part of the trip. Whatever might happen on the rest of the tour, Dylan had already earned enough to put Brinnin financially in the clear; would the thread of responsibility now get even weaker?

As for Dylan, he still had other expenses to meet, including his travel to California, so he would not be banking money for the month with Stravinsky until his last two engagements at Mt Holyoke and Chicago.

Left Adrift: Thursday October 29 – Wednesday November 4

October 29 was the day that John Brinnin wrote himself out of the story. He travelled to New York on the 1pm train, but it was a stay in the city that he did not reveal in his account of Dylan's last days. He spent a few hours working at the Poetry Center, and then, at 8.40pm, compèred a reading by Archibald MacLeish. Afterwards, Brinnin hung about town for a couple of hours before boarding the early morning sleeper to Washington. The day had provided yet another opportunity to assess the deteriorating health of his charge but he did not make contact with Dylan or Reitell.

Even so, he still had more than enough information to have known that Dylan would be put at grave risk during his next seven days in New York. His engagements in the city were over and he was free to do as he wished, until he travelled to Boston on November 5. He was not a man who passed his spare time in art galleries, bookshops or concerts. Both Brinnin and Reitell knew that he would spend it socialising and drinking, all to the further detriment of his health. Brinnin had experienced three earlier tours, and was not short of predictions on what would happen – Laughlin, Caitlin and Capote, and probably others as well, had given warnings. The writing was clearly on the wall for all to see.

Dylan was already dangerously debilitated, through a surfeit of alcohol and a lack of sleep and food - his last proper meal had been on October 22. Exhausted by the demands of his first week, he was now even more vulnerable to infection. He had become a respiratory casualty waiting to happen, a chain smoker with a weakened immune system and a history of chest complaints, living out his life in smoky bars, in a city with badly polluted air. Looking back, Reitell recalled that in these last few days Dylan was "enormously ill", spending much of his time in bed:

> Everything became more difficult for him. Getting to a party, for a meeting, to some pre-arranged event just became increasingly difficult. It was a hardship and more and more frequently he would become truly physically ill...that was a big change from the Dylan who was still able to get around and do things and the Dylan who couldn't...

This later testimony counters the impression that she and Brinnin gave in his account of the death that, towards the end, Dylan suffered from nothing more than hangovers. Ruthven Todd, another old friend from London living in New York, has also warned that Brinnin gave only a partial picture. Although Dylan drank too much during his last weeks, he was also physically ill and, wrote Todd, a sick man before he left London.

What Dylan needed was complete rest, with a wholesome diet, clean air and an environment that held few opportunities to drink. Several of his friends had places in the countryside around New York, including McKenna. Since she was away visiting Brinnin, her house would have been available. Dylan and Reitell could have gone there for a long Halloween weekend, working on *Milk Wood* revisions, filling in the time before he was due to leave for Boston.

It would not have been easy to lever Dylan out of New York, or even to convince him that he needed looking after. But this should have been the moment for devising some stratagem to get him away, perhaps persuading him that time away from the hotel would save money vital to the Stravinsky project. With a little more ingenuity, determination and arm-twisting, the story could so easily have had a different ending.

In the two days after his Cinema 16 appearance, Dylan lunched and partied in his usual liquid style. He met up again with Reinhard Paul Becker, who found him good company but he says nothing of his health. They made fun of America and Americans, and talked of marriage and sex. They went to see *From Here to Eternity*, almost certainly the last film Dylan saw before his own final journey:

> *You didn't think much of it, did you?*
> The audience was deeply moved by the film, and we finally had to leave, because people would have lynched us for laughing at the wrong moments.
> *You also went to a burlesque theatre.*
> We discovered mutually a great fascination with burlesque, almost impossible to admit in better company in America.
> *And the prostitutes, Reinhard?*
> We attempted to invite two very pretty negresses and discovered, to our dismay, when we were already at their rather luxurious apartment on the East Side of Manhattan, that we did not have enough money with us to meet their extremely high price.

Dylan began the weekend of tricking and treating with a dinner party on October 30 at Ruthven Todd's house. Reitell phoned beforehand and asked Todd not to give him whisky. The guests included Herb Hannum and the artists, Dave and Rose Slivka, who were to have walk-on parts in the unfolding drama of Dylan's last days. Also present was a young black novelist, Al Anderson, with whom Dylan spent time discussing writing techniques, drinking beer all evening and making no effort to get drunk.

Afterwards, he went to the White Horse with Reitell and Hannum. A photograph taken in the bar reveals the deterioration

15. Wrecked in the White Horse, October 30 1953

in his health. His face and right hand look bloated. He has a cigarette in his other hand. He is drinking straight whiskies. His money has been flung carelessly aside. He looks thoughtful, even worried. The headlines in the newspaper on the bar scream of atrocities in Korea.

Some of the next day was spent with Harvey Breit of the *New York Times*, interrupted by lunch with Reitell, when Dylan ate next to nothing, merely picking at the dishes he had ordered. In the evening, Breit took him to a dinner party, noting later that he saw nothing about him that was unusual and that he "seemed normally well (or normally unwell)."

Out in the city, air pollution had already risen to above normal levels, and was set to worsen. Dylan arrived drunk at the White Horse at 9pm. He carried on drinking with various friends, including Dave Slivka and the young poet David Wagoner. He returned to his hotel in the early hours of November 1, not long after he had been seen popping pills – a private detective noted he was taking benzedrine, though Wagoner has challenged this report. Dylan woke up at midday and went back to the White Horse, where he drank beer and raw eggs, a diet which had provided his only nourishment for the past few days:

> *George, you saw Dylan at the White Horse that Sunday?*
> Again with Reitell... I must say I never felt at ease in Reitell's company and that of her friends... I think some of them were drug addicts and Dylan himself looked a bit drugged.
> *You were still worried about him?*
> They seemed to be isolating him and introducing him into their set. It wasn't as if they were taking care of him, but rather exploiting his "bohemianism" or their own notion of it.
> *Did he say he was feeling ill?*
> He was complaining of a burnt-up feeling inside and had missed a lunch engagement. He looked sicker and sadder and, when I asked him about Caitlin, answered that he wasn't sure if he still had a wife.
> *You said something earlier about a book...*
> Hannum had a copy of a book by Norman Cameron and Dylan became rather concerned about people dying so young. One had a feeling he was thinking about himself. Reitell then took him off to some party...

Dylan attended not one but two parties, the second of which, after midnight, was at Howard Moss' apartment. Like his good friend Brinnin, Moss was another who took prescription drugs to help his peace of mind – he was also a Feltenstein patient. Dylan read poems to the party and then went with Moss onto the terrace of the apartment. Brinnin suggests that they went to look at a rose bush. Dylan bent to examine it and, the story goes, scratched his eyeball on a thorn.

But why would he go out just to examine a rose? He had never been interested in gardening or flowers, especially in the early hours of the morning while a party was going on. A more likely explanation is that he went outside because he was having trouble with his breathing. It was a warm night, 57°F at midnight.

The party ended about 5am and Dylan and Reitell returned to the Chelsea. A few floors away, the poet John Berryman was hitting the bottle, having recently moved into the hotel from his mother's house. An old friend of Dylan, he was also an old adversary of Brinnin, who thirteen years earlier had competed with him for a Hopwood Award. Berryman had pleaded with Brinnin to withdraw his entry, but he refused and went on to win, leaving Berryman deeply embittered.

Dylan had only a few hours sleep before Ruthven Todd turned up. Although Dylan was not feeling well, they talked, joked and drank beer from cans of Ballantine in the refrigerator. Dylan had been reading a Ray Bradbury paperback. By the bed, lay a bundle of unread copies of the *Times Literary Supplement*. Todd also noted that a bottle of Old Grandad whisky had not been opened, an important observation that would become part of Todd's testimony that Dylan had not drunk himself into a coma on the day of his collapse.

Todd stayed long enough to help Dylan sort out various drafts of his unfinished poem, 'Elegy'. For much of the rest of the day, November 2, Dylan worked on the script of *Under Milk Wood* in preparation for the version to be published in *Mademoiselle*. In the early evening, he decided to go out. This was not the best thing to have done: the temperature was in the sixties and air pollution had reached its highest point for several days. It was now at a level that was considered a health risk to those with respiratory problems.

At the White Horse, old friends were already there, including Slivka and Wagoner, who thought that Dylan was his usual half-morose, half-jovial self, telling jokes and reciting poems, including the lyric to an old music hall number that ended "I have been a nice boy, done what was expected. I shall die an old bum, loved but unrespected."

George Reavey was also amongst the group. He thought that Dylan looked sick and depressed. Reitell talked about Moss' party and implied it had been a rather wild one:

> Christ, I thought, why are they taking him to parties like that. The man can hardly stand on his feet... a week of NY alcohol (it's stronger here) and late nights was already doing damage,

apart from whatever else was going on.
Oscar, you were also in the White Horse.
For some strange reason, although I'd seen Dylan dozens and
dozens of times, we shook hands. And that was the oddest
thing of all, because I never saw him alive again. At least, I
saw him alive, but in a coma.

Dylan and Reitell left the bar and ended up at a dinner at the
Colony Club, where Dylan ate next to nothing. He became ill, and
vomited. Reitell took him to another bar, but he complained he
was hungry, and demanded they return to the Chelsea. They
bought food at a delicatessen but back at the hotel he refused
everything but a bowl of soup. It had not been a good Halloween
for Dylan.

The next day, Tuesday November 3, was election day. Todd
was again amongst the first visitors to the hotel room. Dylan was
not feeling at all well, but they had a beer together. When the hotel
maid came in, Dylan insisted that Todd open the bottle of Old
Grandad and pour her a drink. As for Dylan's health, Feltenstein
had warned him "to go easy on everything – except food, of
which he was to take a great deal more."

Reitell went out to vote, with Todd going along for company.
On her return at about 3pm, she found Dylan in the middle of a
drinking session with Hannum and Wagoner, not exactly what she
had in mind when she had asked them to look after him. Dylan
looked tired but he was doing his best to be amusing, busily invent-
ing a schizoid bar in which one was one's only customer.
According to Brinnin, Reitell broke up the party. Todd has contra-
dicted this, writing that he took everyone off to his basement to
drink beer, because bars in the city were closed for the election.

At some stage that day, a lecture agent had arrived at the hotel.
Dylan signed a contract, guaranteeing a thousand dollars a week
for his services. After the meeting, he lay down on the bed,
exhausted and depressed, a state of mind that may have been
caused by a telegram he received from Caitlin saying, according
to one version, "You have left me no alternative but suicide or the
streets. Hate. Caitlin." Dylan was just hours away from his
whisky-drinking episode in the White Horse; a few days later,
Reitell would claim that the telegram was responsible, and that up
to this point she had been managing his drinking.

In the evening, Dylan and Reitell planned to go to the theatre together, but he felt too ill and they returned to the hotel. He lay on the bed, again totally exhausted, hardly surprising since he had not eaten or slept properly for more than ten days. To Reitell, Dylan's exhaustion seemed as much mental as physical and, barely able to talk, he fell asleep immediately.

She nursed him through the late evening, as he drifted in and out of sleep, waking in tears to speak of his youngest son. Dylan also confided that he and Caitlin could no longer live together. Weeping uncontrollably, he fell asleep again. What occurred next is so well known it hardly merits repeating. Yet there are still many questions to ask about what really happened in the hours before Dylan's collapse.

★ ★ ★

Dylan woke up at about 2am on November 4. It was another warm night – 58°F – and it was probably stuffy in the bedroom. "I've got to have a drink," he told Reitell, "I've got to go out and have a drink. I'll come back in half an hour." But why go out, when there was an almost-full bottle of Old Grandad in the hotel room, and beers in the fridge as well? The most likely answer is that Dylan was already having trouble with his breathing – he also told Reitell that "he just wanted air."

He took a taxi to the White Horse, not the best place to go for fresh air. The men behind the bar were the owner, Ernie Wohlleben, and his two barmen. The next day, Todd asked them what Dylan had been drinking. They thought he had ordered straight whiskies, though they could not be certain,

But in the bar that night had been an acquaintance, the painter John CuRoi. He saw Dylan with eight highballs lined up on his table, though he does not say whether or not he drank them all. CuRoi also noted that Dylan's colour was "horrifying" and that he was very bloated: "The man seemed a monster puppet."

Dylan did not spend all his time drinking. He talked with Wohlleben, and with one of the barmen, Kevin Rooney, a young writer working to make extra money. Dylan also sat with two academic types, who made fun of him by cramming his mouth with cigars.

He made a telephone call from the bar to Len Lye, yet another friend from his London days. Dylan asked if he could borrow a tuxedo that he could take to Hollywood. Lye did not want to be disturbed and told him: "I'm working in the cellar." Dylan replied: "I'm away down below cellar." They talked for a further ten minutes, mostly banter and word play.

Dylan returned to the hotel around 3.30am and, according to Brinnin, told Reitell laconically: "I've had eighteen straight whiskies. I think that's the record." This was the equivalent to thirty-six British singles, enough to kill someone. If he had drunk that much, or anything like it, he would not have been laconic but incoherent, even speechless.

Dylan's boast has been rightly dismissed by his biographers. Todd did some research at the White Horse the very next day. None of the people who had been there had noticed Dylan drinking excessively. Todd found that Dylan averaged a little more than one drink every quarter of an hour i.e. six to eight in all:

> Owing to ABC, the Alcoholic Board of Control in New York, a man can tell exactly how many drinks have been used out of a bottle in the previous evening. In the case of Dylan, he had either six... or he might very well have had eight, but that is all he could have had. Six multiplied by three is eighteen – sounds better, and I suppose Dylan, like a Welshman, was making a good story better.

Helpful though it is, Todd's research still leaves some doubt about how much whisky Dylan actually drank. For straight whisky, bartenders usually poured two ounces, but for highballs they poured only one and a half. Some barmen would benignly reduce these measures if they thought a customer had already drunk too much. Others would charge for two ounces, give the customer one, and keep the other for themselves.

There is no material in Brinnin's account that suggests how drunk Dylan really was. His phone conversation with Lye suggests that we should be cautious about this. He was sufficiently sober to be concerned about the proprieties of going to Hollywood, and to remember that Lye had an over-size tuxedo stored in his basement. He was sober enough to remember, or to look up, Lye's number, and to dial it. And he was also sober enough to carry on an extended, if somewhat surreal, conversation with him.

In fact, Dylan was sober enough to climb the stairs from the lobby of the Chelsea, get the room key out of his pockets, find the key hole and turn the key. He opened the door, walked across to the bed and knelt on the floor, placing his head in Reitell's lap. Brinnin does not report that Reitell had said anything about Dylan's speech being slurred or whether he staggered, swayed or stumbled as he came across the room. Nor does she mention any such behaviour in her 1983 interview.

Dylan had also been sufficiently sober for the barmen to keep on serving him, as Brinnin himself later acknowledged: "I suspect... that the figure of '18 whiskies' is hyperbolic. In his condition, Dylan would not have known how many he had consumed, and I doubt that any bar tender...would have continued to serve him." Todd, who had often been refused drinks in the White Horse, has also made a similar point, writing that Wohlleben would have stopped any marathon drinking: "a dead customer puts no money in the till."

Just two weeks after Dylan's death, Todd wrote a detailed, twelve-page letter describing Dylan's last days, beginning with the morning of November 3. It was written in close collaboration with Reitell, who helped to compose and revise it. If the drinking episode in the White Horse was a key moment in Dylan's collapse, why does the letter say nothing at all about the eighteen whiskies, or even of his visit to the White Horse?

There is only one plausible explanation. When they were writing the letter, they both knew, from Todd's survey of local bars, that Dylan had drunk eight, not eighteen, whiskies and that the visit to the White Horse had had nothing to do with his death. In time, Reitell was prepared to admit the truth: ten years later, she acknowledged that the amount drunk could "have been any number, more or less." Thirty years on, she was more precise: "he probably exaggerated, probably had eight."

But when in 1954 she had sat down with Brinnin to help write his account of how Dylan died, she seems conveniently to have forgotten Todd's survey. Brinnin was happy to publish the story about the eighteen whiskies without any reservation or qualification, as if he himself believed it to be a fact beyond challenge. Yet he knew it to be hyperbolic; he also knew, from Todd's survey, that it was so hyperbolic that it was untrue. The story became part of the cover-up, the classic ploy of blaming the victim.

Dylan and Reitell slept through to mid-morning on November 4, which could justifiably be called the Day of the Strangely Empty Hotel Room. Throughout his stay, Dylan's room was usually full of people coming and going but, remarkably, there is no account of anyone visiting him on November 4. It was the day when everyone was somewhere else, or said they were.

Dylan woke up complaining he was suffocating, that he had to get out into the fresh air straight away. He was feeling so unwell that when Todd telephoned, Dylan told him that he was too ill to meet up with him – Todd thought he sounded "terrible." Reitell recalled that Dylan was feeling "dreadful, just simply dreadful."

Harvey Breit was another to telephone; they had arranged to meet that evening and he wanted to check the appointment still stood. He thought that Dylan sounded "bad." And, as with Wickwire ten days earlier, it is Breit's description of Dylan's voice that catches our attention: it was "low and hoarse." Breit wanted to say "You sound as though from the tomb", but he told him instead that he sounded like Louis Armstrong.

Dylan was now just twelve hours away from his collapse and admission to St Vincent's Hospital, where physical examination and an X-ray would show he had both pneumonia and severe bronchitis. His respiratory difficulties could have been exacerbated by the warm weather, and by rising levels of air pollution in the city during the previous few days. No wonder he sounded like Armstrong or that he felt he was suffocating.

Dylan and Reitell left the hotel. The weather was getting cooler but it was still 50°F outside. They walked a few blocks and ended up at the White Horse. Len Lye was there. They had a couple of beers and Dylan arranged to collect the tuxedo. But he was too sick to stay for long so Reitell took him back to the Chelsea, where he lay on the bed coughing, "ghastly racking spasms", as she was to describe them. At about 2pm, Reitell called Feltenstein, and he injected Dylan with ACTH and also with morphine, which should be given to patients with chest disease only with the greatest caution.

This was probably the moment that Reitell told Feltenstein

about the eighteen whiskies. Dylan's fate was sealed – almost everything that would now occur happened because Feltenstein accepted the story that Dylan had drunk a large amount of whisky. Tragically, both Feltenstein and Reitell would interpret Dylan's developing respiratory illness as confirmation of this.

He slept through the afternoon, occasionally waking to vomit. By this stage, most of the whisky he had drunk in the White Horse during the early hours would have been metabolised from his body. When he woke up, he had another attack of nausea and vomiting. Feltenstein came again to the hotel room. He gave Dylan a lecture about the need for a new medical regime, and insisted that he cancel his next three reading engagements – at long last, someone had recognised that he was too ill to go on working.

After listening to his protests, Feltenstein agreed that he could do one further reading but no more. This meant, as Dylan and Reitell would have realised, that the Stravinsky project would be dead in the water. Feltenstein then injected him with more ACTH and morphine. On his way out, he had a private word with Reitell. He told her that Dylan was "very ill." Later, she recalled that Feltenstein's "prognosis was bad." From another account, it seems that he believed that Dylan was at risk of acute liver failure.

After he had left, Reitell phoned Brinnin at 4-30pm, and told him to cancel Dylan's weekend social appointments. She described his deteriorating condition and Feltenstein's two visits that day to the hotel room. Brinnin heard these reports "with considerable alarm." This was his last opportunity to do something to save Dylan but he chose not to return to New York, only an hour away by air and less than four by train. Had Brinnin done so, he might well have had the chance to get Dylan admitted to hospital. But he had other plans for the evening. A friend had been invited round for dinner; afterwards, they went to the cinema.

Perhaps Brinnin thought that everything was being done to help Dylan. Even if this were true, it was still his responsibility, both to his employers and to Dylan, to return to New York to satisfy himself that his charge was receiving the best possible medical care. But he was so lackadaisical that, between October 25 and November 4, he made just one phone call to the Chelsea hotel, and that was to wish Dylan happy birthday, not to find out about his health. Brinnin's inaction throughout the crisis seems astonishing, given that the most celebrated poet of the time was in his care.

After her phone call to Brinnin, Reitell went out to buy the ingredients for a new diet that Feltenstein had recommended for Dylan. The events of the next five hours or so, between her shopping trip and Feltenstein's third visit to the hotel, remain much of a mystery. Brinnin devotes just seven lines to this critical period, observing only that Dylan slept and vomited. It is known that some friends came to the hotel room – the report of the private detective refers to a "get-together". It seems that this occurred whilst Reitell was out, for the detective then noted "Reitell. Friends left." Had she found that the get-together had turned into a drinking session and thrown them out? Was one of them Harvey Breit, keeping his evening appointment with Dylan? And why did Brinnin not mention this get-together in his book?

Whatever happened in the hotel room, if anything, prompted speculation that it must have been something which was detrimental to Dylan's health, and which Brinnin covered up. But there is one thing we do know about these 'missing' five hours. During this time, Reitell tried to calm Dylan with a quarter grain of phenobarbitone given to her by Feltenstein. But Dylan, says Todd, was unable to keep it down.

George Reavey tells another story. When he met Reitell at the hospital, she talked to him about giving Dylan pills. She referred to "those pills", as if she felt guilty about them. Other friends had also heard Reitell "in a hysterical state moan about pills the first day D.T. was taken to the hospital." Rose Slivka had been heard to say defensively: "We all take pills." The sensitivity about pills continued: a reference to Reitell giving Dylan phenobarbitone on October 21 was removed from the published version of Brinnin's book.

But whatever pills Reitell felt guilty about, they could not have been phenobarbitone. It has a long half-life in the body, measured more in days than hours, and Dylan later tested negative for barbiturates at St Vincent's, as well as for other drugs.

Sometime in the late evening, Dylan complained of seeing things, not animals, he said, but triangles, squares and circles.

Reitell decided that he was having delirium tremens, but she was wrong. People with DTs commonly hallucinate snakes, animals and insects; Dylan hallucinated abstract shapes. Neither did he show other signs associated with DTs, such as seeing and shouting at hallucinated people, picking at the bedclothes and staring wildly. Nor, according to Brinnin's account and Reitell's 1983 interview, did he show any mental confusion, disorientation or terror. There are also other difficulties with Reitell's diagnosis of DTs, which I discuss in a note on page 194.

Reitell's problem in making her assessment of DTs was that she was unable objectively to evaluate what was happening to Dylan. She could think only of an alcohol-based explanation for his hallucinations. She knew nothing of his chest disease. And in the moments of developing crisis, she forgot that a few days earlier she had recognised that his illness was something new, not gout, gastritis or drinking-related.

What Reitell wrongly described as DTs were undoubtedly hallucinations brought on by morphine and fever, as well as an impaired supply of oxygen caused by Dylan's pneumonia and bronchitis. The combined effects of all three would have been exacerbated by his chronic lack of food and sleep.

Reitell immediately summoned Feltenstein back to the hotel. He seems to have accepted her diagnosis of DTs without question, equally blinkered by a narrow perception of his patient as a man with a history of heavy drinking. He examined Dylan and injected him with ACTH and 30mg of morphine, more than three times the dose normally used for pain relief, telling Reitell it was for "the brain episode."

According to Brinnin, Feltenstein then warned that Dylan could become uncontrollable, a curious prediction for someone who had just been heavily sedated. Did Feltenstein really say this or was Brinnin covering up for what was actually said? Thirty years later, Reitell's memory was clear about Feltenstein's warning: "Dr Feltenstein said to me 'Liz, he must have someone with him all the time. He might go into a coma… anything could happen now'." If Reitell's recall is correct, it means that Feltenstein knew full well the risks he was taking in giving Dylan such a large dose of morphine, and that coma was a distinct possibility.

Feltenstein advised Reitell to find someone to help her look after Dylan, who was now in serious trouble as the third injection of morphine began further to depress his breathing. She phoned Todd, but he was out at a crime writers' dinner. So an old friend, the painter Jack Heliker, came over. Feltenstein left the hotel at 11pm, leaving his patient, who he believed was seriously ill, in the care of two people with no medical or even nursing experience. And one of these, Reitell, was close to exhaustion herself, having had only a few hours sleep over the last three nights.

Feltenstein's behaviour on Wednesday November 4 when he attended Dylan at the Chelsea seems extraordinary for an experienced doctor. He believed that Dylan was very ill, with a bad prognosis, possibly because his liver was in danger of failing. He also thought that Dylan had delirium tremens, and that he was at risk of slipping into a coma, or of becoming uncontrollable. Why, then, did he not admit him to hospital immediately?

November 5: A botched emergency

After Feltenstein's third injection of morphine, Dylan became a little more peaceful, and Reitell and Heliker "had some sweet calm talks" with him. At about midnight, she sat beside him and held his hand. She felt his grip stiffen, and there was "the terrible sound of this breathing", a gasping sound from deep inside his throat, which she described as a stoppage of Dylan's normal breathing. Then she saw his face going blue.

Dylan was now in crisis: his pneumonia and bronchitis were affecting his ability to get sufficient oxygen into his blood through his lungs. His body would have tried to compensate by increasing the respiratory rate i.e. breathing faster. But the morphine was working in the other direction, reducing the respiratory rate. Dylan drifted into an oxygen-starved coma, the most significant causes of which were pneumonia, bronchitis and morphine.

His life could possibly have been saved if he had been given immediate medical treatment, but it took almost two hours to get him to a hospital. This botched emergency was one of the most critical incidents in the chain of neglect that led to his death. Instead of phoning for an ambulance, Reitell tried to contact Feltenstein. She has left no clue as to why she did this. We can only guess that it was probably a mixture of panic, inexperience and a paralysing anxiety about the costs of hospital treatment.

Feltenstein seems to have been unavailable, and did not arrive in the hotel room until about 1am, on Thursday morning, November 5 – a whole hour had been wasted in the fight for Dylan's life. Feltenstein immediately phoned for an ambulance which arrived a few minutes later. With the crew was Dr Boyce, on night duty at St Vincent's. They noticed that Dylan's lips were blue, and that his breathing was weak and shallow. They gave him oxygen but they knew it would do him little good because he was no longer breathing properly.

They stretchered him down to the street, and Feltenstein and Reitell climbed into the back of the ambulance with them. But there was yet more delay in getting Dylan to hospital. St Vincent's emergency room was in the Seton Building, just a few blocks from the Chelsea, on the corner of 11th Street and 7th Avenue. It was just some five minutes drive away for an ambulance at night. But Dylan did not arrive until 1.58am, as his medical notes confirm. This further hour's delay has never been adequately explained.

Drs McVeigh and Gilbertson were on duty in the emergency room. They were second-year residents from New York university – junior doctors, with less than three years experience since qualifying. Feltenstein told them that Dylan was a famous poet, who had fallen into a coma after a bout of heavy drinking. It seems that he was slow to mention that he had injected Dylan with morphine. Only after being questioned further and in more detail, did he tell the two doctors that he had injected 30mg of morphine shortly before Dylan went into coma.

Dylan was given Dilantin to calm seizures brought on by the impaired flow of oxygen to his brain. Assisted by a nurse, McVeigh and Gilbertson then worked for over an hour to restore his breathing to normal. It was now around 3.30 in the morning – he had not been breathing properly since midnight, but the doctors were unaware of this.

With the breathing stabilised, they were able to attach a saline and sugar drip, and take body fluid samples for testing. They found that the cerebro-spinal fluid was clear, so they were able to exclude a brain haemorrhage and an infection such as meningitis.

McVeigh and Gilbertson also carried out a physical examination. They noted that Dylan was profoundly comatose, and that both sides of his brain were malfunctioning. When they listened to his chest, they found that "coarse crepitant rales were audible in all areas." This was a sign that Dylan had bronchitis in all parts of the bronchial tree, both left and right sides. They immediately requested an X-ray of the chest.

Outside, Reitell and Todd were in the corridor when Brinnin arrived hotfoot from Boston. He put his arms around Reitell as she wept and tried to tell him about the events of the previous hours. She could only manage to say "Oh, John, why didn't I call the *police*?" No one calls the police, he replied, no one calls the police. Soon after, the swing doors of the corridor were flung open, and Dylan was wheeled past. He was wearing an oxygen mask, his hair limp and wet, his face blotchy with fever. Now began, said Brinnin, the five most dreadful days of his life.

5. In on a Thursday, Dead by the Monday

St Vincent's was neither the best nor the worst hospital in New York, lying somewhere between the elite institutions and the municipal hospitals. Originally a Catholic charity hospital, by the 1950s it expected most patients to pay for their care, either with their own money or through insurance. Paying patients with enough money were given a private room, but those with few or uncertain resources were placed in public wards.

And it was to a public ward that Dylan was sent. After leaving the emergency room, he was taken in the elevator to St Joseph's East, a men's medical ward on the third floor of the Seton Building, with space for some thirty patients.

In most American hospitals at the time, the standard of care for public ward patients was generally inferior. Paying patients in private rooms were guaranteed preferential nursing and medical treatment, having their own attending physician, who also had to be paid, as did any specialists who were called in. But ward patients were usually assigned to less experienced house staff, such as an intern just out of medical school or a junior resident.

Staffing levels were also a problem on public wards in most New York hospitals. Staff shortages and absences, including nurses, technicians, doctors and specialists, were a particular worry on weekends, which were unpopular amongst staff and more expensive for a hospital to fund. Unfortunately, Dylan was a "weekend patient", admitted to a public ward on a Thursday and dead by the Monday.

Dylan's ward was usually well staffed during the day but, as in most hospitals at that time, there were difficulties on the evening and night shifts, for which there were usually just three nurses per shift. Holidays and sickness could make the situation even worse. Priscilla Sassi worked the evening shift in the adjoining St Joseph's West in 1954, which was also a men's medical public ward. I asked her what conditions were like:

> On the evening shift, St Joe's West was usually staffed by a
> registered nurse, a student nurse and an orderly or a nurse's

aid. During my time at St Joe's West, the registered nurse was on vacation. That is why I was there, a senior student nearing graduation.

Were you on your own?

I was helped by a first year student. I don't remember any orderly – maybe he was also on vacation... there was a nursing supervisor who made rounds throughout the hospital to check up on us and who was available for any unusual problems.

What about the patients?

Many were desperately ill. They were the victims of strokes, partially paralysed and unable to speak. Others were recovering from heart attacks or dying from cancer, cirrhosis or other diseases.

It must have been tough.

The work was brutally hard, especially since we had no orderly to help lift the heavier patients. We had to prepare them for the night, change their sheets if necessary, and clean them up. I gave out all the medications; we changed dressings, irrigated bladders and colostomies, managed the IVs and on and on. I never got to write my charts until the night shift came on at midnight...

It's hardly surprising that private nurses were hired to come to St Vincent's to look after Dylan, paid for by his friends, including Brinnin, McKenna and Ruthven Todd who borrowed the money from the White Horse – Dylan would have appreciated the irony that the money he had spent on the 'eighteen whiskies' was being recycled to pay for his nursing care.

As for the doctors, Dylan was seen during his first day, November 5, by a Dr Keating, described in one account as a neurological specialist, but for most of the time McVeigh and Gilbertson continued to look after him. He was, of course, just one of the many patients that the two young doctors had to care for over the weekend. As junior doctors, they should have been supervised by a chief medical resident, but it seems that it was a day and a half before they were able to have a few minutes' discussion with Dr George Pappas, chief resident of neurosurgery at the hospital.

In the meantime, for those first critical thirty-six hours, McVeigh and Gilbertson were supervised by Milton Feltenstein, even though he had no position of authority in the hospital. And from the very outset, he insisted that they accept his diagnosis of acute alcoholic poisoning. They were in no position to argue back: they were junior doctors and he an experienced practitioner. Feltenstein was also a bear of a man, small but robust and barrel-chested, with a dominating physical presence, a "tough talking, take no prisoners type of guy."

Even more startling than Feltenstein's assumption of supervision, was the delay that occurred before the hospital's senior brain specialist examined Dylan – he did not arrive on the ward until the afternoon of November 6, some thirty-six hours after admission. This was Dr C.G. Gutierrez-Mahoney, who had been head of neurosurgery and neurology at St Vincent's since 1945. Dylan would now be looked after by one of the city's best brain specialists, even if he had arrived rather late in the day.

The delay, however, was not the fault of the hospital or Gutierrez-Mahoney. When Feltenstein decided to call in a brain specialist, he tried to hire the chief of neurosurgery at Beth Israel Hospital. But it took another day for Dr Leo Davidoff to reply. He said he was unavailable but that he unreservedly recommended none other than Gutierrez-Mahoney, who was immediately contacted and arrived shortly after at Dylan's bedside.

But why had Feltenstein recommended Davidoff? Feltenstein had admitting rights and privileges at Beth Israel where he had worked for over twenty years – presumably he knew Davidoff as a colleague. It might be that Feltenstein believed that bringing in a specialist he knew would give him more protection in covering-up any mistakes he had made in caring for Dylan. Whatever his reasoning, it resulted in a long delay before Dylan was seen by the hospital's senior brain specialist.

The dripping syringe

Dylan remained in a deep coma throughout the time he was in hospital, and his doctors were never hopeful about his survival. McVeigh and Gilbertson knew virtually nothing of his medical history. When they asked how long Dylan had been unconscious and not breathing properly, both Feltenstein and Reitell were unable, or unwilling, to help. George Reavey knew what was going on:

> *You talked with one of the doctors?*
> He said Dylan did not have a good chance from the beginning.
> *Because?*
> Because there had been no one to tell the hospital the case history or how long he had been in a coma before being brought. He said the people who had brought him had been too 'emotional' and they could not get any facts from them.
> *The hospital doctors obviously knew about the morphine by now.*
> He said that a morphine shot had been given to Dylan by his doctor and that may have been the cause of coma…
> *To be honest, they had very little to go on.*
> The doctor said "We were in the dark… they would have liked to know what happened to Mr. Thomas before he was brought here." This really sent shivers down our spine. After this, I began making notes.

Under Feltenstein's watchful supervision, McVeigh and Gilbertson treated Dylan for acute alcoholic encephalopathy i.e. they assumed that his brain had been directly damaged by a rapid intake of a large amount of alcohol some time prior to admission. This diagnosis was based only on the false information given by Feltenstein and Reitell that Dylan had drunk eighteen whiskies. The doctors were also told that Dylan had, in the past, drunk wood alcohol and also Smoke, a drink made by mixing stove fuel with alcohol.

Today, a patient's blood alcohol level would be measured to confirm any diagnosis made simply on the basis of information provided by others. Cerebrospinal fluid, urine and blood samples were taken some eighty minutes after Dylan was admitted, as soon as his breathing had been restored to normal. But the summaries of the hospital notes – see the appendix – contain no information on the amount of alcohol, if any, found in Dylan's body.

It might be that in 1953 a patient's body fluids were not routinely tested for alcohol. It's also possible that Milton Feltenstein so overawed the doctors with his diagnosis of alcoholic coma that they felt it unnecessary to measure Dylan's alcohol level. Feltenstein's stories about the eighteen whiskies, wood alcohol and Smoke would have served to deflect attention away from his treatment of Dylan, and to lend authority in the eyes of the two junior doctors to his own diagnosis.

It is not known what other steps, if any, McVeigh and Gilbertson took to corroborate Feltenstein's diagnosis. A doctor might look at a number of things to find out if someone had been drinking heavily – a flushed face, dilated pupils, low blood pressure and a rapid pulse. There is no record of a blood pressure reading, but we do know that Dylan's face was not flushed, but had a splotchy red-and-white appearance, and that his pulse was steady and his pupils small.

Doctors would also look for the smell of alcohol on a patient's breath but again there is no record of this in the summaries of the hospital notes. But during one of his several conversations with hospital staff, Reavey was told that alcohol had been detected on Dylan's breath – Reavey's notes tersely record "Dr smelt alcoh."

Four days later, when the hospital's Medical Summary was sent to the post-mortem with the body, the diagnosis of acute alcoholic brain damage was described as nothing more substantial than an "impression". In other words, the doctors had not found anything from body fluid tests or physical examination to support Reitell and Feltenstein's stories about a large alcohol intake prior to admission.

McVeigh and Gilbertson began to learn a little more about Dylan's general condition when the results came back from the laboratory. He tested negative for diabetes, and for poisoning by barbiturates and other drugs. His white cell count was raised, indicating the presence of an infection, undoubtedly that in his lungs. As for Dylan's serum amylase, it was normal, indicating that he probably did not have pancreatitis, often a complication of both acute and chronic alcohol abuse.

The two doctors already knew, from their physical examination, that Dylan had extensive bronchitis. When the chest X-ray results came back, the report indicated that he also had bronchial pneumonia, though a doctor's note on the report "was not strongly stated." This might have been because the pneumonia was at an early stage or because Feltenstein had put pressure on the doctor to moderate his note – it would have been in

Feltenstein's interests to play down the pneumonia, and to play up the alcohol.

No record remains of how the doctors viewed the relationship between Dylan's chest disease and the 30mg of morphine that Feltenstein had injected. Although it would not on its own have been fatal, Dylan's breathing would have already been impaired by his pneumonia and bronchitis.

Had Feltenstein been negligent in giving the morphine? There are three possibilities. First, that he did not examine Dylan properly and failed to diagnose that he had pneumonia and bronchitis. In ignorance of this chest disease, he gave Dylan the morphine. Second, that he knew about the pneumonia, failed to treat it with appropriate drugs and, further, took the extremely hazardous course of injecting morphine. In either case, Feltenstein could be open to criticisms of failing his patient.

Third, that the pneumonia was at such an early stage on November 4 that no doctor could have been expected to detect it. But it was almost as hazardous giving 30mg of morphine to a patient with severe bronchitis. And Dylan's bronchitis would have been resoundingly obvious if Feltenstein had listened to his chest.

There is no evidence from Reitell that Feltenstein examined Dylan's chest in the hotel room. Whether talking to Brinnin or to later biographers, or in subsequent correspondence with them, she has never mentioned that Feltenstein was concerned about Dylan's lungs and his breathing. She has only ever referred to delirium tremens and coma. And Feltenstein himself has suggested that he missed Dylan's chest disease – he later acknowledged to a colleague that Dylan had died because of his failure to carry out diagnostic tests and to prescribe appropriate medication.

An experienced doctor in his late forties, Milton Feltenstein could have been expected to know about the depressing effects of morphine on respiration. Its impact on breathing was well known to medical practitioners in America in 1953. It had been understood since at least the nineteenth century, most notably described in Salter's medical text published in America in 1864.

But what did the textbooks have to say about using morphine to treat DTs? Should Feltenstein have injected it? Apparently not – its use in treating delirium tremens was unequivocally contraindicated in leading American texts at the time, as well as in medical reference books used by doctors. In fact, the standard treatment then for DTs was immediate hospitalisation, with a therapy of glucose, insulin and paraldehyde.

It would be too easy to demonise Feltenstein, the feckless doctor caught with the smoking gun in his hand – or at least, the dripping syringe. But any professional failings on his part must be set against Dylan's long-term indifference to his own well-being. His inability to take his health seriously, to stop smoking, to drink less, and to eat and sleep properly led to a general debilitation which ensured that his chronic and acute bronchitis would lead, through pneumonia, to his death.

If there had been no injections of morphine, Dylan would still have died if his pneumonia had remained undetected and untreated. And without the chest disease, the morphine would have done him little, if any, harm. Feltenstein's real culpability lay not in the injections but in overlooking Dylan's chest disease, and in not admitting him to hospital on November 4 when he believed he was seriously ill.

Conflict at the bedside

As Dylan's tour manager, John Brinnin was at long last taking his duty of care seriously. He worked closely with the doctors over decisions about Dylan's welfare. He also met with Ruthven Todd and Reitell to discuss what else had to be done. Todd was nominated press officer, and also asked to contact James Laughlin, who they believed was the most obvious source of money for hospital expenses.

Brinnin then began phoning people who were close to Dylan. But he did not ring Caitlin. Instead, he arranged to have her notified, as he put it. A telegram arrived later that day, November 5, as she prepared to go to the Laugharne village hall to hear Dylan's pre-recorded talk on the town. It simply told her that Dylan was hospitalised. At the end of the broadcast, the producer stood up and paid tribute to Dylan as a man and poet, comparing him to Shakespeare. Afterwards, Caitlin turned to him and said "Well, that'll do for his obituary."

At the hospital, Feltenstein had by now conferred with

Brinnin, telling him that Dylan had sustained a "severe insult to the brain" due to direct alcoholic poisoning. McVeigh and Gilbertson were becoming increasingly sceptical about this diagnosis but they had little to offer in its place. Raised sugar levels had initially suggested that Dylan may have sustained a diabetic shock, but this idea had soon been discarded.

By mid-morning, Dylan's New York friends began turning up, intent on visiting his bedside but also keen to support Brinnin and Reitell. Todd was already there but then came Howard Moss, Rollie McKenna and Herb Hannum in quick succession. Between them, they patrolled the hospital corridors, protecting both Dylan and each other, standing vigil and vigilant.

That evening, John Berryman came to see Dylan, and stayed well past midnight. He talked to the doctors and was told there was really nothing they could do "except maintain breathing & nutrition, keep him clear of mucus, and administer anticonvulsants."

George Reavey had also arrived at the hospital and later telephoned other friends to alert them that Dylan was on a public ward. In the lobby waiting room, he came across Hannum, Todd and Brinnin; upstairs, he found Reitell in a state of collapse being looked after by McKenna and Rose Slivka:

> They all looked very worried and huddled in groups with a lot of whispering going on…it struck me that the atmosphere of all these people was not only grief for Dylan. They seemed worried about themselves, too.
>
> *And Caitlin?*
>
> Caitlin's arrival was not very welcome… I believe it was hoped that either Caitlin would not come or at least arrive too late. I almost got the impression that they did not want Dylan to wake and talk… I was beginning to realize now that the gang was going to try and isolate Caitlin… Dylan was to be left with Reitell.

The next day, Friday November 6, both McVeigh and Feltenstein vainly sought information about Dylan's past health, even phoning London to see if people there knew anything about his medical history. In Swansea, Dan Jones was doing his bit, firing off telegrams and phone calls to St Vincent's about Dylan's blackouts and drinking. Oscar Williams was an early visitor to the hospital. He, too, was shocked that Dylan was in a public ward and that many friends, as well as strangers, had turned up to view him through a glass partition in the corridor wall:

> *Oscar, you were very upset by what you found.*
> America's public wards in the hospitals are terrible places. And then somebody thought it was too dangerous to move him, so he lay there for three or four days.
> *Did that matter?*
> He was virtually on display, and hundreds of people came, all wanting to see him, and there was no defence. I think that was one of the most terrible things that happened to Dylan, the fact that he was not protected at all from the rabble, or from the consequence of being so famous.

Williams was soon on the phone, ringing Caitlin with details about Dylan's collapse, and complaining about the way he was being looked after. She immediately began making arrangements to leave for America, phoning the long-suffering Margaret Taylor for help in booking a flight.

Caitlin, of course, had little idea of the drama at the hospital. By now, the disagreements between Feltenstein and the two young doctors had broken out into open conflict, and he threatened to wreck their careers if they continued to dispute his alcohol diagnosis. That afternoon, they snatched their first discussion with their supervisor, George Pappas. A little later, Gutierrez-Mahoney arrived on the ward. After discussing the case with Feltenstein, and then with McVeigh and Gilbertson, he summoned Feltenstein to his office and told him he was to take no further part in looking after Dylan.

Gutierrez-Mahoney was now in a dilemma; although he had removed Feltenstein, he could not reject his diagnosis of acute alcoholic damage to the brain. To have adopted the alternative diagnosis – that Dylan's coma had been caused by pneumonia potentiated by morphine – would have implicated Feltenstein in the death, and possibly endangered his career. So Gutierrez-Mahoney continued to insist that Dylan's brain had been damaged by his drinking – the only person to be blamed was the patient himself.

There was also continuing drama in the corridors and waiting-rooms. Williams was so concerned about Dylan that he telephoned Ellen Borden Stevenson. She rang the hospital and those of Dylan's friends who had taken responsibility for his care, offering to pay all the expenses for the best outside specialists and a private room.

But Stevenson's generous offer was refused and she was asked not to interfere. She tried going through the British Embassy in Washington. Soon after, Brinnin was summoned to the phone. It was the Embassy, brief and to the point: "The story down here is that Dylan Thomas is dying and you are denying him proper medical treatment." But Stevenson's efforts were in vain. The rejection of her help, and that of other people who had offered to pay, fuelled Reavey's fears that Brinnin, Feltenstein and Reitell had something to hide, and were apprehensive of independent specialists coming in.

The sculptor Peter Grippe came with his wife to visit. They'd met on Dylan's first tour and then again in 1952. It was Caitlin's absence that the Grippes were most worried about:

> *Tell me what you found at the hospital.*
> When we arrived, we saw Brinnin and then noticed a woman in black sitting in the waiting-room and occasionally walking through to Dylan's bedside. We asked who she was, and some whispered 'That's Dylan's girlfriend.' We were amazed by her proprietary air, acting like Dylan's widow before he was even dead.
> *This was Liz Reitell.*
> Where was Caitlin? Were they trying to keep her away? Why were they making all the decisions about Dylan's care? Did Caitlin know anything at all about it? Had anyone told her that Dylan was close to death? When was she arriving? We found the whole situation quite astonishing.

So did Irene Reavey, undoubtedly aware of how brief – six weeks by this stage – Dylan's relationship with Reitell had been. Irene was in the waiting-room at St Vincent's when she noticed the Slivkas comforting Reitell. She approached Rose and angrily said: "This behaviour is very obscene. There's such a thing as knowing that Caitlin is Dylan's wife and another thing – respecting it."

And the moment for respect was coming. Late on Friday night, David Higham was called out of a performance at

London's Lyric Theatre. It was Dylan's publishing house in New York, which briefed Higham on Dylan's condition, and asked about arrangements for Caitlin's journey to America. Higham reassured him that matters were in hand.

She arrived in London the next day, November 7; although it was a Saturday, Mags Taylor had pulled enough strings to get the American embassy to open up and process the necessary paperwork. The rest of the morning was spent shopping and acquiring sleeping pills until Taylor and Caitlin ended up at a pub for lunch with a mutual friend, Jack Green. Aware that a delay of twenty-four hours could be critical, Green phoned the airline who promised that Caitlin would be put a flight that day. At the airport, she was taken off to be vaccinated and thumb-printed, with the plane revving up on the tarmac waiting for her to come aboard.

Caitlin, Mr Moneybags and the detox clinic

Earlier that morning at St Vincent's, Dylan had been given a tracheotomy to remove mucus and other matter that had been obstructing his breathing; he had then been put in an oxygen tent. Todd came to the hospital, and afterwards he and Reitell went to the Chelsea. In the presence of the manager, Mr Gross, they packed Dylan's bags and papers, which were locked in the hotel storeroom for handing over to the police. The bottle of Old Grandad was given to the bell-captain as a thank-you present. Down in the lobby, Mr Gross opened the hotel safe, in which Dylan had deposited his money, withdrawing cash as and when he needed it. All that remained was a little over $2.

By early afternoon, McVeigh had advised that Dylan was sinking rapidly and that he would die within the next few hours. One of those who came to see him was Kevin Rooney, on a break from serving drinks at the White Horse. He went up to the ward and asked how Dylan was doing. The duty nurse replied: "Oh, it's a good thing your friend Mr Thomas led such a good life and was so healthy. It would have carried most other people off before."

The hospital staff were now trying everything they knew to save Dylan. So was Gene Derwood, a painter and poet. She arrived at the hospital with a large bag which contained the prayer books of every major faith; whatever came to hand, she prayed in accordance with her dip.

Two cables had arrived, one from Caitlin and the other from the Authors' League of America: "May you recover and reach us again." Brinnin had put them on the table by the bed, hoping they would be the first thing Dylan would see if he came out of coma. But there was now little chance of that. He was still in crisis; his fever was high, his breathing troubled and irregular. His temperature rose and fell "in sudden changes that left his face alternately red and perspiring, blue and pallid." The breathing problems were no longer the effect of the morphine, now metabolised from the body, but of the developing chest disease.

It's not known what drugs, if any, Dylan was given to fight the pneumonia. In 1953, most common forms could be treated with penicillin which was being strongly marketed by Pfizer – presumably a sick patient in a hospital would have received it. Dylan's friends and doctors might even have thought it merciful to withhold drugs to allow the pneumonia to run its course. This was certainly Feltenstein's view, telling Brinnin that Dylan's death was not only inevitable but that it was now also to be wished for because of the extent of brain damage.

Brinnin spent most of the evening at Dylan's bedside, as well as making phone calls to ensure that Caitlin was quickly taken through immigration when she arrived. He also journeyed uptown to the Poetry Center to introduce Marianne Moore. It was a difficult occasion; there could hardly have been a person in the audience who wasn't expecting a progress report. Dylan's collapse had been widely reported, and the city was running with rumours about its causes. But Brinnin chose to say nothing at all about him. He returned to the hospital exhausted but was taken away by Howard Moss, who put him to bed with a sedative from his ever-ready medicine bag.

The next day, Sunday November 8, Brinnin woke up with no illusions about the prognosis – "Dylan was doomed." Mindful about money as always, he enlisted help to start a Memorial Fund to pay the funeral expenses and to support Caitlin and the children. But the Fund was also needed, said Brinnin, "to provide for medical fees quite beyond our private means." No wonder he and Reitell had not acted earlier to get Dylan into a hospital.

The idea of a fund was a noble inspiration but Brinnin soon realised he had a personal stake in its success. He had already paid for some of Dylan's medical care; in doing so, he had fallen behind with the rent on his apartment, and the repayments on the loan for his car. He had also misappropriated even more of John Thompson's money. He hoped, he told his long-suffering friend, that some of this expenditure could be claimed back from the Fund.

George Reavey was at the ward before 6am that Sunday morning. He and Oscar Williams then raced to the airport to meet Caitlin. So did Rose and David Slivka, who got there first. But theirs was no ordinary welcoming party – in the back seat were Bob MacGregor from Dylan's publishing house, and Dr Boyce from the hospital. Whilst Caitlin was being rushed through the arrival formalities, MacGregor sought out an airline official to pay a deficit of $119 on her air ticket, which he had raised the previous night by holding a whip-round amongst his friends.

Then the news had to be broken about Dylan's condition. Staff at St Vincent's seem to have been warned about Caitlin's temperament, for Boyce came prepared with sedatives. He had also phoned ahead and learnt that Dylan's condition had worsened, so the airline called the police. Dave Slivka was delighted to screech through New York with a motorcycle escort: "Dylan always gave everyone what they wanted."

As the car sped to the hospital chased by Reavey and Williams in a taxi, Boyce calmly explained exactly what Dylan's condition was. By the time they arrived at St Vincent's, Reitell had discreetly melted away. Up on the ward, Caitlin was struck by the noise of Dylan's breathing which sounded, she said, like the roaring of a winded horse pounding up a slope.

After spending time at his bedside, Caitlin was taken to the Slivkas' house, unaware that they and Ruthven Todd had hatched a plot, as he called it, to make sure that she stayed away from St Vincent's. We all hoped, he wrote with startling ambiguity, that she "would eat a light lunch and then drink enough to put her to sleep." To make sure the plot worked, Todd went round to the White Horse, borrowed a bottle of whisky and delivered it to Dave Slivka. Soon after, Todd and McKenna brought Liz Reitell back to the hospital – "I saw this with my own eyes," reported an astonished Reavey.

Early that afternoon, Irene Reavey phoned Brinnin and asked if Caitlin was returning to the hospital. He, too, was now playing the militant guardian and he told her that Caitlin had been taken out for a drink and was not coming back again. Irene was no easy pushover; she pressed Brinnin further but he was adamant: "She spent 40 minutes with Dylan in the morning and that is sufficient. Now she knows it is real and she isn't coming back anymore." Irene asked to see her but Brinnin refused: "No-one is to see her, she is in good hands."

Irene then phoned the Slivkas, and was eventually allowed to talk with Caitlin, who asked that George Reavey come over to the house. When he arrived, he remonstrated with Dave Slivka about giving Caitlin so much whisky. "That's the way Dylan would have liked it," he replied.

Reavey encouraged her to return to the hospital, hoping that her presence would wake Dylan from the coma. She broke down and wept on Reavey's shoulder, which he thought was better for her than just drinking whisky and making small talk. She went upstairs to take a bath and change – "I want," she announced, "to be like a bride."

Caitlin returned to St Joe's East and was met by Brinnin and McKenna, who took her up to the ward. She saw Dylan for some twenty minutes, before being asked to leave. Then, in a drunken outburst of rage and grief, she threatened to kill Brinnin, shouting at him "All you've been to us is moneybags." He burst into tears, and she attacked him with her fists and feet, recognising clearly his fatal disservice. As she grabbed him round the throat, Rose Slivka shouted "Go for the jugular, baby!"

Brinnin escaped to the ward, but Caitlin followed, screaming in anger. She was taken out to a waiting room, where she sank her teeth into a nurse, demolished pot plants and pulled a crucifix from the wall. Reavey had also arrived, and was now searching for Caitlin. He found McKenna "standing sentinel" by a door. She refused to let Reavey enter, but a matron arrived and let him in:

How was Caitlin?
She was becoming quieter. Then the matron came and said she should see Dylan again – much too soon I feel… with the matron holding one arm and I the other, we went in.

What happened?
The nurse pulled back the sheet revealing Dylan's chest and tummy. Caitlin began feeling him and, growing more excited, her hand began to go towards Dylan's face… then the matron began pulling Caitlin away. I was still holding her other arm and gently urging her towards the door. But the matron was becoming rougher. At the door, Caitlin held on and said she wanted to kiss Dylan, but the matron kept pulling her and then suddenly a couple of men appeared (hospital attendants) and really began shoving her towards the lift.
How did she react?
Caitlin began to struggle. I still had hold of her arm in a sort of daze but was just following the struggling mass into the lift… they had a very tight hold on her and then pushed her along the ground floor corridor into a private room where I suddenly realised that they were going to strap her down on a bed. I and a few others were then pushed out of the room. I asked the matron "Was that necessary?" She replied "I don't understand."

Caitlin now became a victim of the weekend problem. Because it was a Sunday, the hospital "was staffed with nitwits". She was put in a strait-jacket and Brinnin and the Slivkas were summoned to see a "bigoted" and "butter-brained" doctor who asked them to commit her to the municipal psychiatric hospital. They refused and a furious row developed during which the doctor declared that she could not stay at St Vincent's.

Brinnin called in Milton Feltenstein, creating a bizarre situation in which the family doctor of Dylan's lover was now treating his wife, and even consulting the lover about what to do with her. And Feltenstein proved to be no more sagacious in assessing Caitlin than he had been in diagnosing Dylan: he declared that "she was a menace not only to herself but to others, and… that on no account could she be allowed to go free."

Feltenstein sought the opinion of an outside psychiatrist, Dr Adolph Zeckel, who had made a name for himself as an expert on deafness. Feltenstein told Brinnin that Zeckel would be available at short notice, but Brinnin was advised to leave this out of his book because it made Zeckel sound incompetent. And just like Feltenstein, Zeckel had no position or authority in the hospital, but the devout Gutierrez-Mahoney was at Mass.

After further discussion with Brinnin, but none at all with any senior doctor who had been looking after Dylan, Caitlin was sent to River Crest, a private psychiatric clinic on Long Island with a reputation for detox, where Bix Beiderbecke had once gone to recover.

Brinnin was probably anxious about the cost but Feltenstein was prepared. He took a fistful of dollars from his pocket and paid the fee for sending Caitlin there, not just for a night while she calmed down, but for a whole week, a preposterous reaction to the drunken grief of a woman who had just found out that her husband was dying. As the ambulance sped through the falling snow, Caitlin pleaded with Todd to release the straps of the strait-jacket but he refused. With Caitlin on her way to the clinic, Reitell resumed her place at Dylan's bedside.

Caitlin had preoccupied most people's minds that day, but not John Berryman's. He was out of the city at a conference but he and Pearl Kazin bombarded St Vincent's with phone calls. They went out into the country to walk, and Berryman announced he was breathing for Dylan: "if I breathe for him perhaps he will remain alive." At a party that evening, Berryman gave a drunken recital of 'Do Not Go Gentle' and wailed that if Dylan died, poetry would die with him.

The party over, he and Kazin drove back to New York and reached the hospital at midnight. The literary vultures had gone, she said, and a nurse let them into an empty ward. A few days earlier, Dylan had said of Kazin that she had once saved his life but there was nothing she could do for him now. She watched as Berryman, quiet and miserable, stood beside the bed.

The next day, Monday November 9, Todd and Reitell had breakfast together. Milton Feltenstein came along, and joined them. There is no record of what they spoke about.

Reavey was also up early, and discovered that Caitlin was under Feltenstein's supervision. He contacted his lawyer and went round to see the British consul, who demanded her release from River Crest. Gutierrez-Mahoney was now back at the hospital from his weekend break and was outraged that Feltenstein had sent Caitlin to a clinic when she only needed sedation and a night in one of the hospital's private rooms. He immediately phoned to have her released.

As discussions were happening over Caitlin, Brinnin went up to St Joe's East. His first glance told him that Dylan had gone into his final phase. His fever had subsided but his breathing had become almost inaudible: "now and then there would be little gasps and long breathless intervals that threatened to last for ever."

But those around Dylan were still working hard to save him. Tambimuttu, a friend from London since the late 1930s, was now living in New York, and he contacted a British doctor for help. He recommended an alcoholism specialist, James Smith, who came immediately to the hospital. Smith seems to have had a simplistic understanding of the condition of the dying poet. To him, Dylan was just "a classic alcoholic." He believed, bizarrely, that Celtic blood guilt lay behind Dylan's drinking, explaining that there was something that drove the Celts to destroy themselves, as though guilt were hard-wired in the blood.

Whatever his views, Smith had arrived too late and there was nothing at all that he could do to help, as John Berryman was the first to find out. He arrived at the hospital just after 12-30pm and went up to the ward. He found that Dylan was dead, seemingly abandoned by his friends. He shouted for a nurse and staggered along the corridor, hysterical that Dylan had been left on his own during his last moments.

Berryman rushed down to the ground floor to the waiting room, screaming at Brinnin "He's dead! He's dead! Where were you?" Brinnin and Reitell ran to the lift, and got to the ward just as the nurses were dismantling the oxygen tent. Reitell kissed Dylan on the forehead, whispering "See you at the ranch." Later in the waiting room, she was comforted by Rose Slivka. Caitlin was still in the psychiatric clinic.

Todd found Berryman weeping and shaking in a state of collapse. He set him to phone everyone he knew, asking them to contribute to the Memorial Fund, but he collapsed again. Todd then took him off to Chumley's bar, and filled him full enough of martinis to leave him until his mother came to collect him.

James Laughlin had by now returned to New York. Just hours after Dylan's death, he wrote to David Higham that everything was done at the hospital that modern science could do. This was undoubtedly true, though Laughlin would have known nothing about Feltenstein's incompetent treatment. Then innocently repeating what he had heard from Brinnin and Reitell, Laughlin became the very first to pass on, even before the post-mortem had been done, the false information that alcohol had poisoned Dylan's brain. Such were the early beginnings of the story that Dylan had drunk himself to death.

Laughlin and Brinnin met to decide who would carry out the formal identification of Dylan's body. They tossed a coin and Laughlin lost. Brinnin was left with the job of telling close friends that Dylan had died. In Hollywood, Stravinsky received a telegram. He opened it eagerly, hoping it had come from Dylan, with news of his arrival. When he read it, he started to cry.

That evening, Todd had a phone call from Irene Reavey. He gave her short shrift, asking her if she realised that Caitlin was now the widow of a famous man. Irene persisted, and eventually Todd buckled under her pressure, giving her Feltenstein's phone number. When she reached him, she explained they were old friends of Caitlin and wanted to be with her. Feltenstein replied: "She raised such violence we had to restrain her in an institution." No-one, he added, was to see her without his permission, adding that she had a form of illness. Irene was no match for Feltenstein and when she tried to discuss the matter further, he ended the phone call: "A doctor can give orders," he said brusquely.

The next morning, Tuesday November 10, George Reavey and a deputy consul went to River Crest, and brought Caitlin back to the consulate – she had spent two nights in the clinic, the first of which had been in a strait-jacket. The consul talked at length with her and then with Rose Slivka, who had been summoned to the meeting. With a warning that she was to be properly looked after, Slivka took Caitlin back to her home.

Up at Yale, Reinhard Paul Becker was working in his room when a student came in, weeping and silently pointing to a copy of the New York Times. Becker's first reaction was that the Russians had invaded Germany. Then, when he read the headline, he realised that it was something far more serious, a loss for which there was no substitute.

Down in Fort Bliss, a similar scene was played out. A group of men, most of them New Yorkers and college graduates, were sitting in the mess hall. A young private walked in, ashen-faced, and announced that Dylan Thomas had died – "the news that the Korean war had again erupted would have had less impact." Thirty soldiers, some of them in tears, went AWOL. They were eventually found in a library, reading Dylan's poems to each other. They paid with an extra two hours close drill.

Brinnin was also up and about, preparing to go to New York. As he was doing so, a telegram arrived from Caitlin, which seems to have made him decide to take his mother with him. After the flight, he dropped her off at her hotel and made his way to Howard Moss' apartment, where he stayed up late in the night talking.

Just after dawn, November 12, Brinnin was at Pier 90 to meet Edith and Osbert Sitwell as they disembarked from their liner. Then he collected his mother and went to have coffee with Caitlin. She was, he believed, not a wilful or difficult woman but a very sick one, a woman bewildered as to why "that sad hulk of a comatose man should have been the object of so much love & the agent of so much unhappiness." She in turn saw Brinnin as the "devil's pawn", the man responsible for the death of her husband.

The meeting over, Brinnin met up with Reitell, and they went off to have lunch with William Kolodney, presumably to report to him, as their senior manager, the events leading to Dylan's death, and to dwell on any implications it might have for the Poetry Center. A couple of hours later, Brinnin went back to the Sitwells at their hotel, where he told them everything he could remember about Dylan's four days of dying. Now I know, said Edith, what a mother must feel who has lost a child.

Then it was business as usual. Brinnin travelled across to the *Mademoiselle* office to discuss his forthcoming article on Dylan. At 8-40pm, he was back on the stage of the Poetry Center, introducing Katherine Anne Porter to another full house. The following morning, he returned to Boston, sick and exhausted. A distraught Pearl Kazin came by that weekend, wanting to reminisce about Dylan.

Over the next few days, his obituaries appeared. They were the most remarkable his publisher had ever seen for any contemporary writer. The only inquiries into the death were the post-mortem and, much later, the efforts of some, but not all, of

Dylan's biographers to unearth the truth about just how he had died.

Milton Feltenstein continued to practise, and consistently refused to talk about Dylan's death. He died in 1974. In his obituary, the President of Beth Israel Hospital praised his dedication and excellence, noting his integrity and "his steadfast uncompromising with truth as he saw it."

Liz Reitell had saved *Milk Wood* but had lost her lover in the process. She was left with a heavy burden of guilt. Looking back over what had happened, she referred to Feltenstein and observed: "Dylan's medical treatment is something that's caused me enormous suffering...".

She was the most important witness to Dylan's collapse and death but of all the people, after Brinnin, who have written about Dylan, only one carried out a face-to-face interview with her. When Reitell died in 2001, she had never been subject to a rigorous and detailed examination over the events of November 1953.

As for Caitlin, she was still completely in the dark about the circumstances of Dylan's death. Back in Laugharne with Christmas approaching, she wrote to Brinnin: "There is still one thing I want to know very badly, John. What *exactly* was the result of the post-mortem on Dylan – surely I have a right to know."

6. The Post-Mortem

Shortly after Dylan died, Dr William McVeigh completed the Medical Summary which would go with the body to the post-mortem. It was a brief outline of Dylan's condition when he was admitted to hospital, as well as the doctors' diagnosis and treatment – it is reproduced in full in the appendix. It seems likely that, in writing it, McVeigh would have consulted Gutierrez-Mahoney, since Dylan was a public figure who had died in circumstances that could prove embarrassing for the hospital.

McVeigh chose not mention in the Summary that Dylan had pneumonia and extensive bronchitis on admission to hospital. This meant that there was little possibility that the pathologist doing the post-mortem would consider whether or not Feltenstein's injections had played a part in Dylan's death. Was McVeigh's failure to include the data about Dylan's chest disease an innocent oversight or a deliberate attempt, perhaps instigated by Gutierrez-Mahoney, to cover-up the mistakes of a fellow doctor?

Gutierrez-Mahoney had instructed that the post-mortem should be carried out by the City Medical Examiner, a procedure that was required in all deaths where drugs or chemical overdose or poisoning might be a factor, or where death might have been due to criminal violence or criminal neglect. Attendants collected Dylan's body from St Vincent's and drove it across to the mortuary on the second floor of Bellevue hospital, at 29th Street and First Avenue. The examination was carried out by Milton Helpern, who was fast becoming America's leading forensic expert.

Before starting, Helpern read McVeigh's Summary, in which Dylan was described as a patient with a history of heavy alcoholic intake. The doctors' "impression" on admission was of acute alcoholic brain damage. Helpern would have seen there were no body alcohol measurements in the Summary, nor other test results which offered confirmation of this.

When Helpern examined the brain, he noted pial oedema, which I discuss on p.203. He then registered the generalised cerebral oedema – the brain tissue and cells were swollen or congested. The rest of the brain appeared normal: there were no areas of softening or haemorrhage, nor blood clots or tumours – there was no pathology to explain the blackouts that Dylan had experienced.

Most significantly of all, Helpern found nothing to confirm the hospital's diagnosis of alcoholic brain damage. He found no evidence that Dylan's alcohol consumption had caused the oedema in the brain, or damaged the brain in any other way. There were no signs of damage or changes to the structure of the brain associated with long-term alcoholism.

Helpern then took a close look at the lungs, noting "extensive" and "very evident" pneumonia in both that was grey in colour and consolidated. They were also slightly emphysematous. The bronchi – the main air passages to the lungs – were "deeply congested" and infected, indicating that Dylan had acute-on-chronic bronchitis. Helpern also saw that Dylan had acute tracheobronchitis, an infectious disease of the windpipe.

In short, Dylan's respiratory system was badly impaired: an infection had developed in the whole of his respiratory tract from the windpipe down through the left and right bronchi, and into the lung tissue itself in both lungs – pneumonia. This was the infection that had gradually taken hold whilst Dylan had been in America. This was the infection that had made Dylan sound like Louis Armstrong on the morning of November 4. And this was the infection that Milton Feltenstein had failed to diagnose.

Helpern next turned his attention to the heart. What he found was typical of an overweight thirty-nine year old who led a sedentary life and who drank and smoked too much. The coronary arteries had been narrowed by fatty deposit, in one case by fifty percent, with "considerable sclerosis with calcification." Had he lived, Dylan would have been heading for angina and a possible heart attack as one or both arteries became completely blocked.

When Helpern examined Dylan's liver, he noted it was fatty, and both firmer and heavier than normal, all conditions associated with long-term alcohol consumption and a poor diet. There were no signs of alcoholic hepatitis or cirrhosis in the liver. But

Helpern did find dilated veins in the lower end of Dylan's oesophagus, as well as an enlarged spleen, both often indicative of alcoholic liver disease.

There are several references to oedema in Helpern's report (pial and cerebral oedema, oedematous foreskin, puffy face). Some oedema is to be expected as a consequence of the coma but it is also possible that this generalised oedema could have been contributed to, over the long-term, by hypoproteinaemia (low blood protein levels). This is caused by poor diet and/or a malfunctioning liver, with low protein levels in the blood leading to fluid "leaking" out of the blood vessels into the tissues. Hypoproteinaemia is consistent with Dylan's fatty and enlarged liver, and both in turn are consistent with his alcohol consumption and poor diet.

Hypoproteinaemia is also consistent with Dylan's flesh being described as "watery" when he was admitted to St Stephen's hospital in 1946. It is consistent with his puffy appearance being apparent as early as 1951: "an unpleasant pallor and puffy, extremely puffy, for a young man." Other indications of Dylan's possible hypoproteinaemia are given on pp203-04.

If Dylan had hypoproteinaemia, then it could be that his cerebral oedema had been developing over a long period of time, and was not just due to the onset of pneumonia in November 1953. There are, however, no blood test results available to confirm or refute a diagnosis of hypoproteinaemia.

* * *

Helpern concluded that the immediate cause of Dylan's death was oedema of the brain, but the primary cause, he decided, was hypostatic bronchopneumonia, which meant that he believed the pneumonia had developed as a result of Dylan being in coma whilst in hospital. This was wrong, but Helpern cannot be blamed, because the Medical Summary had failed to mention that Dylan had pneumonia on admission to hospital. His immobility in hospital will have exacerbated the pneumonia but it did not cause it.

The distinguished forensic pathologist, Bernard Knight, offers a further opinion on this. Knight, who is Emeritus Professor of

Forensic Pathology at the University of Wales College of Medicine, examined the post-mortem report and concluded that

> death was clearly due to a severe lung infection, with extensive advanced bronchopneumonia. This is often a terminal event to many other underlying causes, but here the pre-existing acute-on-chronic bronchitis could be quite sufficient to flare up into a full-blown pneumonitis... given that Dylan had a history of a cough and chest trouble, confirmed by the autopsy finding of some emphysema, he obviously had chronic bronchitis. This often flares up at intervals into acute-on-chronic bronchitis, especially if he persisted in smoking. One would have to go on his history to a large extent, but the severity of the chest infection, with greyish consolidated areas of well-established pneumonia, suggests that it had started before admission to hospital.

This confirmation by Professor Knight of pre-hospital pneumonia is consistent with Dylan complaining he was suffocating when he woke up on the morning of November 4. It is consistent, too, with many of the details noted in Brinnin's account of Dylan's last days in New York: fever and chills, fatigue, paleness, loss of appetite, nausea and vomiting, shortness of breath and excessive sweating, not to mention the "ghastly racking spasms" noted by Reitell.

Milton Helpern would have seen from the Medical Summary that Dylan had been injected with a half grain of morphine just before going into coma, but he made no comment about its likely effects on Dylan's respiratory system. Presumably, this was because he considered the pneumonia to have been a more potent factor in causing the cerebral oedema than the morphine. Experts have agreed with this view. Sheldon Cohen, one of America's leading chest specialists, has summarised Dylan's life-long history of bronchial troubles, and concluded that the primary cause of death was "respiratory tract disease with consequently impaired oxygenation."

Professor Knight, on looking at the evidence on this matter, also concluded that "there was a mild degree of cerebral oedema terminally, related to the mode of death from a severe chest infection... it sounds as if he was already in very poor health and may well have died, morphine or not." Pathologist Cyril Wecht was of the same opinion: "Given his condition, he probably would have died even without the morphine."

Helpern had found no evidence that Dylan's brain had been directly damaged by alcohol or any other toxic agent. But was alcohol an underlying cause of death? Helpern clearly thought so. Whilst he did not list alcohol, alcoholism or alcoholic poisoning as a cause, when he came to classify the death for official statistics he wrote "Acute and Chronic Ethylism [alcoholism]. Hypostatic Bronchopneumonia." The death certificate also listed "fatty liver" i.e. alcohol, as an antecedent cause, though not as the immediate or primary cause – there is more on fatty liver as a euphemism on p203.

'Acute alcoholism' means that Helpern believed that Dylan had drunk a large amount of alcohol in the hours immediately prior to going into coma. What evidence did Helpern have for this? He himself had not been able to carry out any tests for alcohol – his report noted that Dylan had been "In too long for alcohol studies." The Medical Summary sent to Helpern with the body did not contain any data on Dylan's body alcohol level.

Despite the lack of objective data, Helpern came to the conclusion that Dylan must have been drinking prior to his collapse and admission. Presumably, he based this on the Medical Summary which said that Dylan had a history of a heavy alcoholic intake. This kind of subjective assessment is not unusual in post-mortems. Professor Knight, who found the recorded causes of Dylan's death "a bit woolly", cautioned that post-mortem examinations are not an exact science, and were even less so in the 1950s. The cause of death is

> often rather speculative in many types of case, relying heavily on the known previous history and circumstances, rather than a totally objective decision based on the post-mortem evidence... the inclusion of the alcoholism as an underlying cause was a reasonable, but subjective, addition.

The present history of events for the evening of November 4, as recorded by Brinnin, does not appear to support Helpern's assumption of acute alcoholism. In the early hours of November 4, Dylan drank eight whiskies at the White Horse between 2 and 3.30am. He then had two glasses of beer at lunchtime. But even with a damaged liver, much of this alcohol would have been metabolised from his body by late evening on November 4. According to Brinnin, Dylan did not drink anything alcoholic after the two lunchtime beers.

This history depends wholly on Reitell's account of the evening, as passed on to Brinnin and published in his book. Could Reitell have been mistaken or was she even lying as part of a cover-up? As Dylan lay ill in his hotel room on November 4, did he wheedle any alcohol from her? Did the get-together at the hotel, recorded by the private detective, turn into a drinking session in which Dylan participated?

In the absence of results from body fluid tests for alcohol, we have to rely on individual testimonies, but these are not unequivocal. On the one hand, Jack Heliker said of Dylan and Reitell: "He wanted a drink very badly, but she wouldn't give him one." Ruthven Todd has written that when he went to the hotel room on November 7 to remove Dylan's possessions, the bottle of Old Grandad was at the same level it had been a few days earlier when he had poured some for the hotel maid. In over fifty years, no biographer or other researcher has uncovered any information that contradicts the Brinnin-Reitell account that Dylan drank nothing after his two beers at lunch time on November 4.

On the other hand, Reavey has noted that the doctors at the hospital smelt alcohol on Dylan's breath. This conflict in individual testimonies should caution us to keep an open mind on this matter – it's possible that the effect of Dylan's chest disease in depressing his breathing was aided not just by morphine but also by alcohol.

Helpern's classification of chronic i.e. long-term, alcoholism indicates he believed that Dylan's lifetime of drinking played a part in bringing about his death. Dylan's long-term alcohol consumption would have been a factor, along with smoking, inadequate nourishment and sleep deficiency, in the chronic debilitation that allowed his bronchitis and pneumonia to flourish. It would also have been a factor in any hypoproteinaemia that might have been present.

After the post-mortem, Dylan's brain and liver was sent for chemical analysis, which was done the following day by Alexander Gettler, the City's Principal Chemist, who is acknowledged as one of the founders of modern toxicology. He found no sign of ethyl or methyl alcohol, barbiturates, other volatile poisons or morphine. This is hardly surprising since all these would have been metabolised in the days since Dylan's admission to hospital on November 5.

Finally, Helpern issued a Notice of Death, which said that the hospital's diagnosis of alcoholic brain damage could not be confirmed:

> Comatose upon admission. Never regained consciousness. Hist: (1) heavy alcoholism (2) half grain of morphine administered by a private doctor. Treated in hospital for toxic encephalopathy but diagnosis unconfirmed.

When the examination was over, Helpern's assistants sewed the body back together again. Later that afternoon, James Laughlin arrived at the mortuary to do the formal identification. As he entered the basement, he was struck by the smell of formaldehyde and the confusion of trolleys with their rubber sheets covering the bodies. The old man in charge looked around, trying to remember which was Dylan. He lifted one sheet and then another, asking "Is this him?" No, replied Laughlin, it wasn't. He lifted two more sheets before they finally found him, looking "awful, all bloated."

Laughlin was sent off to a window to confirm the identification. He wrote 'Dylan' on the form because the young woman behind the window had never heard the name before and could not spell it. "What was his profession?" she asked. Laughlin told her that he was a poet. "What's a poet?" He replied that a poet was a person who wrote poems. She typed on the form "Thomas, Dylan. 39yrs. Male. White. Married. Writer" and issued the death certificate at 4-15pm on November 10.

7. The Verdict

Dylan Thomas died from a severe chest infection with extensive and advanced pneumonia, complicated by morphine and possibly alcohol, leading to oxygen starvation and cerebral oedema.

Self-neglect and medical negligence were both implicated. Dylan's smoking, drinking, poor diet and sleep deficit, as well as his reluctance to seek medical help for his various pulmonary ailments, created the circumstances in which bronchitis and pneumonia could develop in the days before he entered hospital. Milton Feltenstein failed to detect Dylan's chest disease and, in ignorance of it, injected morphine, which depressed Dylan's damaged respiratory system still further.

Feltenstein's three injections of morphine would not on their own have killed Dylan; they merely served to hasten a death that his pneumonia would have made inevitable if it had remained undetected and untreated.

Self-protective, distracted, demob-happy and self-absorbed, John Brinnin failed in his duty of care. Both he and Liz Reitell recognised that Dylan's sickness was something new and serious but they chose not to cancel his engagements. They also failed to ensure that Dylan had an appropriate level of medical care in the two weeks before his collapse on November 4.

Feltenstein did not admit Dylan to hospital when he came to see him on November 4, even though he thought that Dylan was seriously ill. When Feltenstein returned to the hotel for a third time, he made a diagnosis of delirium tremens. He also believed there was a danger that Dylan might slip into a coma or become uncontrollable. He still failed to send him to hospital.

After reviewing Dylan's hospital notes, Dr William Murphy concluded: "It remains a mystery how so obviously and gravely ill a person, mentally and physically, could have remained outside a hospital." The hospital's senior brain specialist, Dr C.G. Gutierrez-Mahoney, concurred that "Feltenstein's treatment was extraordinarily inadequate on several counts." Another doctor who knew the case commented that "Dr Feltenstein's failure to have Dylan admitted to hospital earlier was even more culpable than his controversial course of injections."

Reitell and Heliker did not call an ambulance immediately when Dylan fell into coma at midnight on November 4/5, as Reitell wasted almost an hour trying to contact Feltenstein. The ambulance then took a further hour to deliver Dylan to the hospital.

These initial errors were compounded by Feltenstein's failure, and Reitell's, to tell the admitting doctors that Dylan had been unconscious for some two hours before his admission to hospital.

For the first critical day and a half of Dylan's time in hospital, Feltenstein directed Dylan's treatment, overawing and overruling McVeigh and Gilbertson. These two young doctors appear to have been left during this period without adequate supervision, and Feltenstein, who had no position of authority in the hospital, assumed that supervision.

Dr Gutierrez-Mahoney, was not called to examine Dylan until the afternoon of November 6, some thirty-six hours after Dylan's admission. Feltenstein was responsible for this delay.

The story of the death of Dylan Thomas is one of a chain of neglect. It was an early death that could so easily have been prevented.

8. The Aftermath

Dylan's body was taken to a Manhattan clearing house, where the City's health department issued permit H24268 to the undertakers, Daniel MacLean and Son, authorising burial. But getting Dylan buried was no easy undertaking. Money problems still dogged him even in death, and MacLean became anxious that his bill would never be paid. Ruthven Todd arrived quickly to reassure him. Then the police refused, because it was a public holiday, to give MacLean the bag containing Dylan's clothes. He rose to the occasion, and fetched a cheap blue suit and shirt from his store in the Bronx, whilst Todd bought a blue-and-white polka dot bow tie on Broadway. Todd also chose the best of the cheapest coffins (a snip at $100), and ordered a simple name-plate, without dates, in order to save money.

There were still more twists to come. The Welsh Society in New York turned up and solemnly presented Caitlin with a cheque from the Welsh community, whilst others came with gifts of second-hand clothes. Dave Slivka wanted to make a death mask. Whilst Caitlin was receiving visitors, Slivka worked in the basement, helped by Todd:

> I helped... remove the plaster from his face on the death mask... it took two people to take off the plaster – and the floor was cluttered with Colgate's Brushless Shave Cream tubes. You use that to prevent it sticking to the skin... David and I were very glad when we had it in a carton, tucked in the back of the old station wagon and took it away. Neither of us enjoyed ourselves.

A memorial service was held on November 13, attended by some four hundred people. In a grand church that was modestly called St Luke's Chapel, the Reverends Weed and Leach conducted a Protestant Episcopal service, and read from Chapter 15 of St Paul's Epistle to the Corinthians. Noah Greenberg and his Pro Musica Antiqua sang two motets by Thomas Morley,

Agnus Dei and *Primavera.*

Liz Reitell stood in the very back of the church feeling, she said, the loneliest person in the world until William Faulkner came across and held her hand. Quite extraordinarily, Brinnin chose not to attend. He was in New York the night before but got up very early in the morning for a brief teaching session at the University of Connecticut, before returning to Boston.

Caitlin hated the service, knowing that Dylan would have preferred the blood and thunder of Welsh hymns. That evening, she spent a couple of hours with John Berryman; she was still close to hysteria, alternating between bouts of tears and furious anger, as well as, according to Berryman, trying to seduce him – "I would like to see you again," she wrote afterwards.

The weary Todd had a different problem to cope with that evening. A vigorous knocking brought him reluctantly to his front door. Outside were "five black-visaged Welshmen" who he presumed were elders from a chapel in New York. They berated him for not having kept the Welsh community in the city informed of Dylan's progress in hospital. He rounded on them fiercely: "You would have little or nothing to do with him when he was alive or while he was dying, but now he is conveniently dead you all want to wallow in his corpse. Good night."

James Laughlin was also very busy, taking personal responsibility for the Memorial Fund. Some big literary names had backed it, including Arthur Miller and Tennessee Williams, and now Laughlin threw himself into making it a success. Within nine days of the death, $6,000 had already come in, and by the end of December it stood at $15,000 – Laughlin ruefully noted that if only half the people who were now talking about Dylan had bought his books when he was alive, "he would have been on easy street."

Individual donations to the fund were as little as one dollar and as large as a thousand, and some came with poems and stories, including one from the Californian broadcaster, Lewis Hill, who recalled plans that he and Dylan had discussed for a new literary magazine. The Women's Welsh Club in New York collected $10, students raised money in their classrooms and large fundraising events were organised, such as the reading in the Poets' Theater in Cambridge, which thirteen hundred people attended. Dylan was given the Edna St. Vincent Millay Award, though it only produced $100 for the Fund. *Harpers Bazaar* and *Mademoiselle* together contributed $1,100, though this was money they owed for publishing Dylan's work, a bizarre case of a person contributing to his own memorial.

The National Institute of Arts and Letters gave $250, even though it had never before made an award to help a widow, but sympathetic voices squeezed it through committee on the basis that Dylan had been alive when the appeal had been lodged. Everybody was doing their best, including the White Horse which raised $75 and Chumley's bar, whose patrons contributed an astounding $300.

The first calls on the Fund were to repay Feltenstein the $162 he had loaned to get Caitlin into River Crest, as well as money to the Slivkas for looking after her. The worried undertaker had his bill of $780.75 paid – its details are on page 205. That just left St Vincent's. Quite remarkably for a private hospital, it announced that it would waive all its fees for Dylan's treatment.

Caitlin herself got $50 for pocket money in New York, and was furious with Laughlin when he asked for a receipt. The Fund committee wanted to avoid doling out large sums to her. It was also keen to ensure that the three Thomas children benefited, a problem which they raised with the trustees of the British fund: the children should be given every opportunity to escape "the curse that has blasted the lives of their parents."

Back in Wales, others were also concerned about money. The Mayor of Swansea set up a fund to help the Thomas family, as did the *Western Mail*. Both passed the £500 mark by the end of November. Daniel Jones wanted more, and encouraged the vicar of Laugharne to start raising money in the town. In London, other friends were thinking about organising a gala evening in aid of the British fund. Richard Burton agreed to take part and, on January 24 at London's Globe Theatre, he was First Voice in a short extract from *Under Milk Wood*.

The canny Dan Jones was also thinking ahead, wondering how best to plan for the future income that would come from the sale of Dylan's works. Caitlin, he knew, would spend it more quickly than it was earned. By the end of the year, she had agreed to the setting up of a trust, the income from which would be divided between herself and the three children. Jones was made the literary executor, and he became yet another to take on the mantle of the militant guardian. His first decision was to refuse permission to include in the broadcast and publication versions of *Under Milk Wood* that work which Dylan and Reitell had done on the play during his last two weeks in New York.

Dylan's friends were also worried about the funeral, amidst rumours that his body would stay in America. Jones sent a telegram to Gutierrez-Mahoney indicating that it had been Dylan's wish to be buried in Wales. Dylan's old friend, Ralph the Books, was wheeled into action:

> When Dylan died, Dan come up the shop. "Look Ralph," he said, "we'll have to get something done to get his body back." Because we understood that Caitlin was going to leave the body there. So we got hold of John Ormond... really speaking it's through Dan and John, and perhaps myself, that we got the body in this country...
> *What did his American friends feel?*
> The Americans, I understand, wanted to keep the body there, and she was not desperate... John said to me "You get a wreath from a place I know up in Sketty there." And we had a laurel wreath. 'Course, I had to pay for that again, see. They tells me to do these things, you know.

At the undertaker's in New York, Dylan's body orifices were sealed with cotton wool ready for transportation. The coffin was placed inside a water-tight box and taken to the pier for the journey home. Laughlin gathered up the flowers and written tributes that had been sent, and had them delivered to Caitlin on the boat. George Reavey also turned up just before the sailing, and gave her a letter that had arrived that very day from Bill and Helen McAlpine, who had been amongst the closest of Dylan's friends.

A patch of comfy ground

Caitlin and the coffin set sail in the *S.S. United States* bound for Southampton. After a row with the captain about the quality of her cabin, she sat in the hold with a couple of crew members and,

16. Dylan in his coffin

it is said, played cards on the top of the coffin. Before disembark-
ing, she gave an interview to a newspaper reporter, telling him
that she was determined to bring Dylan back to Wales so that
Americans would never have any reason to claim him as one of
their own poets.

Waiting on the quayside to offer their condolences was the
Southampton Cymrodorion Society. Nearby, stood Ebie Williams
of Laugharne with his hearse, Daniel Jones who had taken charge
of the funeral arrangements and a Miss Vera Bevan, an old school
friend of Dylan who now lived in the town. But there were yet
more problems in getting him buried. The sealed container
holding the coffin was too big and too heavy for the hearse. It was
taken off to a local mortuary, prised open and the coffin liberated.

After a long drive through the night, the hearse eventually
reached Laugharne, where Dylan's body was brought to his
mother's home opposite Brown's Hotel. Booda, the town's ferry-
man who had no hearing or speech, took up position by the open

coffin, taking on the role of master of ceremonies as people came to view Dylan's body. As each person looked at the rouged and lip-sticked face, Booda would indicate by signs what he expected of them.

Ebie Williams threw a red carnation into the coffin and was shocked when he saw the body: "When I seen him in the coffin I didn't believe it was him – that's telling you the truth. He was out like a cask." Dylan's Swansea friend, the Rev Leon Atkin, had much the same impression:

> It was hard to believe it, because I'd seen him the night before he went to America. It was so recently I'd seen him that I felt that, well, in a few weeks how could he have changed like this? What the hell have the Yanks done to him? They must have either brainwashed him, or doped him, or inoculated him. They must have changed him.

Dylan was buried in St Martin's church on November 24, with three ministers officiating. It was a beautiful sunny day when birds sang, cocks crowed and the organist played 'Blessed be the pure in heart'. Smoke from the town's chimneys went straight up into the clear air, as if in salute. One mourner wished she'd taken a swim suit – "I would have risked a swim, for the sea was calm and beautiful and the sands golden and summer warm. Or so they seemed."

Nellie Jenkins, who had nursed three generations of Thomases, was impressed by "all the big people" from Swansea, not to mention those from Cardiff and London who had come by car and sleeper. As she watched the funeral leave Pelican, her only regret was that Caitlin was not wearing a hat – "she told them that she was a Catholic, and that Catholics never wear a hat during a funeral. I said, tell her she's a liar, because I'm a Catholic myself, there's no such thing, I said."

The coffin was carried not by the 'big people' but by Dylan's Laugharne friends, a cross-section of the community, including a publican, a taxi-driver, a gunsmith and a milkman. Caitlin came behind, leaning on Daniel Jones' arm, her mother at her side. Then, filling the road and pavements, walked the rest of the villagers, family and friends, including Vernon Watkins holding a white plastic bag with the wreath inside, looking, it seemed to the

17. The funeral procession

Rev Atkin, as though he imagined that, after all, it might not be necessary, and he might have to take it home with him.

The procession to the church was filmed for television. At the graveside, the cameraman clumsily pushed in front, trying to focus on Caitlin. This annoyed Watkins who rebuked him: "Is this really necessary?" Without taking his eyes from the camera, he replied: "'Course it is. Dylan Thomas is news – world news, brother!" When the Rev Atkin leaned across and asked Watkins how much of the service Dylan would have endorsed theologically, he replied "Oh, every word of it."

The burial over, the mourners converged on the town, a black funnel of people, a great wide mass at the church narrowing down to two or three as they pushed their way into Brown's. Every room, passage, stair and corner was soon filled, upstairs and down. People shouted and sang, drowning sorrows that were immediately resuscitated and drowned all over again. Friends wondered whether they had too many memories of Dylan or not enough, whilst others worried that they would never laugh so deeply again. As bottled cockles were swallowed as easily as tales of Dylan escapades, the beer flowed. Old friendships were renewed and lifelong feuds put aside:

> He had an enormous range, had friends in many walks of life and layers of temperament. They very often disliked each other intensely, or tried to like each other because of him and failed. When he died one could see men being polite and even reverent to each other, who had never exchanged a word unless it was a sneer, for years. This was the wreath they placed upon his coffin. It was a beautiful thing to behold.

It had been a day for coining epitaphs, swapping stories and castigating Americans. Brinnin wisely stayed away. He was busy, as usual, with his work. The Poetry Center was "magic again" with packed houses for every session that followed Dylan's death.

A Desperate Heart

As Dylan lay in coma, Brinnin had felt that he was dying with him. But within a week of the death, he was getting stronger, and beginning to understand what Dylan had left him. He felt in himself a new knowledge, "an inheritance I had not thought to possess." But he needed a chance to recuperate. He confirmed his resignation as Director of the Poetry Center, and flew off to the Bahamas, where he rested for several weeks.

He returned with the same burdens, complaining to John Thompson that he was "congenitally broke and on the edge as ever." In March 1954, he met with the Sitwells in New York. Over lunch, they talked about Dylan, and Edith suggested that Brinnin write a book about him. Brinnin was hesitant; the experience, he told her, was still too painful and even the most truthful of accounts could be open to misinterpretations. "You must write two accounts," she replied. "One to set the record straight as only you can, another to be put aside until persons to whom it might give offence are dead and buried…". Osbert agreed with her, noting that when indiscretions became historical, they become discreet.

Brinnin gathered up his Dylan papers as preparation to writing. But as he started the book, his new-found strength soon disappeared. He was, he confided to Thompson, in a hell of a way, with a "nervous system that waits upon pheno-barbital" to calm an inner "constant ravagement". He went to see an analyst. She diagnosed a life-long anxiety centred in a fear of loss, perhaps understanding the effects on Brinnin of three family deaths, as well as those of his friends, his doctor and the poet he had loved but with so much ambivalence and neglect. She also recognised Brinnin's lack of anchorage in the real world, reminding him that there were other levels of understanding than intellectual.

He struggled on, and by the end of July had finished most of the first draft of *Dylan Thomas in America* – barely nine months had passed since Dylan's death. He then went off to Europe for the summer and resumed work on the book on his return. By January 1955, he had found a publisher, and was sending drafts of his manuscript to the Sitwells for their comments. Sustained by alcohol, benezedrine and three packs of cigarettes a day, he kept up the writing, in the face of many doubts, self-recriminations and streaks of guilt, as he put it.

Most of all, he found it hard to write about the last weeks of Dylan's life, and feared being overwhelmed by migraine and other forms of collapse. But with the help of two typists in high gear, he pounded through "the tortuous last pages", not so much concluding the book, he said, but abandoning it. He rewarded himself with a new car and another excursion to Europe, travelling in style in a First Class cabin.

But Dylan and the book continued to haunt him. Brinnin returned a month before its November publication and was thrown into a state of nervous depression as he tried to deal with all the pre-publication work that lay on his desk. He was brought down by the one thing he had most wanted to avoid, having to relive the experience he felt he had exorcised. Involvement in the book had turned, he said, into a misery, as he spent day after day in a drunken stupor, falling into bouts of uncontrollable weeping.

A visit to a doctor and a therapist pulled him through, thanks largely to a prescription for the new wonder drug, Miltown. This was meprobamate, a tranquilliser that was soon popularly known as "the happiness pill." Just to make sure, Brinnin flew off to Nassau for two months, even though he was now aware that his old faith in travel as a solution to his problems was false.

Within weeks of his return in February 1956, Brinnin found himself again reliving, for real this time, Dylan's last days. He was rushed to the emergency ward in Boston's Beth Israel, where he was found to have an ulcer and a major intestinal problem. He recovered after a regime of intravenous feeding, as well as drugs that made him temporarily blind.

But, just like Dylan, he had no insurance. Anxious about the costs, he persuaded the doctors to discharge him. After eight days in hospital, he owed more than a $1,000 dollars. He confessed that the sight of a penniless, sunburned patient, who had summered in Europe and wintered in Nassau, was not a flattering self-portrait. He turned to his usual miracle-worker, John Thompson, to whom he already owed $600. Brinnin's solution was to offer up as collateral his collection of Dylan's papers and letters.

He came out of hospital, declaring that the experience had made him a new man. For the first time, he was able to look outwards and to forget himself, delighting in what he called a new appreciation and care for people. Unfortunately, it was just a little too late for Dylan.

Come the summer, it was Europe as usual. In London, he became fast friends with Emlyn Williams, cavorted with Eric Ambler and was impressed by the young Dannie Abse. Brinnin also went to Edinburgh to see *Under Milk Wood*. With his new-found appreciation of life outside his head, he discovered that kilts created a special tone, declaring that neither Copenhagen nor Amsterdam should be too bold about their precedence as cities of special masculine interest and freedom.

He ended up staying with the Sitwells in Derbyshire, where he celebrated his fortieth birthday. Dame Edith sent in a note with his breakfast, reassuring him that her critical review of *Dylan Thomas in America* had not been intended as a personal attack; Brinnin was relieved because he, too, had begun "to wonder just what was the truth of things."

It was left, not to Dame Edith, but to the exotic Gladys LaFlamme to make the more perceptive comment on Brinnin:

despite his Boswellian intimacy with Dylan, he had succeeded in writing a book that was only a book about himself. Dylan moved through it, she wrote, as little more than a shadow of the real man and even that shadow was distorted.

That same year, Brinnin's book had a completely unforesee-able consequence. Sylvia Plath was on holiday in Europe with her boyfriend, Gordon Lameyer. They discussed Brinnin's account of Dylan's last weeks. She vehemently argued that Brinnin should and could have prevented the poet's death. Lameyer disagreed as strongly, and the conflict severed a friendship that was already in trouble. He decided he wanted to be rid of her and, in April 1956, Plath returned to England, straight into the arms of Ted Hughes.

Within two months, she was married to him, a man and a poet she saw as Dylan Thomas incarnate. Too much like Thomas, warned Olive Prouty, her benefactor. Whilst Caitlin had been wonderful about Dylan's behaviour, would she, Plath, be able to put up with Hughes' philandering? Prouty also reminded Plath that she herself had told her about his aggression, cruelty and unkindness. Six years later, Plath left Hughes and in 1963, the year that marked the tenth anniversary of Dylan's death, she killed herself.

From hearse to bandwagon

The day after Dylan's funeral, the *News Chronicle* predicted that "Now will begin the Dylan cult and Laugharne will become a shrine." After all, the town had everything it took to make a perfect shrine: the poet's grave, his work hut, his favourite pub and a ready-priested shore, all in a magnificent estuary setting. Brinnin gave the bandwagon a good push, providing in his book the first published descriptions of the town and Dylan's life there.

Not everyone wanted to live in a shrine but eventually, after many years, the pennies began to drop. A Mr Oriel was asked to keep the grave and Boat House tidy, and was paid five shillings a week for doing so. The cliff path to the Boat House was renamed as 'Dylan's Walk'. This was followed by the opening of the Boat House and by the founding of the Dylan Thomas Society, which promptly made its first annual outing to Laugharne.

And, as with any proper shrine, there would inevitably be relics. In 1978, a professor of medicine was the first to show an interest in Dylan's bones, wondering if his repeated fractures were due, not to drunken falls, but to hereditary bone disease. He did not ask for the body to be exhumed, but contented himself with a request for Dylan's X-rays.

That same year, the twenty-fifth anniversary of Dylan's death, three Swansea businessmen enticed Dylan fans to journey on "up market pilgrimages" to the shrine. Chauffeured Bentleys and Mercedes took parties on trips to Laugharne, stopping for champagne receptions, cordon bleu dinners and poetry readings. This promotion was part of a marketing blitz from the Welsh Tourist Board, who believed that Dylan could soon be one of the biggest attractions for foreign tourists to Wales.

Within months of Dylan's death, twenty-five thousand copies of the British edition of *Under Milk Wood* had been sold. The world-wide popularity of the play went hand-in-hand with the enshrining of Laugharne, and in time few would remember that *Milk Wood* had been mostly written in New Quay, South Leigh and America – only some three hundred lines, about seventeen percent, had been written in Laugharne, and many of these could well have been done in Harry Locke's Hammersmith house.

The White Horse also became a shrine; its walls soon boasted Dylan articles, photographs and paintings, and a trickle of pilgrims grew into a healthy trade. On the fifteenth anniversary of Dylan's death, a burly, six-foot five-inch Texan in a long suede coat walked into the bar, carrying a bunch of flowers. He asked Eddie Brennan, the new owner, where Dylan used to sit. Brennan, who had had the occasional drink with Dylan back in the 1950s, pointed to the table. The Texan went across, and ordered three triple vodkas. And then he ordered more, and yet more again. Brennan remembered

> eighteen vodkas in two hours. He was trying to emulate the shots that Thomas had... and he put the flowers in the vase on the table, which I left there as long as I could. He said "I promised myself in school that I would do that." The kid left and I never seen or heard from him again. He was paying respects... that's all he wanted to do. That's one of my more vivid memories. That was the most touching.

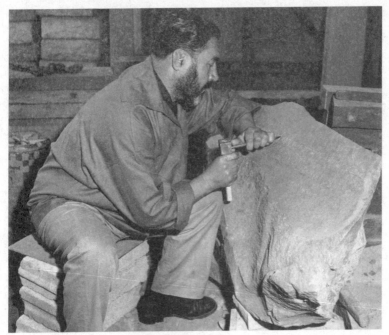

18. Ron Cour carving the Cwmdonkin memorial stone

Other respects were also paid, sooner or later. Dylan took his place in Poets' Corner in Westminster Abbey, and also found a spot in the affections of Presidents Carter and Clinton. Swansea got its Dylan Thomas Centre as well as a statue, a theatre, a square, a school, a bookshop and a Dylan pub. More modestly, New Quay boasts its Dylan Thomas Trail. Wales has its Dylan Thomas Prize, a handsome £60,000 awarded for the first time in 2006 to the Rhondda writer Rachel Trezise for her collection of short stories, *Fresh Apples*.

Homage has been paid in other ways, notably through property. There's a Blue Plaque on Dylan's lodging place in Delancey Street, north London. Number 5 Cwmdonkin Drive has passed through many hands but is now being shrined up; once it is restored to its original Edwardian splendour, people will be able to holiday there. Down in Laugharne, the actor Neil Morrissey bought up Brown's, as well as another hotel and a pub. In New Quay, Majoda has been modernised, and the patient owners smile kindly on the Dylan pilgrims who beat a path along the coast to their door.

In time, two of his Swansea friends got together to talk about a memorial. Vernon Watkins and the sculptor Ron Cour wondered about something in Cwmdonkin Park. They travelled across to Cwmrhydyceirw quarry and, after much searching, found a suitable chunk of blue pennant stone. It was not, Cour was at pains to stress, a municipal memorial but a private one, sponsored by Dylan's American record company, Caedmon. But the municipal tip-of-the-hat eventually came, a Memorial Public Shelter erected in 1977 in the park, from which wild boys could cheek the park-keeper, throw stones at the swans and feel the first slow boiling of a poem.

The only tribute missing was a major movie about Dylan, but this was put right in 2007 when filming started in New Quay on *The Edge of Love*. It starred Keira Knightley, Sienna Miller, Matthew Rhys and Cillian Murphy. The producer was Rebekah Gilbertson, the granddaughter of William Killick, the disaffected soldier whose actions were at the beginning of events in Dylan's terminal decline.

But what of Liz Reitell and Caitlin? And John Brinnin? Reitell continued to work on *Under Milk Wood*. She prepared the script of the play that was published in *Mademoiselle*, and also wrote a television treatment for the NBC *Omnibus* programme. Then she retreated back into the familiar territory of art and design until, in 1958, she returned to the literary world, working as a secretary, editor and organiser for various writers. Whilst doing these jobs, she came to realise that working with Dylan on *Under Milk Wood* had given her the confidence to see her future as a writer.

It was in 1958, too, that she married Herb Hannum. The ceremony took place in her mother's church in Wysox, a township in the Endless Mountains region of northeast Pennsylvania, with the family minister officiating. Some saw this as a moment of healing, the basis of a fresh start. But the marriage ended as quickly as the previous two.

In 1962, Reitell finally found, after a lifetime of seeking, a place in which she felt completely settled. She left New York for the mountains of Montana, not to the ranch that she and Dylan had fantasised about, but to the job of publications specialist at

19. Thinking of what might have been, Reitell in New York, 1983

the university's school of forestry, doing what her mother had been good at.

But she also followed in her father's footsteps, becoming wholly involved in environmental schemes as a writer, editor and activist – the zealous saviour had found another good cause. She helped found the Wildlife Society and, in time, joined the boards of other wilderness organisations, taking on the role of President and Vice-President in several of them, including the Montana Wilderness Association. In 1972, she was given the Hilliard Award for outstanding environmental achievement.

Reitell's last job took her even closer to her father's environmental interests when she moved to Oregon to work on an Inter-Tribal Fish Commission, dealing with water and fish issues affecting the well-being of Native Americans. For a time, she lived with a Native American man before moving back to Montana, where she was promptly divorced by her fourth husband.

In 1983, she travelled to New York to make a television programme, in which she was re-united with John Brinnin and the 1953 cast of *Under Milk Wood*. She returned to Montana and was sent a video of the programme; from then on she spoke constantly of Dylan as "the love of my life". Wherever she went, she took the video with her, showing it "to any group even if we had seen it five times before... this video seemed to somehow validate her whole life."

In retirement, Reitell's health slowly deteriorated. She was forced to turn to social security for help; her parents had decided she was too unstable to leave her their substantial wealth, fearing she would fritter it away. Just like Caitlin, she was subjected to the ignominy of a trust fund, which doled out small sums of money for the rest of her life. She ended up, as had her mother thirty years earlier, as a patient with brain disease in a care home; one of her last visitors was the fishing writer, David James Duncan:

> Sally went in to read Thomas poems...The woman's eyes, when we first saw her, were staring straight ahead at a white curtain. When Sally greeted her, then introduced me, her face never changed expression and her gaze never swerved. The Dylan Thomas poems commenced. The gaze didn't change. So much for poetry in the face of mysteries intelligible only as mystery.

After giving up the Boat House, Caitlin left Laugharne for a new life in Italy; she wrote three books on her time with Dylan, became a grandmother and also a mother again after she married Giuseppe Fazio – they had a son, Francesco, born in 1963. Late motherhood took up her time, but Caitlin also threw herself into legal disputes with the trust set up to handle the money earned by Dylan's works. There was much to play for – within a few years, the trust's annual income had reached £20,000 and rose by the 1990s to some £100,000. Ferris published his biography of her in 1993; she died the following year, at the age of eighty-one.

As for Brinnin, he went from strength to strength. Two years after Dylan's death, the Poetry Society of America awarded him its Gold Medal for Distinguished Service to Poetry. After leaving the Poetry Center, he continued to enjoy a successful career as an academic and author. He retired to Florida, where he wrote about transatlantic liners, played poker on the beach and held weekly anagram parties with Leonard Bernstein and other friends. He died on June 25 1998, aged eighty-one. He coined his own epitaph: "I think I am as well known as I deserve to be."

Brinnin was well-known for many things. Yet somehow he managed never to be known as the man who helped send a famous poet to an early and avoidable death.

The milch cow comes home

The New York productions of *Under Milk* played a part in killing off its author, but the play was soon a success. Within days of Dylan's death, BBC producer Douglas Cleverdon began planning a broadcast on the Third Programme. Uunknown to him, Dylan's former colleague at the BBC, Erich Fried, was asked to produce at great speed a translation which could be broadcast in German.

Both men were given warnings. Cleverdon was cautioned that some parts of the play were not fit for broadcasting. He tried to resist the censorship but relented, eventually agreeing to a number of small cuts – the "two tits and a bum" cuts as they became known.

Fried was advised the play was untranslatable, but he took up the challenge. He enjoyed working to tight deadlines, and he was already familiar with Dylan's work. He had previously translated 'A Visit to Grandpa's' which had been published in 1948 in *Neue Auslese*, as part of the country's denazification programme. He had also been working in his own time on translating several of Dylan's poems.

Fried laboured day and night but Cleverdon beat him to it. The first broadcast of the play was made on the Third Programme on January 25 1954, and repeated two days later. But there was a complaint that reception in Wales was so bad that few people had heard the broadcast, and it had been particularly inaudible in Laugharne.

The Welsh Home Service would have reached a much larger audience, but it resisted attempts to broadcast the "lusty, Rabelaisian and uninhibited" play, which it thought unsuitable for "family or home listening... Controller Wales reacts more strongly to it than I do, and his reasoning is only too sound in the context of this region as we know it."

As a result, German listeners got to hear the play before most of those in Wales. Fried's translation, *Unter dem Milchwald*, was broadcast on March 10 1954 and then, on German radio stations, on September 20. Eight days later, the sensitive listeners of Wales were allowed to hear their *Milk Wood* on the Welsh Home Service.

Within three years of Dylan's death, *Under Milk Wood* was published, put on the stage, produced on television and released as a long-playing record. In time, it would come out as a film with Richard Burton and be turned into a musical with Anthony Hopkins. It would be translated into almost every major language and many of the minor ones as well. It even became an examination set text, with performances by school dramatic societies, tits and bums and all. With it, Dylan had secured the future of his three young children. The financial objectives of his last visit to America had been achieved.

9. The Cover-Up

In the wake of Dylan's death, there were four worried people: Feltenstein, who was at risk of a civil action for damages or even criminal charges; Gutierrez-Mahoney, who knew what Feltenstein had done and was worried about the reputation of St Vincent's; Brinnin, who had failed in his duty of care; and Reitell, who feared she might be sued – "No lawyers after me yet", she wrote a few months after Dylan's death.

They had good reason to be worried. John Berryman had decided to seek independent medical advice about Dylan's illness and treatment. George Reavey had already gleaned enough information from hospital staff to make him suspicious of Feltenstein's and Reitell's involvement.

Reavey's letters, sent just after Dylan's death, are full of grief and anger. But shorn of their emotional content, they provide useful data not contained in Brinnin's account. Reavey was an eye witness to what happened in St Vincent's hospital. He and Irene visited Dylan every day, except on the morning of his death, and talked with his doctors and nurses. He should be recognised as the first to report, though his letters, Feltenstein's use of morphine, the two-hour delay in getting Dylan to hospital and the shameful treatment of Caitlin.

John Davenport in London was amongst the first that Reavey contacted, alerting him that there was a 'gang' operating to conceal the facts of Dylan's death and the role played by Reitell; and to prevent any scandal touching the YM/YWHA. Reavey warned that "the gang is working hard to put a nice smooth version across." His letter had the intended effect and, on the day of Dylan's funeral, Davenport and other friends sat in a pub in "silent fury that they couldn't have taken better care of him in the States."

Reavey also wrote to David Higham, that it was apparent that there was "some mystery surrounding Dylan's state of coma and that a gang of people were trying to hush things up and keep control of the situation." Bill and Helen McAlpine, who were old friends of both Dylan and Reavey, were the next to hear from him. He did not pull any punches:

> We haven't recovered yet from the ghastly and gruesome events here and still feel sick from enforced contacts with ghouls, vampires, carrion crows, jackals and hyenas!
> *You keep mentioning a gang……*
> Ruthven Todd… and Reitell were as thick as thieves. She was spending her time between the hospital and Todd's house (sometimes the Slivkas' too) and seemed to be very much running affairs…
> *You'd already warned the McAlpines in June that something was up?*
> I had a very bad feeling since May and particularly on this visit on what was happening to Dylan. He had got mixed up in very bad company when he was already feeling sick and weak, and they just finished him off.
> *And Brinnin?*
> Just a weak, calculating man who may have felt guilty about using Dylan as a showpiece and wanted to avoid scandal…

The Reaveys were doing all they could to make sure that the truth, as they saw it, came out in the open. A few days earlier, Irene Reavey had composed a signed statement detailing the events they had witnessed in the hospital. She sent a copy to Caitlin and to a solicitor whom the Reaveys thought had represented Dylan.

But Brinnin and the 'gang' were also quick off the mark. His reputation, and that of the Poetry Center, was on the line. Not only did the intimate triangle between himself, Dylan and Reitell threaten a scandal, but any investigation into Dylan's death could also expose the details of Brinnin's varied and hectic love life. And he had a good deal to lose. A scandal could endanger the tenured university post he was about to be offered, and possibly ruin the academic career he so desperately wanted. Amidst growing concern that Dylan's American friends had been responsible for his death, Brinnin launched his part of the cover-up strategy. He spent much of the weekend of November 13 with Bill Read, composing letters that would carry re-assurances to British friends that Dylan had received the best possible care. Five days later in New York, he met up with Wynford Vaughan Thomas and "a group of Englishmen" to talk about Dylan and his death.

Brinnin's carefully crafted letters were posted off to Louis MacNeice and T.S. Eliot, who had heard so many unpleasant stories about the causes of the death that he was "comforted" to have received Brinnin's witness, as he put it.

Brinnin also wrote to John Davenport, telling him that everything in the realm of medical science that might have saved Dylan was employed. Brinnin also toed the hospital line that the only person responsible for the death was Dylan himself, who "was driven by other stresses to continued excess." Brinnin told Davenport, falsely, that the post-mortem had confirmed "a diagnosis of 'a severe insult to the brain' caused by direct alcoholic toxicity in brain tissue and cells". This was an astonishing untruth, for the post-mortem report said no such thing – Brinnin was merely parroting what Feltenstein had told him on Dylan's very first day at the hospital.

Ruthven Todd gave the most exhaustive account, sending a twelve-page letter to MacNeice, just two weeks after Dylan's death. Todd told him that "Dylan received all the best attention we could muster and we cannot blame either the doctors or the hospital for the outcome." Todd also wrote that Reitell had called the police and that an ambulance had immediately transferred Dylan to hospital, both untrue.

Todd went on to praise Feltenstein, assuring MacNeice that morphine had played no part in Dylan's death. This was clear duplicity because, at the very same time, Todd and Reitell were "indignantly" telling at least one of Dylan's New York friends that Feltenstein "had mis-diagnosed his trouble, given him a shot of morphine, and that that had killed him."

Todd's letter, of course, was part of the cover-up. He told MacNeice that his letter had been composed at a meeting with Reitell and Rose Slivka, and that Reitell had also seen a final draft which she had vetted. A copy found its way to Daniel Jones. He later dismissed the letter, declaring that it was clearly the result of a conference between those associated with the circumstances preceding Dylan's death. MacNeice, however, was not as scrupulous in his appraisal of Todd's letter. He wrote immediately to warn Dylan's Swansea solicitor, that

There appears to be a gang of intellectuals... seizing this

occasion for gang warfare & circulating rumours that Dylan was treated wrongly etc. It seems pretty clear that those concerned did do everything they could for him, so all such rumours should be spiked.

Dr Gutierrez-Mahoney, too, was writing letters as part of an extensive public relations job. Alarmed that "busybodies" and people "of unsound mind" were writing to Caitlin to tell her what had really happened, he wrote to Daniel Jones that there was no indication of foul play. The letter purported to summarise the post-mortem report. But Gutierrez-Mahoney did not mention Dylan's pre-existing pneumonia and bronchitis or that pneumonia was the primary cause of death. Nor did he say anything about Feltenstein's injections of morphine, or the delay in getting Dylan to hospital.

Gutierrez-Mahoney could no longer go on telling people that Dylan had died of alcoholic brain damage, because that had not been confirmed by the post-mortem. He was forced to backtrack. Choosing his words carefully, he told Jones that the death was brought about by chronic alcoholic poisoning; in other words, Dylan's body had been poisoned by alcohol over a long period of time. It is difficult to know what he meant by this because the phrase 'chronic alcoholic poisoning' fell out of use amongst doctors many decades ago and is now considered archaic. It is a term that does not appear in Dylan's hospital notes nor the post-mortem report, though it would sound a convincing explanation to anyone who knew that Dylan liked his pint.

In private, Gutierrez-Mahoney was more honest. He told one of his senior colleagues, George Pappas, that Dylan did not have any neurological problems and was not really an alcoholic. Pappas' appraisal of Gutierrez-Mahoney's role in the cover-up was sympathetic:

> I guess Dr Mahoney had a painful decision to take. He knew what Feltenstein had done, but he also knew Dylan Thomas died unnecessarily in his hospital... he had to decide whether or not to let the outside world know what had been going on. It was hard for him. He was proud of his hospital and no member of his own staff was in any way to blame.

By now, Caitlin was back on the scene. Brinnin had written to her, asking if she had seen a medical account of the death, though he doesn't specify what he was referring to. Her reply was forthright, expressing suspicions about a cover-up being put in place, saying she had not read it, expressing contempt for the doctors as "those fucking bastards" and dismissing the account as "pure, undiluted, and professionally bolstered bugger all…"

In autumn 1955, Brinnin published his book on Dylan's trips to America. Brinnin was content to pass on the story, which he knew to be untrue, that Dylan had drunk eighteen whiskies. He also repeated Feltenstein's self-serving diagnosis that Dylan had died of a severe insult to the brain due to direct alcoholic poisoning. The idea that Dylan had drunk himself to death would now become firmly lodged in the public mind, nurtured by a romantic fantasy that this was a sexy way for a poet to die.

Brinnin's detailed account of the death put across the "nice smooth version" – he offered not the slightest criticism of Feltenstein or Reitell; nor did he mention the morphine, the findings of the post-mortem nor that the Notice of Death had said that the hospital's diagnosis of alcoholic brain damage could not be confirmed.

He also covered up the two-hour delay in getting Dylan to hospital, writing that within minutes of going into coma "a quick call to Dr Feltenstein brought an ambulance that took Dylan to St Vincent's hospital." Brinnin even contrived to suggest that Dylan had been given his own private room – he chose not to mention that Dylan was on a public ward but referred (on eight occasions) to Dylan's "room in the St Joseph's division of the hospital."

There can be no doubt that Brinnin used his book to conceal the truth. It was not just a memoir of Dylan, he acknowledged, but also a portrait of himself and he was concerned that it might have been written with his "best face forward." In his unpublished memoir, Ruthven Todd also gives the game away, apparently having forgotten his own role in the cover-up:

> John's account, in *Dylan Thomas in America*, is not only inaccurate but also, I am afraid, prejudiced. I can forgive the latter for John was, as his book shows, deeply emotionally involved with Dylan while being out of sympathy with Cait. I do feel, however, that he should have made a better cover-up

story or one, at least, that might have been plausible and accepted by those of us who had the misfortune to be present and involved.

But Brinnin's book was a best-seller in both America and Britain and so the cover-up must have seemed complete and successful, with Feltenstein's and Reitell's reputations intact, and St Vincent's spared any embarrassing revelations. Reitell was especially pleased, but still apprehensive about what the critics might say.

She need not have worried. Although most British reviewers gave the book a hostile reception, nothing was said about her. But they went to town on Brinnin, criticising him not just for giving a partial picture of Dylan's time in America but also for writing it in such a way that he, Brinnin, emerged both as hero and martyr. They also swallowed the drink story of the death, except for one more perceptive reviewer who thought that Dylan had died of conscientiousness. The tragedy of Brinnin's book, he said, was the spectacle of a man of genius who was overworked, overstrained and overdriven by material pressure, but who was trying to do his best for a public that appreciated him for all the wrong reasons.

A case of cold feet revisited

In 1963, Constantine FitzGibbon, a former American intelligence officer, advertised far and wide that he was writing the authorised biography of Dylan Thomas. He appealed for information. George Reavey, concerned that FitzGibbon should not be taken in by Brinnin's book, responded, writing that he was very unhappy about Brinnin's incorrect description of Dylan's last days.

Reitell also wrote to FitzGibbon, declaring that Brinnin's account of the last weeks was substantially true, and that she had found no errors of fact or misinterpretation. This was hardly surprising since she had both supplied Brinnin with his material, and vetted the book in draft. As to why Dylan had died, Reitell stuck to the party line, telling FitzGibbon that Dylan had been killed by alcohol, and that the incidents of his last days could have been taken from a textbook on alcoholism. But just a few months later, she expressed her worries about how FitzGibbon might deal with her role in the death: "I shudder at what he may have done with me."

Another of FitzGibbon's correspondents was Dr William Murphy, who had long been fascinated by Dylan Thomas' death. He first wrote in July 1964, and for the next five months they corresponded, largely discussing Murphy's psychoanalytic theories about Dylan's life and death. But FitzGibbon also sent Murphy a draft of his biography. Murphy responded with detailed comments and then, a few letters later, he mentioned that he would be going to New York to look at Dylan's medical records. He promised to let FitzGibbon know what he found.

Murphy travelled to St Vincent's on December 3 1964. After reading Dylan's notes, he had sherry and lunch in Gutierrez-Mahoney's apartment. Murphy found him to be a most intelligent, cultured, and friendly person. Gutierrez-Mahoney's charm won Murphy over, and he uncritically accepted the doctor's claim that it was "definite" that Dylan had had delirium tremens, and that he had died of acute poisoning on chronic alcoholism.

Murphy returned to Maryland, and typed out a memorandum, reviewing the hospital notes and his interview with Gutierrez-Mahoney – the medical data from the memorandum are given in the appendix. For as long as the hospital refused access to Dylan's records, Murphy's memorandum would become the single most important medical document relating to Dylan's health, surpassing even the post-mortem report. It was the only document, apart from the hospital records, that contained information on Dylan's state of health made at the time of, or just after, his admission to hospital, and therefore of his health in the days running up to his collapse.

In writing the memorandum, Murphy pulled no punches as far as Milton Feltenstein was concerned. He was, he said, at a loss to understand why Feltenstein had given Dylan the morphine and ACTH:

> the rationale of this form of medication escapes me... there seemed to be no sane rationale for the ACTH, and it would seem to me to represent a hazard to the patient. There was no indication for an injection of morphine at the time he got it

and, furthermore, Dr Mahoney agreed that a man in delirium tremens should be hospitalised, whether he wishes to be hospitalised or not. Dr Feltenstein failed to do this.

But Murphy also became part of the cover-up. Gutierrez-Mahoney had agreed with him that Feltenstein's treatment of Dylan was inadequate on several counts, but it was going to be a problem, wrote Murphy, to

> interpret this information to the several friends and wife of the dead man. As of now, I feel no good can come from revealing the inadequate treatment administered by Dr Feltenstein... it appeared that Dylan was permitted to destroy himself publicly not only by his friends, but also by his medical advisor at the time... however, there is no point in getting involved in a rancorous and, possibly, litigious situation, at this stage of things.

FitzGibbon received Murphy's memorandum in late December 1964, and there followed a quick exchange of letters and telegrams about Feltenstein, ACTH and morphine. FitzGibbon now had more than enough time to include the medical data in his biography – he was still revising the typescript in January 1965. This was his golden opportunity to dish the alcohol stories about the death that had grown apace in the ten years since Brinnin had published his flawed account.

FitzGibbon's book came out in early autumn 1965. He got off to a good start by dismissing the story of the eighteen whiskies. But then, in his meagre one-page treatment of Dylan's death, FitzGibbon wrote that Dylan's pneumonia had been contracted whilst in coma, a statement which he must have known, from Murphy's memorandum, to be untrue. FitzGibbon also neglected to mention Dylan's extensive bronchitis.

When it came to Feltenstein and the injections of morphine, FitzGibbon was equally feeble. He did not mention Feltenstein by name, referring only to "the doctor". Whilst he did refer to the last morphine injection, FitzGibbon did not attribute this information to the hospital notes seen by Murphy, but merely said he had been "told" it was morphine. Neither did FitzGibbon mention that this last injection of morphine had been given not long before Dylan went into coma, and he said nothing at all to highlight the hazards of morphine when given to a patient with chest disease. And his criticisms of "the doctor" for failing to have Dylan immediately transferred to hospital were removed, and did not appear in the book.

Ignoring Reavey's warning, FitzGibbon blindly copied Brinnin's account and gave the cause of death as an "Insult to the brain" i.e. it had been directly damaged by alcohol. But FitzGibbon went one step further than Brinnin, and boldly claimed that the phrase "insult to the brain" had been in the post-mortem report. FitzGibbon must have been aware that this was completely false, since he had been given a copy of the report in mid-1964.

The one saving grace of FitzGibbon's account is that he was the first and only biographer to point to the part that the production of *Under Milk Wood* had played in the death, including the way Dylan had been made to rehearse the play on the very night of his arrival in New York. FitzGibbon noted that Reitell immediately "took charge", even though the strain on Dylan was "too great" and that "he was in a state of near collapse." FitzGibbon suggested that Reitell had put her responsibility to the Poetry Center before that she owed Dylan.

Feltenstein, Brinnin, Gutierrez-Mahoney and even Reitell must have been delighted – the cover-up was still mostly intact and the alcohol stories became even more entrenched. But how did FitzGibbon, who had not been advised of any libel difficulties with what he had drafted, come to publish such a bizarre account of the death?

After sending him the memorandum, Murphy began to worry about how FitzGibbon would use it in his biography. So he wrote to FitzGibbon on January 4 1965. After discussing Feltenstein's use of ACTH and morphine, Murphy indicated that he and the hospital were closing ranks around Feltenstein:

> I assume you have read my letter and rough notes (uncor-rected) concerning the medical data... it is easy to criticise him, and after the St Vincent's visit, I felt very critical... I hope you don't intend to make an issue of Feltenstein's efforts... I have sent you this data on the understanding you don't disclose it... I owe Feltenstein nothing but I did promise Dr Mahoney I would not stir up unpleasantness

based on access to his hospital records... I know you have other sources of data e.g. the autopsy report.

Murphy had secured Caitlin's permission to examine the hospital notes and was committed to sending her a report. But he reassured FitzGibbon that the report would be "without reference to debatable matters." Murphy wrote to him again on February 5:

> I was very pleased to hear from you, not knowing what you had in mind worried me. I agree with you essentially and don't feel Feltenstein deserves shielding but I would deplore opening old wounds and inflicting new ones on Caitlin & the children. I didn't tell Caitlin my views on Dr F. I don't want to embarrass or antagonise Dr Mahoney whom I like and respect & who has enough troubles at the hospital without my betraying his confidence.

FitzGibbon duly obliged; he stayed silent about the medical data that Murphy had given him. Of course, Murphy had asked him not to disclose the data, but biographers can usually find a way around such difficulties. And, ironically, when Murphy read FitzGibbon's biography he was angry that the material he had provided had been disregarded. In autumn 1965, he wrote to a friend:

> I feel disturbed about FitzGibbon's account of Dylan's last days. In this, he lied, in a fashion I can believe could only be conscious and deliberate. I sent him the essential information from D's hospital records and autopsy report... Another distortion is his report D. developed pneumonia after being in hospital – clinical examination and the X-ray report showed signs indicating bronchopneumonia on admission. Again FitzGibbon knew this & I know he did because I told him... C.F.'s truth is a distortion, maintained by disregard of reliable data he didn't want to know.

In 1968, Murphy wrote an account of Dylan's mental and physical health. Most of the paper presented a Freudian analysis of Dylan's death, a portrait of a man tormented by his inner demons, and overwhelmed by drink. Murphy neglected to pass on the data from the medical records. But he did write that there were "physical and radiological signs" of pneumonia on admission, but this vital piece of information, buried deep in a morass of psychoanalytic theorising, passed all of us by.

Had FitzGibbon found a way to publish the information from the medical notes, we would have known in 1965 about both the morphine and Dylan's pre-existing chest disease. These two pieces of data would have done much to abate the lurid speculation about the causes of his death.

But it was not to be; FitzGibbon's silence perpetuated the disinformation of Brinnin's cover-up. Between them, they created a knowledge vacuum in which the numerous myths, falsehoods and half-truths about the death would continue to flourish. Some of Dylan's later biographers tried hard to fill the vacuum with fact, but they were only partly successful – the hospital refused to release Dylan's medical notes, and they all overlooked Murphy's memorandum. How that could have happened is the story of the next chapter.

10. Biographer's Droop

Between 1967 and 1974, FitzGibbon deposited his material on Dylan, including Murphy's memorandum, in the archive he had created in the University of Texas. Cataloguing of the entire FitzGibbon collection was completed in 1974. In the years after, several major biographies on Dylan were published. Why did none of their authors uncover Murphy's memorandum?

The answer to this question lies partly in the nature of biography – biographers often seem to work chronologically, usually leaving until last the death of the person they are writing about. With their publisher's deadline approaching, they may find themselves with little time to examine the death thoroughly. Some may also think that their readers are more likely to be interested in the life than its ending, and, as far as Dylan Thomas is concerned, there may even be a conviction that the story is already known – it was the booze, stupid.

Then there's the matter of biographer's droop, an occupational hazard that can blight the last pages of even the most well-researched biography. In trying to be exhaustive for much of a subject's life, the biographer risks becoming exhausted or, worse still, just simply bored and fed up, and so the death can bring a merciful release – this was certainly the way that FitzGibbon felt about his work on Dylan:

> Norman Douglas used to say that he preferred to taste his friends not eat them. For two years now I have, in many ways, been eating Dylan, and I shall be glad when at last I can rise from this table.

Money and time are also important. The major collection of material relating to Dylan is in the University of Texas, but there are also Dylan collections in at least ten other university libraries in America. Before setting out, the biographer has to work out how much time and money can be devoted to these archives. A plane ticket has to be bought, which almost certainly will have a return date on it – and that is the first constraint on visiting biographers, because they are now racing against the clock, working out how much time can be devoted to the various collections before the date of the plane home.

The Texas archive will probably be everyone's first port of call. But now the difficult choices begin. There's not just the main Dylan collection, but also those of his friends such as George Reavey, and his agent David Higham. Given the range of material available, it would hardly be surprising if the time-pressed biographer gave least priority to the FitzGibbon collection. Surely anything of value in it would already have been published by FitzGibbon in his 1965 book?

Even if a biographer finds time to look at the FitzGibbon archive, further challenges lie ahead. The catalogue consists of some two thousand cards covering all aspects of FitzGibbon's life's work and, of these, fewer than two hundred relate to Dylan. These Dylan cards are not assembled in one convenient section but are spread in dribs and drabs throughout the entire catalogue, so hunting them down can be a laborious process – especially for the researcher whose time is running out.

But if the card relating to the Murphy memorandum is found, then its importance is at once crystal clear: "Murphy's account of Dylan Thomas medical records and interview with doctor concerning Thomas death." A few cards away, there is a list of Murphy's letters to FitzGibbon, and a copy of Dylan's notes from St Stephen's hospital.

From Ferris to Tremlett

Andrew Sinclair was the next British writer after FitzGibbon, adding nothing of interest on the death. He was followed by Paul Ferris, who started work in mid-1974 and published some three years later. Ferris identified the two hour delay in getting Dylan to hospital, as well as the time it took in the emergency room to restore his breathing to normal. He was the first to make use of the post-mortem report. He was also the first to mention Milton Feltenstein by name, and the first to publish from the medical record that Feltenstein had injected Dylan with morphine just prior to his collapse.

But whilst the morphine was a large dose, it would not on its own have been lethal. What Ferris needed to show was that Dylan had chest disease when Feltenstein had injected him. But Ferris was not able to do this because he had neither the hospital notes nor Murphy's memorandum. Ferris was forced back on specula- tion, suggesting "it is *possible* that the pneumonia which soon developed had begun already… *if* Thomas was suffering from any difficulty in breathing, the effect of half a grain of morphine could be catastrophic." (my emphases).

Almost thirty years later, Ferris wondered why the truth about Dylan's death would never catch on. His answer was that people liked the alcohol stories because drinking oneself to death seemed a suitable end for a poet. There's a good deal of truth in this, but I'm inclined to feel that biographers have also failed to be persua- sive enough in their arguments. Ferris is a case in point – even without Murphy's memorandum, he could have produced a much stronger body of evidence about Dylan's breathing difficul- ties because the post-mortem report showed that Dylan had emphysema and chronic bronchitis.

Ferris also knew that Dylan was using an inhaler. But he marshalled neither the emphysema, the bronchitis nor the inhaler to support a thesis that Dylan had pre-existing chest problems. In the end, Ferris left his readers with only his speculations about breathing difficulties, and these were not enough to put an end to the stories that Dylan had drunk himself to death.

Nevertheless, Ferris passed on an important gift to future biographers – his speculations should have been an attractive lure to those following him to prove that Dylan's breathing was impaired when Feltenstein injected him with morphine. But the lure was not seen or, if it were, it was ignored. Daniel Jones also published in 1977 but he said more about the funeral than the death. Two years later, Dylan scholar John Ackerman skirted around the issues though he, more than most, recognised the cumulative toll on Dylan's health of his four American tours:

> those gruesome academic gatherings and parties that
> followed the readings, the insensitive (and often not very
> intelligent) questioning of the captive poet, the pedagogic
> longeurs, the impertinent demands for his already exhausted
> attention. It is no wonder that he was driven to drink and

rude comment. But more destructive still was the loneliness, homesickness and sense of isolation.

Gwen Watkins published her portrait of Dylan in 1983 and stayed well clear of the death, unlike Rob Gittins, three years later, whose book was the first 'necrography' of Dylan, focussing solely on his last days. Gittins talked with Reitell and Brinnin, and provided valuable pieces of information, such as Feltenstein's predictions of liver failure and coma, as well Dylan's quest for fresh air in the early hours of November 4.

Two more biographies emerged in the early 1990s, the first by George Tremlett, followed two years later by Jonathan Fryer. Their accounts of the death were cursory and took us no further forward. In 1997, Tremlett tried again, this time teaming up with an American neurosurgeon, James Nashold. Their book, the second necrography to appear, was the most important break-through since Ferris in unravelling the truth about why and how Dylan died.

Nashold and Tremlett were the first to interview some of the doctors involved, including 'Turnbull' and Pappas, but not Feltenstein or Gutierrez-Mahoney, who had both died. Nashold and Tremlett did not gain access to the hospital data, but they were allowed to ask questions of St Vincent's staff, who replied by consulting Dylan's notes.

Although their book is weakened by their use of imaginative reconstruction, it nevertheless provided the first description of Dylan's time in hospital that was largely independent of the Brinnin account. Their book told us more about the delay in getting Dylan to St Vincent's. It also revealed that Milton Feltenstein had no position of authority in the hospital, and described how he took control of Dylan's care in the first thirty-six hours of his admission, bullying the two junior doctors into accepting his diagnosis of alcoholic coma. Finally, Nashold and Tremlett discovered that Feltenstein had given three injections of morphine on November 4, not just the one identified by Ferris from the Medical Summary.

Nashold and Tremlett were in no doubt about what had killed Dylan – they followed the post-mortem report that pneumonia and swelling of the brain caused by oxygen starvation were the cause of death. But, unfortunately, not only did they miss

Murphy's memorandum, they also introduced a large red herring in the form of diabetes, which press and public happily gnawed upon for many years. This is a matter that can now be quickly disposed of.

Nashold and Tremlett argued that Dylan was an undiagnosed diabetic, writing that the sugar levels in the blood taken from Dylan at around 3am on November 5 were "sky high". If Dylan's blood sugar levels were raised, then this would almost certainly have been the result of the three injections of ACTH that Dylan had received from mid-day onwards on the previous day, November 4. Ferris also suggests other reasons why the sugar levels could have been high. In other words, the high sugar levels reported by Nashold and Tremlett could have been a temporary condition, and in themselves did not mean that Dylan was diabetic or in a state of diabetic shock.

Indeed, the salient evidence points the other way: sugar was not found in Dylan's urine when it was tested at St Stephen's hospital in 1946. Dylan's case notes from St Vincent's also record that Dylan tested negatively for diabetes. Dr William Murphy, writing in December 1964 two weeks after examining Dylan's hospital records, told FitzGibbon that "Laboratory findings prior to death ruled out diabetes... there was nothing to suggest he had... diabetes or other toxic condition."

Nashold and Tremlett, who were not allowed to read Dylan's hospital notes, claim that details of Dylan's diabetes were sanitised from his medical records, though they do not say what evidence or sources they have for this allegation, nor what motive anyone might have. In the same December letter to FitzGibbon, Murphy reported that he had seen no evidence that portions of the medical records had been removed or altered.

There is certainly enough biographical material available that points to the possibility that Dylan had problems with his blood sugar levels, though this does not necessarily mean he was an undiagnosed diabetic. Even if he were, diabetes did not bring about his death. Both Dylan's coma and death were due entirely to pneumonia, oxygen starvation and cerebral oedema, as Nashold and Tremlett have themselves conceded at three separate points in their book.

And Ferris to Lycett

The next opportunities that came to re-examine Dylan's death were not taken. James Davies published his *Reference Companion* in 1998, but followed Ferris' 1977 account. Sinclair tried again in 1999 but added nothing. That same year, Ferris brought out a second edition of his biography. He wrote a new introduction, but changed little in the text. In his chapter on the death, he added an extended footnote, in which he took Nashold and Tremlett to task for their theorising about diabetes.

Ferris published a third edition in 2006, but his thirty-year old speculations of the 1977 edition about breathing difficulties remained intact. This was disappointing since Ferris could have removed them and, in their place, given his readers the medical data about Dylan's pre-existing chest disease that had since become available – the hospital information from Murphy's memorandum had been published in 2004 and then again in 2005. Ferris' unchanged 2006 edition must count as another missed opportunity to disseminate the medical facts about Dylan's death to an even wider readership.

In the autumn of 2003, Andrew Lycett published his *New Life*, timed to coincide with the fiftieth anniversary of the death. It vividly captures the circus of people and events during Dylan's last days, an aspect mostly neglected by previous biographers. But, regrettably, Lycett's brief analysis of the death itself adds nothing to previous accounts because he simply reprises the old alcohol story.

Lycett holds Dylan responsible for his death, a flawed man finding "solace in drink" whose "troubles seemed self-inflicted" and who, at the end, was overwhelmed by "chronic alcoholism" and "alcoholic damage". He claims that Dylan's doctors were clear that he was suffering from acute alcohol poisoning, ignoring the evidence presented by Nashold and Tremlett that the doctors were far from clear or agreed about anything, and that there was a bitter dispute between them about their diagnoses.

The immediate cause of death, says Lycett, was pneumonia, though the death certificate says it was oedema of the brain. Merely hinting at Feltenstein's incompetence, Lycett says nothing about Reitell's part in delaying Dylan's admission to hospital. He tells us that Dylan was in hospital "within minutes", and that the police were involved in calling the ambulance, ignoring Reitell's plaintive cry to Brinnin: "Oh, John, why didn't I call the *police*?"

Lycett displays great diligence in unearthing fresh material on his subjects, but he became the last in a long line of biographers to overlook Murphy's memorandum. For Dylan's death, he relied almost wholly on John Brinnin's 1955 book. Lycett also cites Reitell's diary, but it contains nothing about the death or the circumstances leading to it.

His other cited source on the causes of the death is the letter from Gutierrez-Mahoney to Daniel Jones in January 1954 – see page 134 above. Lycett is persuaded by Gutierrez-Mahoney's archaism that Dylan's death was caused by chronic alcoholic poisoning which led, claims Lycett but not Gutierrez-Mahoney, to a build-up of cerebro-spinal fluid that put pressure on Dylan's brain. But the hospital's Medical Summary – see the appendix – indicates that Dylan's cerebro-spinal fluid pressure was, for an obese man, at the upper limit of normal. Even if it were considered to be somewhat raised – and the morphine would undoubtedly have had an elevating effect – the intracranial pressure would still not have been high enough to have caused Dylan's coma in its own right.

Lycett further speculates that Dylan was suffering from alcoholic brain disease, overlooking evidence from the post-mortem that none was found – Milton Helpern did not find any sign of direct alcoholic toxicity in the brain tissue or cells, nor any damage or changes to the structure of the brain associated with chronic alcoholism, as the Notice of Death made plain. The evidence is clear: the damage to Dylan's brain was caused by an insufficient supply of oxygen brought about by his pneumonia and bronchitis, and precipitated by morphine.

One of Lycett's specific suggestions is that Dylan was suffering from Korsakoff Syndrome, a psychosis that affects chronic alcoholics. The syndrome can include a decline in the capacity for thinking and learning, mental confusion, confabulation, impaired vision, eyelid drooping, muscle atrophy, speech impairment, incontinence and memory loss. But Lycett produces only one sign, an apparent confabulation by Dylan about a girl in a taxi. This is problematic for a number of reasons: one sign does not make a syndrome, and this particular sign could just as well be related to other clinical conditions. For example, Nashold and Tremlett use it to support their case that diabetes was affecting Dylan's brain.

Alcoholic brain damage would not suddenly strike Dylan down in those two weeks in New York. It is a long-term degenerative process and its range of signs, if Dylan was afflicted by it, would have been very apparent back home in Laugharne. In New York, Dylan's mind was functioning perfectly well during his professional and social engagements. He displayed none of the signs of the neurocognitive deficits of alcoholism, not even those associated with mild alcoholism such as impaired memory, a declining capacity for abstract thought, attention deficit and concentration difficulties.

Dusting off the truth

In 2003, I began to write a chapter on Dylan's death for inclusion in volume two of *Dylan Remembered*. I wrote to St Vincent's asking to see Dylan's medical notes. The hospital ignored my letters and phone calls. Dylan's daughter, Aeronwy, was legally entitled to see her father's medical records and she kindly wrote requesting them. When her letters were also ignored, I persuaded a friendly New York lawyer to contact the hospital, which eventually conceded they still had Dylan's notes. But there was one problem – they were unable to find them without knowing the patient number assigned to him when he was admitted. Fine, we replied, how do we get that number? The only place to find it, they said, would be on his medical notes.

I was about to give up when an email came from Mary Edwards. She was clearing out the office of her husband, Colin, and had come across some old correspondence. None of it looked relevant to the editing of his tapes that I was doing for *Dylan Remembered*, so she was minded to throw it out. Never throw anything out, I replied. A week later, an envelope arrived with the last bits and pieces of Colin's files. Amongst his 1960s correspondence were letters from William Murphy which indicated that he had visited St Vincent's and had sent his findings to Constantine

FitzGibbon. I asked the University of Texas for a copy of the catalogue of the FitzGibbon archive and within weeks I had Murphy's memorandum in front of me.

There was one more piece of the jigsaw to put in place. When, in his 1977 biography, Ferris referred to the hospital's Medical Summary, he mentioned only that part relating to coma and morphine. There was other information in the Summary, but McVeigh's handwriting was impossible for me to understand. I asked the current Chief Medical Examiner in New York to decipher it, and he told me immediately what was there.

The discovery of Murphy's memorandum, taken together with the complete data from the Medical Summary, meant that we now had the best ever information, outside the full hospital notes, on Dylan's health at the point of his admission to St Vincent's. We also had Murphy's correspondence with FitzGibbon that revealed the nature of the cover-up put in place after Dylan's death. All this had taken more than fifty years to emerge, but a fuller telling of the story of who and what killed Dylan Thomas could now be written, thanks to Mary Edwards' spring-cleaning.

11. How to Kill a Poet in Ten Steps

In the middle of life's journey
in the middle of New York
in the middle of the century
of prose and penicillin
barring accidents and tyrants
a poet is not easy to kill.

First, he must be endowed
with a weakness: the ghost of Keats
coughing like Carabosse over his cradle.
Second, he must grow up to be a child
over everything but words – live on
sweets and treats and smokes.

Third, he must take care to marry
another as silly as himself,
a drunken dancer who will not feed him.
Fourth, there is still the danger
his friends might look out for him
so they have to be hypnotised –

Then, when he vomits blood
when he blacks out
when his coughing racks him
shakes him off his feet
when he brushes all this aside
they stare, then shrug – another round?

All this will not suffice.
A doctor must be summoned:
Feltenstein, Physician to the Stars,
with his little needle
and his big assumptions
about the sickness of celebrities.

Fatal Neglect: Who Killed Dylan Thomas?

And now the poet is in coma.
Even so, more must be done.
Sixth, seventh and eighth
the dithering friends, the strange silences,
the scenic route to the hospital.
Is any brain here functioning?

Ninth – a master stroke –
he nosedives just before
a weekend, when the hospital
has only a skeleton staff.
Still the poet lives. But the poetry
has long since sputtered out.

So maybe it doesn't matter,
the finishing touch –
the day and a half of drift
before the specialist is called.
Or that a crowd is allowed
to watch the great bard gutter.

What-ifs are pointless
but irresistible. Would the years
have tempered him to an RS
or dumbed him down
to a Wordsworthian dotage?
Enough! We have Fern Hill.

Stevie Krayer

Appendix
Dylan Thomas' Medical Notes
and Post-Mortem Report

1. Notes from St Stephen's hospital, London, 1946, held in the Constantine FitzGibbon archive, Harry Ransom Center, University of Texas at Austin.

Dylan was admitted to St Stephen's Hospital, London, in the early afternoon of March 10 1946. He was taken to Ward 7-B where he gave his address as 39, Markham Square, Chelsea, his religion as non-conformist, and his occupation as writer, poet, journalist and BBC worker. The admitting doctor's letter is not with the notes but it appears, from a letter to FitzGibbon from a Consultant, that Dylan was admitted to the hospital as a case of haematemesis i.e. vomiting blood. The notes record:

> Urine sugar NIL
> Recurrent bouts of depression. Recurrent bouts of alcoholic & smokers [next word unclear]. Recurrent bouts of vomiting & paroxysmal morning cough. Recent attack 3 weeks duration. Apprehensive ++ Pulse high tension BP [blood pressure] 160/98. Tremor. Shaking hands. Obesity. Watery flesh. Dilated pupils. Sympathetictonia[?]. Chest: NAD [Nothing Abnormal Discovered when examined by a doctor]. Heart NAD – Tachycardia [rapid pulse]. CNS [central nervous system] overactive ++. Liver ↓ 2 fingers Tender. Throat Dry granular
> = Anxiety.

By March 12, Dylan's blood pressure had fallen to 132/96. He was also seen that day by a psychiatrist who recorded: "Depression consists mostly of *reactive* depression with elements of hypercritical attitude. Finds sleep aided by drink – *habit +*".

Dylan was discharged as "recovered" on March 15 with a final diagnosis of "gastritis", and was given a prescription for phenobarbitone to be taken three times a day.

Comments on the notes

The liver was not only tender but also enlarged since it was found two fingers down from the ribs. Three liver tests were done; there is nothing in the notes that any damage was found. Both the chest and heart were normal when examined by a doctor. A chest X-ray was done but there is no record in the notes that it revealed anything wrong. Dylan's urine was tested for sugar but none was found. No mention is made in the medical notes of diabetes, nor of any drugs or diet to treat diabetes. As for medication, Dylan was given only phenobarbitone, as a way of calming him. The notes record that he was put on a normal diet.

Reactive depression is that occasioned directly by events in the external world e.g. a loss of a loved one, and is an extension of normal feelings of loss or grief. That the psychiatrist underlined "reactive" may suggest he had found sufficient reasons in Dylan's external circumstances for a state of depression, though we do not know what these might have been. Neither is it clear whether the phrase "hypercritical attitude" means that Dylan was hypercritical of himself or of people or circumstances around him.

There is nothing in these incomplete notes to support a diagnosis of gastritis, let alone one of alcoholic gastritis as put forward by FitzGibbon – if the hospital had suspected alcoholic gastritis, they would certainly have put Dylan on a special diet and given him appropriate medication.

The vomited blood could have been the result of a Malloy-Weiss tear i.e. a tear in the lining of the stomach wall that can be caused by vigorous vomiting. Ingestion of excess alcohol and drugs can produce bouts of violent vomiting. Vomited blood could also come from a rupture of an oesophageal vein – there is more on this in the section on the post-mortem report.

The collection of signs recorded in the medical notes (apprehension, raised blood pressure, tremor, shaking hands, dilated pupils, fast pulse rate, overactive central nervous system and dry throat) led the doctors to conclude "anxiety". It was the first anniversary of the Majoda shooting – see pp12-14. These signs are also sometimes suggestive of other factors including the use of amphetamines, such as benzedrine.

On the facts available about this admission, Dylan had

– an enlarged liver probably due to long-term alcohol abuse and poor diet, but no damage to the liver was detected.
– an anxiety state of unknown cause, possibly brought about by the first anniversary of the Majoda shooting or possibly induced by amphetamines (which also cause loss of appetite and can cause vomiting).
– raised blood pressure, which is not unexpected in an obese, sedentary smoker who drank.
– depression.

I also conclude that he did not have diabetes in 1946.

2. St Vincent's hospital, New York, 1953. A memorandum made by Dr William Murphy after a visit to the hospital on December 3 1964, held in the Constantine FitzGibbon archive, Harry Ransom Center, University of Texas at Austin.

The medical notes, as summarised in Murphy's memorandum, record that prior to admission Dylan

– had delirium tremens before falling into a coma, and that he had had delirium tremens "several times in the past." [this information could have come only from Feltenstein or Reitell and should be treated with caution. I discuss and dismiss the diagnosis on p194.]
– had been given half a grain of morphine and eight units of ACTH approximately half an hour before lapsing into coma [Feltenstein left the hotel at about 11pm on November 4. In a letter of January 4 1965, Murphy refers to "80 units" of ACTH, which was undoubtedly the dosage given.]

The notes then went on to say that on admission Dylan

– had seizures and was placed on Dilantin. [This is the brand name of phenytoin, an anti-epileptic drug. It was given to calm seizures, which in Dylan's case were induced by the insufficient supply of oxygen to the brain.]

– was "profoundly comatose", in that "he had extensor plantar response bilaterally." [When a doctor runs a hard object down the sole of the foot, the toes curl downwards – a plantar response. If they curl the other way – an extensor response – it means there is damage in the 'long tracts' of nerves which run up to the brain and back to the foot muscles. Somewhere along that distance is a problem, and when associated with coma, the problem is likely to be in the brain. In Dylan's case, it was bilateral (both feet), so both sides of the brain were malfunctioning.]

– had coarse crepitant rales audible in all areas of his chest. [These are noises associated with bronchitis.]

– had bronchial pneumonia as shown by a chest film.

– had a red blood cell count of 5,100,000 and a white cell count of 21,050. [The red cell count was normal but the white cell count is raised, which is associated with an infection, in this case, bronchopneumonia.]

– tested negative for diabetes.

– tested negative for poisoning by barbiturates and other drugs.

Finally, the admitting doctors noted "in their rather scanty history", as Murphy described it, that Dylan

– suffered from a stomach ulcer three years prior to admission. [the post-mortem found no sign of ulceration.]

– attempted suicide with Siconal in 1951. [Sicanol is the trade name for chemicals, made by a Belgian company, that are used in the beverages industry. I believe that it is a typing error, and that the writer intended Seconal, a barbiturate often used in suicides in combination with alcohol. Murphy records that the medical notes give no further information about this incident. See also the note on p168]

– had old scars, about four, "over the dorsal aspect of both wrists."

– had drunk "smoke", as well as "wood alcohol in the past". [Smoke is a cocktail that was once served in some New York bars; it mixed alcohol with Sterno, a stove fuel. This information about smoke and wood alcohol could have come only from Feltenstein, Reitell or Brinnin and should be treated with caution. I discuss this on pp87-88]

3. The Medical Summary

The other main source of data available to us on Dylan's condition is the Medical Summary completed on November 9 by Dr William McVeigh for the purposes of the post-mortem. It described the circumstances of Dylan's admission, diagnosis and treatment at St Vincent's:

> Admitted 5th day of November 1953 at 1.58am by ambulance from the Hotel Chelsea 23rd St.& 7th Ave. Examined by F. Gilbertson MD
> Pt. Brought into Hosp in coma at 1.58am 11/5/53. Remained in coma during Hosp stay. History of heavy alcoholic intake. Received gn.1/2 of M.S. [morphine sulphate] shortly before admission. CSF [cerebrospinal fluid] clear on 2 occasions, press 260mm/H2O, Protein 34 mg %. Urine neg for barbiturates. Serum Amylase normal.
> No history of injury.
>
> LUMBAR PUNCTURE 11/5/53   11/8/53
> Impression on admission was Acute Alcoholic Encephalopathy – for which patient was treated without response. Expired after 4+ days in coma.
>
> W. B. McVeigh MD

Comments on the notes

Dylan was injected with half a grain (30mg) of morphine shortly before admission. Morphine can cause coma, and can contribute to it. It can also cause respiratory depression, which can lead to hypoxia (insufficient oxygen in the blood stream), especially in someone with a pre-existing lung disease. Hypoxia can lead to coma, permanent brain damage and death. Morphine is usually metabolised by the liver, but this would be delayed in a person whose liver was damaged so that a course of injections in one day, such as Dylan received, would lead to a build-up of morphine in the body.

The CSF pressure was at the upper limit of normal for an obese man, allowing for some elevation having been caused by the morphine. The fact that the CSF was clear rules out many causes of coma, including sub-arachnoid haemorrhage, major trauma to the head and infection i.e. meningitis. The protein measurement in the CSF of 34 mg % was within the normal range, 18 to 58 mg per dL, but it is also within the range known to occur in acute alcoholism, 13 to 88 mg per dL, so it does not rule in, nor rule out, acute alcoholism, nor most other diagnoses for coma.

Dylan's urine had tested negative for barbiturates, so that an overdose of barbiturates was not the cause of his coma.

Raised serum amylase is diagnostic of pancreatitis, often a complication of acute and chronic alcohol abuse. But the result was normal.

The lumbar punctures were carried out to extract the cerebro-spinal fluid for diagnostic tests.

4. Other data from St Vincent's

Nashold and Tremlett (1997) also provide data which they obtained from the questions they put to hospital staff. On admission, Dylan was severely dehydrated (p172) and that blood sugar tests on November 5 "showed a level of over 500 milligrammes against a norm of between 100 and 120 milligrammes" (p159). They were also told that Dylan's heartbeat was faint; his pulse weak but steady; his face "dry and clammy with blue lips and a splotchy, red and white, bloated face"; and the pupils of his eyes were small, not dilated (p155). Nashold and Tremlett report that Dylan was found to have anaemia (p115), but this is not borne out by the blood cell count described in Murphy's memorandum. However, the blood cell count on admission would have been done on concentrated blood, since Dylan was dehydrated. After the blood volume had been restored by administering fluids, that figure would have dropped because the blood would have been more dilute. This fall in red blood cell concentration could have brought the figure below normal, which is the definition of anaemia. It was probably for this condition that Dylan was given a blood transfusion, described by Brinnin, in the early hours of November 5.

Post-Mortem Report

Reproduced faithfully, including American spellings and typing errors.

AUTOPSY

Approximate Age   **39 years**   Approximate Weight   **180 lbs.**
Height   **5'5"**

Identified by   Residence

Stenographer   **William J. Burke**   Residence   **(Book #304)**

I hereby certify that I   **Milton Helpern, MD** have performed an autopsy on the body of   **DYLAN THOMAS**   at   **City Mortuary**   on the **10th** day of **November** **1953** **dictation begun** hours after the death, and the said autopsy revealed   **@ 2:40 p.m.**

AUTOPSY PERFORMED BY DR MILTON HELPERN
DEPUTY CHIEF MEDICAL EXAMINER
(In the presence of Drs. DiMaio & Mathus)

EXTERNAL INSPECTION:

Adult white male appearing to be about 40 years of age; 5'5" tall; estimated weight 180lb.; obese trunk; puffy face; wavy brown hair on head; moderate frontal baldness; brown eyes; unshaven face; several days growth of brown hair; teeth in upper jaw irregular in alignment, rather widely spaced – in the lower jaw also show some irregularity – all teeth show discoloration – several teeth missing in the left lower jaw; rigor mortis is complete; foreskin short somewhat edematous; purplish post mortem lividity present posteriorly; needle puncture marks with slight ecchymosis of skin over dorsum left hand; lumbar puncture mark posteriorly; mottled purple lividity; skin anteriorly somewhat pale; faint blue lividity of face; slight rosacea of cheeks; small scar 3/4" above outer end of the right eyebrow and also linear scar of the left eyebrow. No other signs of traumatic injury.

ON SECTION OF THE HEAD:

On reflecting the scalp no evidence of injury in the galea. Cavarium 1/8" to 5/16" in thickness. Dura intact.

Brain shows considerable pial edema over vertex with increase in cerebrospinal fluid lifting up piarachnoid. No hemorrhages noted between meninges which are clear. Arteries at the base appear normal. Brain heavy, 1,600 grams; on section shows only congested; no areas of softening or hemorrhage made out anywhere. Lateral ventricles contain clear fluid. Basal ganglions intact. Pons, cerebellum, brain stem grossly normal. No injuries at the base of the skull. Dura strips fairly easily.

ON SECTION OF THE TRUNK:

Panniculus up to 1½" in thickness; recti muscles fairly well developed; considerable excess fat in the mesenteric, omental retroperitoneal fatty depots; fat is rather firm and lobulations are exaggerated. Peritoneum everywhere smooth and shiny. On opening the chest cartilages are slightly calcified. Diaphragm at the level of the 4th rib right, 4th space on the left.

LUNGS: Lie in the posterior portion of the pleural cavities which contain no fluid. Anteriorly, lungs slightly emphysematous; posteriorly somewhat atelectatic and also lumpy in consistency with many small punctuate hemorrhages in the pleura over the collapsed lumpy portions of the lung posteriorly.
Bronchi deeply congested and also covered with patchy fibrinopurulent membrane. Lungs heavy for their size – left one, 750 grams – right one 700 grams. On section, parenchyma dark red in color; markedly dimished aeration with a patchy bronchpneumonia very evidence on the cut surface especially in the depednent portions. Lower lobes – pneumonic areas gray in color somewhat raised. All of the lobes appear to be involved in this bronchopneumonic process.

HEART: Lies free in the pericadial sac; increased fat over anterior surface of pericadium and also in the superior media stinum. Heart weighs 330 grams. Chambers contain dark red fluid and soft clotted blood, also some chicken fat clot. Valves on the right side flexible and natural. Fossa ovalis closed. Some atheroma in the anterior leaflet of mitral valve. Aortic valve cusps normal.
Proximal segment of left anterior descending coronary artery shows considerable sclerosis with calcification and narrowing of

the lumen to about 50 per cent of its original size. Right coronary shows only slight atheromatous change. Myocardium flabby, uniformly light brown in color. Aorta throughout its length fairly smooth and elastic.

NECK ORGANS: Larynx removed. Air passages not obstructed. There is considerable reddening with irritation of mucuous membrane upper part of trachea extending down from vocal cords. Thyroid dull red in color.

G.I. TRACT: Esophagus – several fine varices in the lower part of the esophagus.
Stomach dilated; mucuous membrane bile-stained; contents consist of some green turbid fluid about 1 liter with small particles of food in it; mucous membrane soft and slimy; no evidence of ulceration made out.
Duodenum is grossly normal.
Small Intestine contains light yellowish green liquid content, turbid, in considerable amount; farther long more mushy, fecal in character.
Appendix present.
Large Bowel contains mushy greenish brown feces; abundant excess pericolic fat.

LIVER: Smooth, light yellowish brown in color; weighs 2,400 grams; on section, color is similar; markings regular; consistency somewhat firmer than normal; fairly evident fatty infiltration.
Gall Bladder: Contains about 20 c.c. of thin green turbid bile.

SPLEEN: Moderately enlarged; weighs 260 grams; smooth; pulp soft, dark red in color.

PANCREAS: Shows considerable fatty infiltration, surrounded and concealed by fat; on section, lobulations are fairly well preserved; no evidence of fat necrosis or old pancreatitis but considerable fat between the lobules.

ADRENALS: Show well differentiated cortex and medulla.

KIDNEYS: Normal in size; light brown in color; together, 350 grams; marking somewhat indistinct. Pelves and ureters natural.

URINARY BLADDER: Empty; mucosa shows several hemorrhages in the region of fundus evidently associated with catheretization.

PROSTATE, SEMINAL VESICLES, TESTICLES: Grossly normal.

No injuries of SPINE, RIBS, BONES of EXTREMITIES.

Note: There is a transverse tracheotomy – enters the upper part of trachea.

ANATOMICAL DIAGNOSIS: Enlarged fatty liver:
Fatty kidneys:
Pial edema:
Pulmonary congestion, atelectasis:
Extensive hypostatic bronchopneumonia, bilaterals
Tracheotomy:
Acute tracheobronchitis:
In too long for alcohol studies:
Portion of brain and liver taken for chemical analysis (#2396).

CAUSE OF DEATH: PIAL EDEMA:
FATTY LIVER:
HYPOSTATIC   BRONCHOPNEU-
MONIA.

IDENTIFICATION:
Body of deceased identified to Miss L. Hirsch, stenographer, at the City Mortuary, about 4.15, Nov. 10, 1953, by:
JAMES LAUGHLIN, FRIEND 20 YEARS, 333 SIXTH AVE., N.Y.C.

Classify as
Acute & Chronic Ethylism
Hypostatic Bronchopneumonia
M.H.

Notes

The following abbreviations have been used:

Libraries:

NLW	National Library of Wales, Aberystwyth
CE/NLW	The Colin Edwards Archive, National Library of Wales
DMT/NLW	Dylan Thomas Archive, National Library of Wales
RT/NLS	Ruthven Todd Archive, National Library of Scotland, Edinburgh
CF/Texas	Constantine FitzGibbon Collection, Harry Ransom Humanities Research Center (HRC), the University of Texas at Austin
DMT/Texas	Dylan Thomas Collection, HRC
GR/Texas	George Reavey Collection, HRC
Minnesota	John Berryman Collection, University of Minnesota
JMB/Delaware	John Malcolm Brinnin Collection, University of Delaware
JMB/JHT	Letters from John Brinnin to John H. Thompson, Delaware
JMB/UPM	Brinnin's unpublished memoir, *A Passing of Papers*, Delaware
ND/Harvard	New Directions Collection, Houghton Library, Harvard

Books and papers:

Brinnin	John Malcolm Brinnin, *Dylan Thomas in America*, 1965, Dent
DNT 2004	David N. Thomas, *Dylan Remembered 1935-1953*, vol 2, 2004, Seren
GTD/RG	Transcripts of interviews carried out by Geraint Talfan Davies and Rob Gittins in New York in September 1983, and in the possession of Gittins. A small portion of the interviews was used in a HTV documentary *The*

	Far-Ago Land, broadcast in November 1983. See Davies 2008 pp75-77 for an account of the filming.
Ferris	Paul Ferris, *Dylan Thomas: The Biography*, 1999, Dent.
FitzGibbon	Constantine FitzGibbon, *The Life of Dylan Thomas*, 1965, Atlantic
Lycett	Andrew Lycett, *Dylan Thomas: A New Life*, 2003, Weidenfeld and Nicholson.
N and T	James Nashold and George Tremlett, *The Death of Dylan Thomas*, 1997, Mainstream Publishing

No chapter or page numbers are given for Ruthven Todd's unpublished memoir of Dylan Thomas because they vary from one draft to another. The memoir was written in the late 1950s and early 1960s as the first authorised biography. Todd gave up in 1962 and FitzGibbon was asked to take over.

John Brinnin's unpublished memoir has no page numbering. Brinnin started gathering material for the memoir in the 1950s and worked on it over the years, right up until his death.

The Colin Edwards archive at the NLW comprises some 150 taped interviews with Dylan's friends and family, most done in the 1960s and early 1970s. They have been transcribed and edited, and appear in Thomas 2003 and 2004.

QCE means that the questions asked in the interviews reproduced in this book were posed by Colin Edwards.

QDNT means that I have inserted the questions in an interview, memoir or letter as a device to make the material more readable, but the interviewee's, or letter writer's, words are exactly the same as they appear in the original. This can be checked against the reference given for the original.

1. A Case of Cold Feet

p7 *Helpern*: see Houts 1968 and Helpern 1979.
scars on wrists: see the appendix.
p8 *causes of death etc*: death certificate, DMT/NLW.
Murphy's memorandum: see the appendix.

2. Dylan's Bucking Broncho

p9 *brain haemorrhage, mugging*: Brinnin p238.
p10 *bronchitis and laryngitis*: to Caitlin, April or May 1937.

weak lungs: to the Royal Literary Fund, August 26 1938.

Samuel Barber: see Heyman 1992, p375 and Coleman 1958. The money was to come from Barber's patron, Mary Bok Zimbalist.

unreliable lung: to James Laughlin, June 20 1940.

huge cough, itching feet, mumps and gout: letters of February 3 1940, September 1943, July 27 1944 respectively.

vomiting: see, for example, Elizabeth Ruby Milton and Rayner Heppinstall, interviews, CE/NLW.

p11 *Conquest of a Germ, food-losing cough etc*: to Caitlin, ?1943 and Donald Taylor, ?1943.

p12 *for a description of New Quay when Dylan was there*: see Thomas, 2002b.

Dylan in New Quay, the local doctor etc: see Thomas 2000 and 2002a.

the Killicks, shooting incident etc: see chapters 1 to 4 in Thomas 2000 and pp97-104 in Thomas 2002a.

p14 *history of the writing of Under Milk Wood*: see DNT 2004, chapter 2.

letters from New Quay: to Donald Taylor March 28 1945 and to an unknown woman May 21 1945.

Under Milk Wood in London: see Davin 1985, p126; also quoted in DNT 2004, p292

Welsh Carmarthenshire: to Blaencwm, halfway between Llangain and Llansteffan in Carmarthenshire. The dampness was noted in the *Rural Housing Inspection Report, 1945.*

living in America: to Oscar Williams, July 30 1945.

swampy place: Jack Lindsay 1968, pp18-19.

broadcasts: he made 48 in 1946 and 25 between 1937 and 1945, including those for which he had written scripts. FitzGibbon, 1965 pp347-50.

p15 *laid out with a haemorrhage*: the friends were Bill and Helen McAlpine – see a letter from Bill to Constantine FitzGibbon, May 15 1964, CF/Texas.

St. Stephen's hospital: see the appendix for the hospital notes. Case of haematemesis: see p153. Failed to keep appointment: reported by Lindsay (1968) and in a letter from a Consultant to FitzGibbon, CF/Texas.

harking back: to John Ormond, May 30 1946.

asthmatic son: Llewelyn, who lived with his grandmother in the "flat, damp New Forest district." He lived at the Cherwell hut from January 1947 until the trip to Italy in April – see Dylan's letter to his parents, January 12 1947.

£1000 from Laughlin: see Laughlin's own account of this in the collection of his writings edited by Epler and Javitch 2006, p298. Dylan went

to Laughlin's room at Claridge's, and Laughlin immediately took him to a bank and had the £1000 counted out into Dylan's hand. Dylan owned up a few days later and repaid the money through his royalties. The incident was probably during Laughlin's visit to London in 1946 – see Dylan's letter to him of November 24, which also refers to the plans for America.

Lutyens and Walton etc: see Lutyens 1972 p154 and Dylan's letter to his parents of January 12 1947.

p16 *snow and great flood of 1947*: see Wainwright, 2007 for details.

British weather: these data, and those that follow, come from newspaper reports and T.A. Harley's excellent British weather homepage.

hut damaged etc: letter to Vernon Watkins, March 16 1947.

icicles on his cough: Edith Sitwell to Maurice Bowra, March 24 1947 in *Selected Letters*, 1970.

good health in Italy: Piero Bigongiari interview, CE/NLW and DNT 2004,

Under Milk Wood in Elba: DNT 2004, pp293-94.

a man who passes on earth: Augusto Livi interview, CE/NLW and DNT 2004.

flooded fields: Bill Green interview, CE/NLW and DNT 2004.

low, sodden etc: to Hector MacIver, February 17 1949. A visitor described how she walked "along the broken and muddy path leading to his house, isolated and lost in a large, foggy meadow…" Roussillat 1954, p10.

p17 *health at South Leigh*: see Bill Green, Bill Mitchell (station master) and Dosh Murray interviews in CE/NLW and in DNT 2004.

reading 'Extraordinary Cough' on the radio, fog etc: November 15 1948.

cycling in the fog: letter to Vernon Watkins, November 23 1948.

enveloping fog: from November 26, lasting for almost five days.

deaths from the fog: see Logan, 1949.

orchestral asthma: to Vernon Watkins, November 23 1948.

wheezing etc in Prague: Jirina Haukova in DNT 2004, p161; and Josef Nesvadba interview CE/NLW, also in DNT 2004.

Under Milk Wood in Prague: see DNT 2004, chapter 2, pp295-97.

bronchial heronry: to Oscar Williams, October 8 1952.

flu, invitation from Brinnin etc: letter from Dylan to Brinnin, May 28 1949. Brinnin had been appointed on April 4 1949. Brinnin offered $500 for travel to, but not back from, America and the fee for the reading on February 23 1950 at the Poetry Center, and then $150 for each of the readings at the Center on February 25 and May 15 (Brinnin's financial papers, JMB/Delaware). The return passage of $260 was deducted from Dylan's earnings. For the 1952 and 1953 trips, Dylan had to fund his passage to and from America from his fees, as Brinnin's financial accounts make clear.

agent's fee: Brinnin says in his book (p53) that his fee was ten percent. But his financial accounts at Delaware, as well as his letter of March 14 1951 to Dylan's accountant, state that it was fifteen percent. It later rose to 25%.

p18 *no place for a rest-cure:* to the McAlpines, November 12 1949.

debts, breakdown etc: letter to John Davenport, July 30 1949.

condition of Boat House: an inspection carried out in March 1946 found it to be in good repair, with no dampness or any other defects, except for the absence of lead flashing on the chimney stacks. (*Rural Housing Inspection Report*). It's unlikely the condition of the house changed greatly between 1946 and 1949, as it was occupied until 1948.

doctor's prescription: Laugharne chemist private prescription book, July 28 and 29 1949. He prescribed aspirin, camphor, sodium chloride and sodium bicarbonate for the chest.

list of medicines: linctus: reverse of a letter to John Brinnin, DMT/NLW; balsam: letter to David Higham, February 6 1953; Fenox, codeine and codis: a memo Dylan wrote on the back of a cheque book, where the codeine and codis are mentioned as being for his chest and the Fenox to relieve congestion in his nose. The memo also refers to Takazyma for his stomach acidity and calomel for his liver, a medicine that was later found to have been responsible for many deaths (DMT/NLW).

gout, gastritis, phlegm etc: see various letters May 28 to November 28, 1949.

Caitlin ill with pneumonia: Dr David Hughes interview, CE/NLW.

Caitlin on Dylan's coughing fits at Laugharne: Caitlin Thomas 1986, pp67-68, 175.

Aeronwy Thomas: interview, CE/NLW and DNT 2004.

p19 *Florence Thomas:* interview, CE/NLW.

visit to sanatorium: to see Griff Jenkins Senior. The sanatorium was at Talgarth, Brecon, and Dylan used to visit Jenkins in 1944 and 1945. See a letter from the hospital secretary to FitzGibbon April 13 1964, CF/Texas. I have written about Dylan's friendship with Jenkins in Thomas 2000.

deaths in the family: death certificates.

smoking as a cure: the uncle was Evan Williams of Llwyngwyn farm, Llangain – see chapter 1 of Thomas 2003, which has an extensive account of Dylan's family tree.

Dylan's eating and poor diet: see the Index of DNT 2004, p403, for testimonies on this. Ice cream and beer: FitzGibbon, 1965, p81. Beer and

cake: Mervyn Levy interview, CE/NLW and in DNT 2004. Breakfast at
Cwmdonkin: Dylan to Hansford Johnson, January 1934. Not eating in
South Leigh: Bill Mitchell interview, CE/NLW and in DNT 2004. Not
eating in Laugharne: John Morgan Dark interview, CE/NLW. Not eating
at the Etoile: David Higham, a memoir of Dylan, CF/Texas.

p20 *Dylan and sleeping*: see the Index of DNT 2004, p403. He also had
bouts of insomnia as a young man. See his letters to Pamela Hansford
Johnson, week of November 11 1933; and May 9 and 27, 1934.

St Stephen's notes re sleeping: see the appendix.

Caitlin on sleep and anxiety: see Caitlin Thomas 1986, p175, and 1957,
p64.

sedatives at the Boat House: Laugharne chemist private prescription book,
May 25 1949. We do not know for how long Caitlin took phenobarbitone
because free prescriptions became available soon after, and no records
survive.

Seconal: from Dylan's St Vincent's hospital notes, as summarised in
William Murphy's 1964 memorandum, CF/Texas, and see the appendix
above. Both Ferris (p278) and Lutyens (1972, pp202-04) give accounts
of the incident that took place in the autumn of 1951 when Dylan threatened to kill himself after a row with Caitlin.

Barber's address: letter to Princess Caetani, February 12 1950.

cooked too long: Milton 1993.

a very sick man: Reuben Brown, Amherst college, to Brinnin, March 17
1950, JMB/Delaware.

Bryn Mawr etc: see Augustine, 1950. Dylan looked terribly ill: email from
Jane Augustine, May 5 2008.

p21 *reading at Urbana*: see Craft 1959, pp77-78 and 1972 p16. The
pamphlet for the Festival notes a "Concert of Compositions by Igor
Stravinsky" (University of Illinois archives).

coughing, vomiting and blood: Brinnin, pp6, 11, 16, 18, 19 and 36.

sleeping in America: letter to Caitlin, March 15 1950: "I never seem to
sleep in a bed any more, only on planes & trains." Sleeping pills: letter to
Caitlin, February 25 1950.

Brinnin gives sedative and calls doctor: Brinnin, pp19, 20.

sleeping pills: David Daiches 1954 p58.

fed him pills and capsules: Brinnin, p64.

Dylan in Iowa: see West 1972.

wonderful but impossible etc: JMB/JHT, April 2, May 27 1950.

p22 *scared of everything etc*: JMB/UPM, no page numbers.

friends and lovers etc: see Brinnin p60 and letter from Harvard professor
F.O. Matthiessen, quoted in JMB/UPM.

fee of $810: see the note on p169 below.
Studebaker convertible: JMB/UPM.
dabbled in gay sex: see Ferris, p117.
I want him: quoted in Lycett p284.
p23 *Brinnin kissing Dylan*: S. Kaplan-Williams, *The Life and Death of Oscar Williams*, website.
flood of tears etc: Brinnin, p67.
impulse, obsession etc: JMB/UPM.
dead to the world etc: Caitlin Thomas 1986, p140.
American earnings 1950: **total earnings** $5400/£1928 (£1=$2.80). **Total expenses** $3482/£1243. **Net earnings** $1918/£685, on some of which Dylan still had to pay British income tax. Expenses accounted for 64% of total earnings. These expenses comprised living and travelling costs of $2460, USA income tax $212 and Brinnin's fee of $810. (From Brinnin's reply to Dylan's accountant, Leslie Andrews, March 14 1951, in Brinnin's financial papers, JMB/Delaware. The net earnings of $1918 correspond with the figure Brinnin gives in his book of $2000 – see p54). Brinnin's accounts make it clear that Dylan had to pay his internal travel costs, his return passage to the UK, and hotel bills. Of Dylan's earnings, $800 was smuggled in a handbag by Brinnin to Caitlin (Brinnin p67); $300 was posted to her, and some $200 was in Dylan's wallet when he left New York (letter to Leslie Andrews from Brinnin, May 7 1951). The information about the $200 in his wallet had been supplied by Dylan himself in his letter to Brinnin of April 12 1951.
Lena Horne, looking after Dylan, limping home, silken thread, Florence and Venice etc: JMB/JHT, September 3 and 30 1950.
p24 *dancing with McKenna, meets her in Venice, masculine glow*: JMB/UPM and JMB/JHT, February 10 1951. Brinnin's memoir describes other romantic interludes with McKenna.
Brinnin in Paris, Florence, Venice etc: JMB/JHT, September 3 and 30 1950 and JMB/UPM.
Brinnin's money problems: Grubb Street – January 12 1953; controlled and defeated by money – January 29 1952. See also October 7 1950 ("chronic poverty"), March 18 1951 ("hanging on by my teeth"), June 30 1951 ("razor's edge"), March 10 1953 ("hanging on by the nails"), February 27 1954 ("congenitally broke and on the edge as ever"). All JMB/JHT.
begging letters to Thompson: see those of January 5, September 3 and 30 1950; January ? (behind on car repayments), January 21 (court order for a debt), April 3 (owing tax), June 30 and September 16 1951; October 11 and December 6 1952; February 28 (owing tax) 1953.

JMB/Delaware. Brinnin and John Hinsdale Thompson had met as undergraduates at Michigan and remained life-long and intimate friends until Thompson's death in 1973. Thompson taught at Stephens College in Columbia, Missouri.

much-abused miracle: JMB/JHT, January 26 1951.

expensive tastes, Europe, liners etc: see his letters to John Thompson, 1950 to 1957, JMB/Delaware. In 1950, for example, he rented a house for most of June, July and early August in Pigeon Cove, Mass., before leaving to spend six weeks in Europe

rich people: "Youth and the intellectuals travel tourist, really rich people travel cabin, while Hollywood and the State Department travel first, along with a few declasse oil barons and buyers for Henri Bendel." JMB/JHT, December 25 1950.

soaking up a lifestyle, living beyond his means: JMB/JHT, September 3 1950.

pleurisy and pneumonia: Pearl Kazin to Brinnin, quoted in Brinnin, p77. Dylan also described the illness to Princess Caetani: "lots of chills, and they jaundiced me, and I lay snarling at the edge of pleurisy." November 11 1950.

visit to a doctor: Lycett, p310.

p25 *Dylan in Iran*: see Thomas 2000, chapter 6.

Brinnin in anguish: JMB/JHT January ?, January 21, April 3 1951.

Read looks for woman, Sandy etc: JMB/UPM.

visits McKenna: JMB/UPM and JMB/JHT February 10 1951.

Capri, Cannes etc: JMB/JHT, August 23 and September 3 1951.

present pace etc: Laughlin to Brinnin, August 21 1951, JMB/Delaware, quoted in Lycett p319.

bronchitis, fits etc: letter to Oscar Williams, October or November 1951.

listened to The Rake's Progress: Craft 1959, pp77-78. The premiere was on September 11 1951.

Michael Powell etc: see Craft 1959, Powell 1992.

p26 *McKenna, Thornedale*: JMB/UPM and JMB/JHT, February 10 1951.

Katzenjammer Kids, entrepreneurial enterprise etc: JMB/UPM.

at least once a month: JMB/JHT, February 19 1952.

Broyard meets him: see Broyard, 1997, p123.

ill in America, sleeping pills etc: letter to Sophie Wilkins, February 21 1952.

strained, tired etc: LaFlamme, 1956.

alternating chills and fevers: Bogorad, 1956.

barbiturates and atropine at Vermont: LaFlamme, 1956. Gladys LaFlamme was a poet and teacher and married to Francis Colburn (1909-1984), a humourist, raconteur and artist in residence at Vermont since 1942.

rasher of bacon: Eberhart 1954 p56.

pleurisy: letter to David Higham, June 28 1952.

p27 *fatal disservice etc*: Caitlin to Brinnin, May 10 1952, JMB/Delaware. Misdated and probably sent on May 16 or 17. The ship had left New York on May 16.

3. A Fatal Disservice Done

p28 *tired of job*: Brinnin had decided by September 1950 that he wished to give up, or seriously curb, his work with the Poetry Center. JMB/JHT, September 30 and October 7 1950.

Reitell appointment: JMB/JHT, July 30 and October 11, 1952 ("spectacularly good at the job").

1952 tour, Goyen, Sitwells, MacNeice, Moss, gay club etc: JMB/JHT, April 8, July 2 and 30, August 17 and 24 1952. Bum voyage etc – details in JMB/UPM.

north London pub, together and sick again etc: Brinnin, p149ff.

p29 *simper and spindles*: Dylan to Oscar Williams, October 8 1952.

borrowed $300: JMB/JHT, October 11 1952.

drizzle over Boat House: Dylan, November 6, 1952, to Princess Caetani. It was the day that a deepening depression moved across Britain, bringing rain, winds and heavy snow, with drifts in the Welsh valleys that stopped trains running.

slippered crow: Dylan to A.G. Prys-Jones, November 21 1952. Bronchitis: three letters on November 21 1952. Dylan had been in London for a week, and appeared in *The Shadow of Cain* on November 16.

Donald Hall visit etc: see Hall 1992. Hall gives an interesting account of Dylan at Harvard in 1950, as well as in Laugharne, London and Oxford 1951/52. It seeems the reading at Oxford was on October 15 1952 – see Dylan's letter to Douglas Cleverdon, October 9.

deaths: Marged Stepney-Howard was the patron, Norman Cameron and Idris Davies the friends. Another friend called Helen also died.

murder: that of Elizabeth Thomas, battered and stabbed to death on January 10 1953. See Thomas 2000, chapter 5.

p30 *London air pollution levels*: see Hunt 2003 and Bell 2004. There was a 14-fold increase in deaths from bronchitis, 5-fold from pneumonia and 9-fold for other respiratory conditions. The total number of excess deaths caused by the Great Smog was in excess of 5,000. Dylan appeared in *The Shadow of Cain* on January 13, returned to Swansea and then went back to London to stay there whilst Caitlin had her abortion.

ill returning from London: letters February 6 1953.

grieve and sneeze: to Joan Bowles, February 15 1953.

London in late February: see his letters February 16 to March 2 1953.

severe smog: newspaper reports.

Billy Williams and Mably Owen: CE/NLW and in DNT 2004, QDNT. Williams dates the incident to seven months before Dylan died. The interviewer, QDNT, is me and, in other interviews, Colin Edwards. For more on QDNT and Edwards, see p164.

first-class noodle, planning Europe trip: JMB/JHT, February 28 1953.

clear-eyed etc: Brinnin p156.

p31 *cold American girls*: quote from Ferris p301.

political office etc: Dorothy Bradley, a friend in Montana since 1970, email February 21 2007. Reitell helped Bradley get elected to the Montana House of Representatives. Reitell gave her "brilliant assistance every step of the way with speeches, press releases and campaign strategy. I probably would not have been bold enough to do this without her fierce brazenness and confidence."

Sioux chief: Talfan Davies 2008, p76.

Reitell highly emotional, no restraint etc: Cecil Garland, a Montana friend for over twenty-five years, letter February 12 2007: "with almost no personal restraints in her devotion to a cause."

no experience etc: Reitell said it was her first literary job – to Gittins December 9 1984. I haven't found any evidence that Reitell had had any previous production experience. At Bennington, she majored in design. Her student experience was in design and dancing – see drama programmes 1939 and 1941, Crossett Library, Bennington.

Reitell's logical mind, vocabulary and concise expression: family memoir by her uncle, Richard Evans Myer, in the possession of Rob Gittins and Lois Gridley, Reitell's cousin.

brilliant wordsmith: Dorothy Bradley, email February 21 2007. Another friend also thought Reitell was "phenomenal" with words: Harriet Marble, a friend in Montana since 1965, email February 1 2007.

Miller on Reitell: quoted in N and T pp205-06. Reitell claimed that she also looked after Marilyn Monroe during the filming of *The Misfits*: email, Harriet Marble; letter, Cecil Garland, February 12 2007; and Reitell's obituary, *Bozeman Daily Chronicle*, February 21 2001.

things in common, good at bad behaviour, Sitwell, ranch fantasy etc: Reitell interview, GTD/RG.

p32 *Haverford April 24*: letters to Brinnin from John A. Lester of the college, professor of English, March 30 and April 13 1953, JMB/Delaware. See also the note on p177 about the Haverford reading.

John Ashby Lester Sr, 1871-1969: Googling brings up his cricket career.

Bennington: see Anon. 1953.

met Jackson and Hyman 1953: David Griffith Rees, email February 22 2008. Rees, who is Special Advisor to the President of the college, had been told this by the then President. Hyman had a teaching post at the college, and the couple lived in Bennington, having moved there from Westport where the 1950 supper had taken place.

Weep for Adonais: see Oppenheimer 1989 pp150-152 for an account of Jackson's three pieces written about Dylan.

Syracuse: letters to Brinnin from Mary Marshall at the university, December 24 1952 and April 14 1953, JMB/Delaware. See also Osborn 1953.

Williamstown reading: see McGowan 1953.

harried by Reitell: Brinnin pp165 and 173.

p33 *Duke reading*: see Divine 1953.

Dylan at Connecticut: Brinnin p173.

Dylan returned exhausted: see Brinnin pp172-73.

Liz Reitell and Under Milk Wood etc: Brinnin, chapter 6 but see also DNT 2004, chapter 2.

ill and weary: Brinnin, p174.

simply can't do this: Reitell, BBC programme on Dylan, 1963, BBC archives, Caversham.

devastating denial: Brinnin, p183.

self-protective policy: see Brinnin, p160: "Wary of useless involvement, I had come to pay little attention to his habits or his movements... I was really taking care of myself." See also the notes on pp178-79. In fact, Brinnin had resolved as early as Dylan's 1950's trip to stop looking after him – see Brinnin pp59-60.

inhaler: N and T, p419.

Reitell's family doctor: interview, GTD/RG.

ACTH: Dylan seems to have had at least four injections of ACTH in May 1953 whilst in America.

morphine and gout: Nashold and Tremlett report on p125 that Milton Feltenstein gave Dylan morphine to ease the pain from the gout, but they do not give their source for this.

Oscar Williams: interview, CE/NLW and some in DNT 2004, QDNT.

p34 *Amherst, MacNeice etc*: see Anon. May 18 1953.

New England, meets Stravinsky etc: Brinnin pp175-182 and Craft 1959.

p35 *probably morphine*: Lycett, p354, refers to an analgesic or narcotic. No source is given, but presumably it comes from Reitell's diary.

friends from Vermont, very ill etc: see LaFlamme 1956, who uses the words "guards" to describe Reitell and Brinnin. LaFlamme's account contradicts Brinnin's timing of events that evening. Readings at the Poetry Center always started at 8.40pm. The performance of *Under Milk Wood* would have been over by 10.30pm. Brinnin says he took Dylan straight back to the hotel but LaFlamme has put this at midnight. Other discrepancies in Brinnin's account of this night are given by van Ghent, 1956. Van Ghent also quotes from a private note of LaFlamme which describes how Dylan was ill during and after the performance.

absolute deliverance: Brinnin, p184.

lunch with Barber etc: Brinnin p185.

Dylan ill, phone call to Brinnin etc: Lycett, p355, no source given.

Plath etc: she was a student at Smith College and had won a month's internship as a guest editor, June 1-26 1953. For more on this, see Alexander 1991 p114, Kirk 2004 p50 and Gordon 2003. For a wider picture on Plath at the magazine see Hammer 2001. Dylan refers to the meeting with Abels and Bolster in his letter to Abels of June 20 1953.

loved more than life: Gordon Lameyer in Butscher 1979 p33.

p36 *Feltenstein's career, marriage, children, college record etc*: from the Columbia College of Physicians and Surgeons archives; City College archives; the Medical Directory of New York; Feltenstein's obituaries in the *New York Times*, September 3 and 4, 1974; and his wife's in the same paper, April 11 1999.

Feltenstein's cv: born April 12 1901 to Hyman and Annie Feltenstein. Brought up in the Bronx (Union Avenue) and the borough of Queens (New Haven Avenue), New York. *1926*: gained his B.A. after attending City College of New York and Columbia College. *1931*: graduated with M.D. from Columbia University College of Physicians and Surgeons. *1931-32*: internship at Beth Israel Hospital, Manhattan. *1932 to his retirement*: staff member at Beth Israel and private practice at 44 Gramercy Park, New York. Retired from Beth Israel as an Associate Attending Physician. *July 26 1959*: bought 45 Water Lane, Free Acres, Berkeley Heights, New Jersey. *Married*: (1) name not known (2) Pat Liveright (1910-1999), a portrait photographer. There were two daughters, Isabel (married a Scharff) and Evelyn Ann, both from Feltenstein's first marriage, as well as two sons, John Henry King and Jeffry Howard King, from Liveright's first marriage. The sons' marriages led to three children: Tammy Jeanne, Heather and Jeff Jr. Milton Feltenstein died September 1 1974.

Feltenstein's parents etc: his father was Hyman Feltenstein, age in 1910 about 39, born Germany. Hyman's father's and mother's birth place: Russia. Hyman's year of immigration: 1884. Occupation: millinery salesman. Other household members: Annie Feltenstein, mother of Milton, age 29; Elfred Paul Feltenstein, 2, brother of Milton. Source: 1910 census, Bronx Assembly District 34, New York, which also shows Milton D. Feltenstein, age 9. In the 1920 census, the family is in the borough of Queens and Hyman is now listed as a "Manufacturer of Ladies' Hats." This census also provides the further information that Annie had Polish parents, was born in English-speaking Canada, and that Hyman's parents were Polish-speaking Russians.

writers and artists as patients: Todd to Louis MacNeice, November 23 1953 CF/Texas.

Pat related to Horace Liveright: Joe Romano, a Free Acres historian and neighbour of the Feltensteins, email August 12 2007. Information given to him by Pat Feltenstein, though no documentary confirmation.

p37 *son-in-law spoke Mandarin, visit to China etc*: Pat Liveright Feltenstein, letter to *Time* magazine, October 11 1976.

Feltenstein painter and sculptor etc: Terry Connor, friend and Free Acres neighbour, emails May 30 and 31 2007.

p38 *Welsh Zionist*: interview with Mary Ellin Barrett, April 27 1954.

Dylan and Jews: see DNT 2004, the index, pp401, 402; and *New Welsh Review*, spring 2005, p122.

Dylan on Feltenstein: letter to Reitell, June 16 1953.

Feltenstein as outspoken, gregarious etc: emails Terry Connor, May 30 and 31 2007.

swear in front of women etc: email Terry Connor, May 31 2007.

right thing, wrong place: Professors Linus and Tetsuo Yemane, emails May 29 and 31 2007.

p39 *been through hard times*: Joe Romano, email August 14 2007: "She'd been through some hard times personally. It was in her eyes. Whatever had happened it seemed to me that she'd made a connection with Milt, had accepted him whole, good points and bad, and made the most of whatever closeness they had." Romano remembered her as "a short, smart, outgoing woman who always seemed to be laughing or smiling. She called Milt "my bear"… Pat was sophisticated and well-travelled, and she looked a bit Asian." Email, June 3 2007.

Feltenstein a bastard: Professor Daryl Maslow Hafter, ex-Free Acre resident, email August 28 2007.

Feltenstein's Will: October 24 1973: "I intentionally make no provision under this my Will for my daughter, Evelyn Ann Feltenstein." After making provision for his wife, Feltenstein shared his estate between his other daughter, Isabel, and his wife's son, Jeffry Howard King.

generous doctor, popular in Chinatown etc: Linus and Tetsuo Yemane, emails May 29 and 31 2007.

shortcuts: email Terry Connor, May 31 2007. He once sewed up Conner's cut hand without giving him any Novocain, "laughing and telling me to bite on my leather belt!"

Reitell on the wild doctor: quoted in Ferris, p321.

made waves, brash, overbearing, unapproachable etc: Professor Daryl Maslow Hafter, email June 1 2007.

exhausted and shattered etc: Caitlin Thomas 1986, p176.

not financially rewarding etc: Brinnin, p171.

American earnings 1952, four months: **total earnings** $5572/£1990. **Total expenses** $5179/£1849. **Net earnings** $393/£140, before British income tax. Expenses accounted for 92% of total earnings. These expenses comprised Brinnin's fee of $1393; travel $1986, including trans-atlantic fares; living costs $1800 e.g. hotels, food, drink, shopping, laundry, tips, entertainments etc. Brinnin's financial papers, JMB/Delaware, with a summary on p40 above.

American earnings, spring 1953, six weeks: based on Brinnin's final accounts, as follows: **total earnings** $2555/£912. **Total expenses** $2287.95/£817. **Net earnings** $267.05/£95, before British income tax. Expenses accounted for 89% of total earnings. These expenses comprised Brinnin's fee of $638.75; travel $855.50, including trans-atlantic fares; living costs (defined as in above note) $615, of which about $150 were for hotels; medical expenses $178.70 (Brinnin's financial papers, JMB/Delaware, and see p40 above). Brinnin omitted the medical expenses from his final account but they were included in the earlier accounts of June 1 prepared for American income tax (DMT/Texas) and I have included them here – for details of these expenses see the note on p189. **NB**: In addition to the $2555, Dylan also earned, but might not have received, another $764.19 but this sum had disappeared from the final accounts and I have not included it here as part of his total earnings – see the sixth note below after this one.

earned more than Dylan, fee of twenty-five percent etc: Brinnin's financial papers, JMB/Delaware. He earned $2031 in fees from the 1952 and spring 1953 trips, whereas Dylan's net earnings totalled $660.05. With minimal expenses as an agent (only postage and telephone, some of which he claimed back from Dylan's earnings), Brinnin would have still earned more (net) than Dylan from the two trips even with a fee of fifteen percent.

p40 *Chancellor of the Exchequer*: JMB/JHT, January 26 1952.

p41 *signed blank cheques*: West (1972) describes his horror at finding Dylan with such a cheque book.

Dylan's accountant: Leslie Andrews and Co. of Horsham, Sussex.

Brinnin claims plane fare: Brinnin's accounts show that he claimed $35/£12.50 (= £253 today) from Dylan's earnings for Dylan's fare from Haverford to Boston. A letter from John A. Lester at the college on April 25 1953 told Brinnin the college had paid: "We had a grand evening with Dylan Thomas last night... [Haverford] has paid to get him on by plane to his next assignment in Boston." JMB/Delaware.

fees not in final spring 1953 accounts: the sum of $764.19/£272 (=£5,516 today) not entered in the accounts is explained as follows: a) Brinnin's accounts of June 1 1953 (see p178 for details) show that Dylan earned a total of $3255. But Brinnin gives the total as $2855, thus "losing" $400. b) when Brinnin did his final accounts (see p40 above), he gave Dylan's total earnings as $2555, losing another $300. c) The Poets' Theatre paid Dylan $364.19 for his appearances on May 1 and 3 but Brinnin entered only $300 – see a letter from the Theatre to Brinnin, July 15 1953 confirming the $364.19 as a fee and a share of the proceeds of the gate. Sources: a) June 1 accounts: DMT/Texas. These accounts were prepared for the visit of Dylan and Liz Reitell on June 1 to the American tax authorities to fill in his Departing Alien tax return. b) Final accounts and Poets' Theatre letter: Brinnin's financial papers, JMB/Delaware. There is also a further puzzle in Brinnin's accounts: the fee of $80 from the university of Connecticut, where Brinnin worked, is well below that from Dylan's other venues, and almost half that he received from the university ($150) on his 1952 trip. See Fig. 20, on page 178.

part of the cost, agent's fees, hanging by the nails, madness: JMB/JHT, March 10, February 28 and June 16 1953. The Center had agreed to pay a quarter.

nervous exhaustion: JMB/JHT, March 28 1953; bladder infection, July 31 and October 15 1953. Penicillin and sulphadiazine were often used to treat venereal disease. In his letter, Brinnin used the word 'sulfa.'

doctor's suicide: JMB/JHT, October 15 1953.

Brinnin's trip to Europe: JMB/JHT, August 8, 24 and September 13 1953.

Capote and Coward: JMB/JHT, September 13 1953.

p42 *chided by Capote*: Brinnin 1981 pp69-70.

little short of the truth: see Dylan's letter to Oscar Williams of June 22 1953 in which he writes that October 6 or 7 had been pencilled in for *Under Milk Wood* in New York.

reading of Under Milk Wood: at Porthcawl, south Wales – see interview with Thomas Taig, CE/NLW and DNT 2004.

p43 *visit to a doctor*: Wynford Vaughan Thomas went with Dylan to the doctor's, and mentioned the visit to Brinnin, who dates it as "two months before his final visit to New York." See Brinnin to FitzGibbon, February

UNIVERSITY & LECTURE FEES FOR DYLAN THOMAS June 1, 1953	
Haverford College	$225.00
Bennington College	150.00
Syracuse University	200.00
Williams College	150.00
Randolph-Macon College	150.00
Duke University	225.00
Amherst College	200.00
Boston University	300.00
University of Connecticut	80.00
Institute of Contemporary Arts	150.00
Massachusetts Institute of Technology	150.00
Young Men & Young Women Hebrew Association: Educational Department	800.00
Harvard University: Poets Theatre	200.00
Harvard University: Poets Theatre	100.00
Philadelphia Arts Council: Educational Council Seminar	175.00
TOTAL INCOME	$2,855.00

20. Dylan's American tour earnings, spring 1953, June 1 accounts

26 1964, CF/Texas. The blood clot and blackout are mentioned in Lycett, p371, without citation. Lycett dates the incident as eight weeks before Dylan's final visit.

hand-in-hand: Brinnin p189.

p44 *self-protective etc*: Brinnin interview, GTD/RG.

stopped his life etc: Brinnin interview, GTD/RG. Brinnin had made the same point in his book on p193.

bored with Dylan etc: Brinnin, p160, writing of his feelings in April 1953 at the start of Dylan's third trip.

Dylan damaging Brinnin's reputation: David Wagoner, email April 1 2007.

Brinnin in Laugharne, Stravinsky, purpose of trip to make money: Brinnin, pp194-96, 205-06.

finally off his hands: Brinnin interview, GTD/RG: "there was an agent who finally would take him off my hands... that was a sense of relief for me."

five other engagements: City College of New York, Cinema 16 Symposium on Art, Wheaton College, MIT and Mt Holyoke. See Brinnin p228 on the last three which were not fulfilled.

p45 *letter to Stravinsky*: September 22 1953. Dylan would be staying in the Chelsea hotel from his arrival on October 20 to his departure on November 5 for his reading at Wheaton College on November 6, from where he would go to Boston to stay with Brinnin for five days, before going on to Chicago, sometime before his engagement there on November 13. The stay in the Chelsea would have cost about $90 for the eighteen days. Dylan had to fund his fare to Chicago and then to California (and that back to New York) and daily expenses but not his accommodation, which Stravinsky was providing.

Phil Richards, Ivy and Ebie Williams: interviews, CE/NLW and in DNT 2004, QDNT.

new tooth: John Morgan Dark, interview, CE/NLW and in DNT 2004.

haircut: Jane Dark interview, CE/NLW and in DNT 2004.

tea with a minister: at the Manse, Llansteffan, Wynford Edwards note, CE/NLW.

arts club: at Tenby on October 2. See Garlick, 1995.

farewell party, blackouts: John Morgan Dark, interview, CE/NLW and in DNT 2004.

p46 *David Hughes*: interview, CE/NLW and in DNT 2004.

Florence's explanation: interview, CE/NLW.

Watkins on Dylan's heath: Watkins 1956. The diet sheet was found amongst Dylan's possessions in his hotel room. Watkins also wrote to John Berryman: November 28 1953, Minnesota: "He was not well before he left..."

frenzy of writing: Laurence Gilliam interview, CE/NLW. See also Locke, CE/NLW and DNT 2004, on Dylan writing *Under Milk Wood* in Locke's Hammersmith House.

Harry Locke, Philip Burton: interviews, CE/NLW and in DNT 2004.
looking sick before he left: London friends to Ruthven Todd, memoir
RT/NLS. The memoir was written in the years before 1962.
depressed and gloomy etc: the friend was Constantine FitzGibbon. See
CE/NLW and in DNT 2004, and also FitzGibbon p343.
p47 *Sean Treacy and Gaston Berlemont*: interviews, CE/NLW and in
DNT 2004, QDNT.
another blackout: in the company of Louis MacNeice – letter to John
Brinnin, November 30 1953, JMB/Delaware.
London doctor. The doctor was C.W.E.B. Greaves. He sent Dylan a letter
with the certificate. The letter, sent from 14, Oakley Square, NW1 and
dated October 19 1953, is signed "Evelyn" (DMT/NLW). The letter
advised Dylan to contact Greaves' friend, the American film director
Edgar G. Ulmer. *The Medical Directory* gives the doctor's full name as
Charles William Evelyn Branch Greaves.
Locke on not coming back: CE/NLW and in DNT 2004. Locke also told
FitzGibbon that "Dylan was sober, depressed and quiet." (FitzGibbon,
p344.
Lampeter. June 20 1953 DMT/Texas

4. The Final Weeks

p48 *money drives, contols etc*: JMB/JHT January 29 1952.
S.S. Atlantic, birthday etc: JMB/JHT, September 13 1953. Brinnin arrived
home on September 18.
fearfully busy, doing what I can etc: JMB/JHT, October 15 1953. He
described the Center's programme as "our biggest yet."
performances of Milk Wood etc: in New York - October 24 and 25,
December 12 and 13. In Chicago – November 13, put on by the Modern
Poetry Association. Poetry reading in New York: December 17.
five other engagements: see note on p179 above.
earnings October 20 to November 13 1953: The following are estimates:
total earnings $1450. **Total expenses** $1192.25. **Net earnings**
$257.75/£92.05, before British income tax. Expenses would have
accounted for 82% of total earnings. Total earnings comprise $600 for
three performances of *Milk Wood* (Dylan was paid $200 per perform-
ance in May 1953 at the Poetry Center, and I've assumed the same fee
for the Center on October 24 and 25, and at Chicago on November 13)
and $850 for the five other engagements, at $170 each, Dylan's average
fee for readings on his spring 1953 trip. Total expenses comprise
Brinnin's fee of $362.50 at 25% of Dylan's gross earnings; travel $470,

including $295 London to New York (actual cost) and $175 Boston to Chicago to California, estimated from Brinnin's 1950 accounts; living costs e.g. hotels, food, drink, shopping, laundry, tips, entertainments etc. $360, based on twenty-four days at Brinnin's figure of $15 per day for hotel and all other daily expenses. Data taken from Brinnin's financial accounts 1950-53, JMB/Delaware. The accounts make clear that Dylan's trans-atlantic and internal fares were paid from his earnings. Lycett (p367) writes that the publisher Victor Weybright also gave Dylan an advance of $500 on October 30, but Lycett gives no sources for this. Dylan had only $2 left in the hotel safe when it was opened on November 7 – see p94 above. Dylan was also expecting fees for articles scheduled to be published in *Mademoiselle* (February 1954) and *Harper's Bazaar* (December 1953) but it is extremely unlikely he would have received these in time for the California trip.

$10 a day: $257.75 for 27 days = $9.54 per day, assuming Dylan arrived in California on November 14, the day after his Chicago reading, and left on December 11 for his New York *Milk Wood* performance on the 12th. This would be just enough to live on, with accommodation provided free. He had averaged $11 a day on his spring 1953 trip, excluding his hotel costs (around $5 a night). Taken from Brinnin's financial accounts, JMB/Delaware.

Stravinsky's efforts: he wrote to Dylan in September 1953 to say that he would ask his friends Aldous Huxley and Christopher Isherwood to set up some lectures. Quoted in Shavelson, 2003.

p49 *earnings December 1953*: the following are estimates for what Dylan would have earned had he not died: **total earnings** $600, for three sessions at the Poetry Center (December 12, 13, 17) based on $200 per performance in May 1953. **Total expenses** $725. **Net loss** $125. Total expenses comprise Brinnin's fee of $150; travel $470, including California to New York at $175 and New York to London at $295; living costs (as defined in the above note) $105 for seven days, based on Brinnin's figure of $15 per day. Data from Brinnin's financial accounts, JMB/Delaware.

resignation, tenure, Europe etc: JMB/JHT October 15 (which notes his decision to resign), November 17 1953, February 3 1954. Brinnin dates the actual handing in of his resignation to sometime after November 12 – see his *Sextet*, p198.

leisurely day, Old Howard etc: Brinnin's journal, JMB/Delaware.

Brinnin's cv: John Malcolm Brinnin, poet, biographer, teacher, editor, critic and anthologist, was born at 78, Spring Garden Road, Halifax, Nova Scotia, September 13 1916, to John Thomas Brinnin (1890-1936, a theatre scenic artist, of Irish Catholic descent) and Frances Malcolm Brinnin (1891-1992, of Scottish descent). John Malcolm was brought up in Detroit from the age of four, living in his early teens in 13026 Houston Avenue. Enrolled Wayne University but dropped out and worked in three bookshops. *1934-35*: co-editor with G. Smith of *Prelude*. *1936-38*: co-editor with J.H. Thompson of *Signatures*. *1937-1942*: university of Michigan, winning three Hopwood Awards 1938-40; edited *Perspectives*, a monthly magazine of student writing; summer 1940, dance scholarship at Bennington College. Graduated from Michigan with a BA in English, followed by graduate study at Harvard. Later taught at Vassar, Boston, Connecticut and Harvard. *1947*: collaboration with Henri Cartier-Bresson. *1949-1953*: Director of the Poetry Center at the New York YM/YW Hebrew Association. *1954-56*: Consultant to the Poetry Center. *1955*: Poetry Society of America Gold Medal for Distinguished Service to Poetry. *1963*: Centennial Medal for Distinction in Literature, university of Michigan. *1971*: Emeritus Professor, university of Boston. *1978*: elected to the American Academy of Arts and Letters. *Published*: six books of poetry, three of biography, two of social history, four of criticism, as well as two anthologies and a book for children. Died June 26 1998 at his home in Key West, Florida (information on the Brinnin family 1930 census from Dick Tague, USGenWeb Census).

p50 *Brinnin's early childhood, Nova Scotia, love of the sea etc*: see Brinnin 1986 and 1982.

Brinnin's student days, left-wing etc: see Wald 2002, Miller 1989 and Cifelli 1997 and material in the Brinnin Supplement, Delaware. Student data from the *Alumni Records File* and *The Michiganensian*.

p51 *Europe in the late 1930s*: travel documents at JMB/Delaware and see *The Gargoyle*, November 1940, University of Michigan. He visited Paris in 1935 when he was just nineteen – Brinnin 1981, p237 and 1982, p10.

Brinnin and Auden: see Miller 1989, pp1-4 and *The Gargoyle*, November 1940, University of Michigan.

Valerie Bettis etc: see Foote 2004, pp53-54 with more detail on www.ickl.org/conf01_proceedings/ICKL01_243_250.pdf

Cartier-Bresson: see Brinnin's account in his *Sextet*, 1982.

arrogant, literary pecking order: David Wagoner, email April 1 2007.

determined to be a success, name-dropping etc: JMB/JHT, 1953 and 1954.

stratosphere of his own: Caitlin Thomas 1957, p72.

Brinnin not interested in real life: Richard Wilbur in Brinnin's obituary, *New York Times*, June 30 1998.

not touching land: JMB/JHT, May 24, 1954.

p52 *Fiasco Kid*: JMB/JHT, February 27 1954.

hot soup: Brinnin's obituary, *New York Times*, June 30 1998.

cared little about other people: see p122 above.

migraine: Brinnin, p125.

arthritis: Caitlin to Brinnin, December 19, 1953 and JMB/JHT, February 7 and March ? 1954. He was diagnosed with advanced rheumatoid arthritis in 1955 – JMB/JHT, November 19. Ten years later, Brinnin had lengthy periods in hospital after two operations – Brinnin to FitzGibbon, February 26 1964, CF/Texas.

case of medicines: Caitlin Thomas 1957, p72: "a suitcase of magic tablets." Brinnin called it his "trunk of medications" – JMB/JHT, July 28 1951. Dylan wrote to Oscar Williams on February 27 1953: "I hardly dare write to Brinnin to say it is all too difficult, but must do so quickly or he will need a hundred new kinds of pills all big as roc eggs."

health problems: dependent on phenobarbitone, JMB/JHT, May 24 1954. And see the note on p206 below.

open relationship: JMB/UPM and his letters to John Thompson at Delaware.

Brinnin and Dylan never lovers: Brinnin interviewed by N and T, p245: "I loved Dylan, but we were never lovers."

Brinnin letter on Dylan and sex etc: letter from Brinnin to Kimon Friar, January 16 1957, The Friar-Brinnin Collection, University of Delaware.

details on the Reitells: Liz Reitell's uncle's family memoir, and letter from Liz Reitell's cousin, Lois Gridley, November 23 2007.

p54 *missionary great-aunt*: Harriet Myer Laird, born 1803 in Wysox, Pennsylvania, a young woman with "intense religious zeal." In November 1833, she and her husband, Matthew Laird, sailed for Africa but died within a year.

Jane Reitell's writing: see Books and Articles, pp213-14. Her cousin, Lois Gridley, also has the following dates for stories in *The Saturday Evening Post*: August 11, October 16 and December 18 1943. Jane Reitell also wrote a review of W.E. Burghardt DuBois' book, *The Dark Princess*, in the *Annals of the American Academy of Political and Social Science*, vol. 140, November 1928. There might also be an article in a 1936 issue of *Scribner's*, and a poem in *The Saturday Evening Post* titled "My Mother's Braided Rugs."

Charles Reitell's academic books: see entry in Books and Articles, p213, for a small sample but Google to obtain more.

Fish Commissioner: foreword to *Let's Go Fishing*.

Reitell's high school: Lincoln School of Teachers College, Columbia University, funded by John D. Rockefeller Jnr, and attended by his children.

Martha Hill on Reitell: from Reitell's college record, email from David Griffith Rees, Bennington, February 22 2008. Hill was one of the influential figures in American dance, and founder of the Bennington School of the Dance. Reitell also studied at Bennington with Wallace Fowlie, Francis Fergusson, Arch Lauterer, Lewis Webster Jones and Jose Limon, a remarkable group of teachers.

Liz Reitell's cv: born September 11 1920, the only child of Jane Myer (1892-1972) and Charles Ervin Reitell (1887-1967) of Elmira, New York, married June 7 1916. Liz Reitell came to New York in 1934 when her father started teaching at Columbia university. She attended private schools in Pittsburgh (where her father was professor of economics) and Harrisburg. *1933*: Western High School, Washington D.C. *1934-1937*: Lincoln School of Teachers College, Columbia University, New York. *1937-1941*: Bennington College, Vermont, with a degree in theatre design, dance and drama literature, with two student placements, 1940 and 1941, designing costumes for Hanya Holm. *1943-46*: First Lieutenant, Women's Army Co., working in administration, information and education. *1946-51*: art student at Cooper Union, New York; Skowhegan School of Painting and Sculpture, Maine; Colorado Springs Fine Art Center; Detroit; University of Aix-Marseilles, France. *1947*: AAUW award for oil painting, Detroit Art Institute. *1951-52*: art teacher, YM/YM Hebrew Association, New York. *July 1952-54*: administrative assistant then assistant director at the Poetry Center, YM/YM Hebrew Association. *1954-58*: free-lance display and exhibit artist, including producing the Cambodian exhibit at the 1957 World Trade Fair. *1958-59*: literary secretary to Ilka Chase, writer and novelist. *1959-61*: assistant to Frank Taylor, editorial director of Dell Books and film producer e.g. *The Misfits*. *1961-62*: secretary to Arthur Miller and editor for Howard Moss. *1962-67*: publications specialist, school of forestry, university of Montana. *1965-1980*: free-lance writer and editor, wildlife activist, board member and trustee in wilderness organisations. *1972*: Hilliard Award for outstanding environmental achievement. *1980*: public information officer, Columbia River Inter-tribal Fish Commission, Portland, Oregon. *Married*: 1941, Adolph Green, lyricist and entertainer. 1945, Clement Stabolepszy, engineer and army officer. 1958, Herb Hannum, architect. 1967, Eldon Smith, biologist and, later, metalsmith and jeweller. All ending in divorce. No children. She died February 13 2001.

p55 *Kachadoorian and Bryan etc*: Reitell obituary, *Bozeman Daily Chronicle*, February 21 2001: "dearest lifelong friends."

her father's disapproval: Harriet Marble, a friend in Montana since 1965, email February 1 2007.

Reitell's intimate record: just after Dylan's death, Reitell told Todd that "she is going to try to write an account of Dylan's last days." (Todd to Louis MacNeice, November 23 1953, CF/Texas). Brinnin referred to Reitell's "intimate record" in a letter to FitzGibbon, February 26 1964, CF/Texas. Reitell and Brinnin to Ferris, May-July 1975, from Ferris' notebook, in an email to David Thomas, October 29 2006. Reitell met with Brinnin on a weekend in early spring 1955, and then twice in June 1955 (JMB/JHT, May 5 and June 27 1955).

Reitell on draft: draft of Brinnin's book with corrections by Reitell, JMB/Delaware.

1983 interview with Reitell: GTD/RG, see details above on pp163-64. Gittins and Talfan Davies were with Reitell for a week in New York. Gittins' 1986 book drew on these interviews, done both on- and off-camera, conversations and later phone calls with, and letters from, Reitell.

my book: interview, GTD/RG.

p56 *errors, falsifications, second-rate poet etc*: Dorothy van Ghent 1956.

others came forward: for example, the poet Allen Curnow, who has described Brinnin's account of Dylan's Harvard engagements (at which Curnow was present but Brinnin was not) as 'false' and his book as a whole as ill-balanced and ill-informed. See Curnow 1982. The biographies of Ferris, Tremlett and Lycett also take Brinnin to task.

swelling with joy: interview, GTD/RG.

three-week romance: Dylan arrived in New York on April 21 and stayed until April 25, during which time he and Reitell were not at ease – they had taken an instant dislike to each other. He then left the city, returning on May 8, but then left again the next day, and did not come back until May 14, the day of the first performance of *Under Milk Wood*. Drawing on Reitell's diary, Lycett also dates the start of the romance to May 14. Dylan left New York on June 3.

p57 *shocked at Idlewild, Dylan changed, ill in the Fall etc*: Reitell interview, GTD/RG. *Milk Wood* actor, Roy Poole, also thought that Dylan had been in "great shape" during the spring visit – interview on the HTV programme, *The Far-Ago Land*, 1983. Two other close friends also noticed that Dylan was unwell when he arrived. Oscar Williams thought "Dylan really was a sick person when he came to the United States." Rollie McKenna, considered that Dylan looked "ghastly. Very bad... he was in particularly bad shape." Oscar Williams and Rollie McKenna: interviews, CE/NLW and in DNT 2004.

complaining of the heat: Brinnin, p207.

temperature details: taken from the *New York Times*, which gave the temperature for each hour of the day and night.

problems with stuffy hotel rooms: see Dylan's letter to Caitlin of February 25 1950, and David Daiches 1954 p58.

air pollution: as measured in daily smokeshade values (coefficient of haze units) – see Greenburg et al 1962. Air pollution rose from October 31, and remained until November 4 appreciably above the average values for November in the years 1950-52 and 1954-56. On November 2, air pollution peaked at 3 coefficient of haze units. Readings above 2 units are considered unhealthy for sensitive groups, such as those, like Dylan, with respiratory problems. Values on November 1, 3 and 4 were 2.75, 2.50 and 1.25 respectively, as calculated visually from Greenburg's graph. Average values for these dates in November 1950-52 and 1954-56 were at or below two units.

some two hundred killed: air pollution averaged 8.38 Coh units on November 20, Greenburg et al 1962. See also Johnston 2002.

p58 *fresh air a constant theme*: Gittins, email January 21 2007: "I do know it was a constant theme of Dylan's on that last trip and Liz referred to it on more than one occasion both in interviews and on occasions when we simply talked off camera."

quite wretched, air and light: Reitell interview, GTD/RG.

Reavey in White Horse: Reavey to McAlpines, November 21 1953, CF/Texas.

phenobarbitone: Lycett, p363, taken from Reitell's diary: "I gave him half gr of pheno and left him." Lycett interprets "gr" as gram but it should be grain. In a draft of his book, Brinnin wrote that Reitell gave Dylan a mild sedative but this was removed from the final version (JMB/Delaware).

Reitell on nurse role, dreadful illness, suicide etc: interview, GTD/RG; interview on the HTV programme, *The Far-Ago Land*, 1983; and Brinnin p209.

most important factor: the actor Roy Poole in Gittins 1986, p73 and Poole to Gittins, May 14 1983.

not well much of the time: Roy Poole, on the HTV programme, *The Far-Ago Land*, 1983.

last proper meal: Brinnin, p209. Impossible to get him to eat: Reitell, interview, *The Far-Ago Land*, as above.

Brinnin arrives in New York, out on the town etc: Brinnin's journal. JMB/Delaware.

third rehearsal, exhausted, Hannum etc: Brinnin, p210ff.

p59 *short-term prop*: Brinnin p213 "…the injection was but a temporary boost – a prop that would help him get through the next few days…"

benzedrine prescription: both Nashold and Tremlett, p142 and Lycett, p363 claim that Feltenstein prescribed benzedrine for Dylan, but neither book gives a source. Lycett believes he took it from Nashold and Tremlett (email December 4 2006, which also confirms that there is nothing in Reitell's diary, now in Lycett's possession, about benzedrine.) Reitell has also written: "Dylan was not taking benzedrine. I could not pretend absolute certainty on this, for Dylan was secretive as you know. I'm sure for myself that he wasn't, and I'm sure that Feltenstein didn't prescribe them or give them to him (for I did the drugstore purchasing etc) – but – I cannot *swear* that he wasn't, I'm just certain he wasn't." (to Bill Read, February 20 1965, DMT/Texas).

collapse at third rehearsal: Brinnin p210-11.

attack, stroke etc: Brinnin draft, JMB/Delaware.

physical spasm: Brinnin interview, GTD/RG.

Brinnin shocked at fourth rehearsal, new and dreadful: Brinnin, pp213-14.

something radically wrong: Brinnin interview, GTD/RG.

talked only briefly: Brinnin p214.

p60 *meets Kolodney*: Brinnin's journal, JMB/Delaware.

turned in on himself, absorbed etc: Brinnin pp213-19.

German poet and critic: Reinhard Paul Becker, memoir, CF/Texas. In 1947, a British army officer had given Becker a copy of *Deaths and Entrances* to illustrate "that modern English lyric poetry was utterly bloodless, insincere, artificial and void of common sense." But Becker was so taken with the poems that he began translating them. In 1951, he presented his manuscript to one of the most distinguished literary circles of southern Germany, the celebrated Sunday afternoon 'jours' of Marianne Weber, the widow of Max Weber. The architect Rudolf Steinbach gave a lecture on Dylan's work and read selections from Becker's translation. The following year, it was published as *Tode und Tore*. Becker was at Yale in the autumn of 1953.

Dylan and Reitell come to see Brinnin, depression, McKenna etc: Brinnin pp215-16.

Dylan ill at October 25 performance: Nancy Wickwire interview, September 1967, CE/NLW, pp12, 13 and 25. Part in DNT 2004, QDNT. The October 25 performance was the only one done in the afternoon. In describing how ill Dylan was, Wickwire mentions his arm was in a sling; this was an error on her part – his arm was in a sling during the May 28 reading.

p61 *bad condition, ginger ale*: Poole to Gittins, May 14 1985.

bewildered, upset, alarmed, serious illness etc: Brinnin's own words in a draft of his book, *Dylan Thomas in America*, JMB/Delaware. "Alarmed" also in Brinnin pp214-15.

Brinnin's salary to be halved, income tax troubles: JMB/JHT, February 28 1953.

p62 *Brinnin buys plane ticket*: invoice for $295 dated October 15 1953 sent to Brinnin's home address from his travel agent in Cambridge Mass., and marked as paid. He had also paid in advance for the 1952 tickets, describing it as a loan to Dylan (Brinnin's financial accounts, JMB/Delaware).

misappropriation etc: JMB/JHT, November 17 1953. Thompson had entrusted Brinnin with $340 (equivalent to several thousand dollars today) as a deposit on a cruise they were going on. Brinnin explained that "Dylan arrived broke and I broke into it until such time as his lecture fees would return to me, as his agent, a like amount. Since this will not now be realised and since, in the circumstances of his illness, I had to make out payments immediately, I ate up not only what I had left that was rightfully yours, but into my rent and car payment, too." The saga of the $340 is also detailed in letters to Thompson from March 28 to June 16 1953. It also appears in a letter from Brinnin to Thompson on February 27 1954: "without warrant, I used your money and mine when it was crucially needed." Brinnin told Thompson (November 17) that he intended to apply to the Memorial Fund for reimbursement of part of the money he had spent on Dylan. Brinnin had probably paid Dylan's hotel bill in advance, and given him spending money, as he had done for the 1952 visit – see Brinnin pp118-19.

Europe trip expensive: the trip took in Spain, France, Belgium, Italy, London and Laugharne. See JMB/JHT, August 8 to September 13 1953.

funding most of it himself: JMB/JHT, June 16 1953.

temporary boost etc: Brinnin, p213 and see the note on p186 above.

Brinnin's New York doctor: a doctor treated his migraines when he was in the city. He took Dylan, who was suffering from a gum infection, to see this doctor during his 1952 trip (Brinnin p135). There was also Dr Anny Baumann to whom Caitlin was taken for treatment on this visit, and whose bill of $16 had still not been paid by May 21 1953 (I am grateful to Andrew Lycett for this information about the unpaid bill, taken from a letter in DMT/NLW.) Lycett p324 says she was Pearl Kazin's doctor.

token fee: Feltenstein's fee for medical treatment during Dylan's third visit was $93.70, of which $66 was a fee, and the rest the cost of medications (June 1, American income tax statement prepared by Brinnin, in DMT/Texas). But on June 4, Reitell wrote to Brinnin to say that she had also paid Feltenstein another $30. Reitell told Brinnin that $20 was for drugs and medications and the remaining $10 "is just sort of a token." June 4 1953, quoted in N and T p23. See also the comment about

Chinatown on p39 re reduced fees.

too much faith in Feltenstein, only doctor she knew: Reitell interview, GTD/RG.

Reitell's periods of illness: see note on p190.

p63 *Brinnin and Reitell pay Feltenstein's bill*: for Brinnin, see June 1 accounts, DMT/Texas, and for Reitell, see her letter to Brinnin June 4 1953, reproduced in N and T, p23. Reitell was owed $262 by June 4, though not all this would have been for medical treatment. She gave Dylan four cheques between May 19 and 31 1953, for amounts ranging between $10 and $75 (Christie's auction catalogue, 1997).

$2 a day: his net earnings of $257 (see the note on ppp180-81 above) would have been reduced to $57 if one cancellation of *Milk Wood* had taken place, leaving him just $2.11 a day for the 27-day visit to California. His medical bills on the spring 1953 trip had been $178 (see the note below); incurring such a level of costs again would have reduced his daily allowance in California to $2.92.

medical bills, spring 1953: Milton Feltenstein: $93.70. Dr L. Bleidin, orthopedist: $75. Dr Friedman, X-ray: $8. Total of $178.70 (Brinnin's June 1 accounts, DMT/Texas. $2 error in total is Brinnin's).

save Dylan's life: Reitell to FitzGibbon, March 6 1964, CF/Texas.

militant guardian: interview with Rose Slivka by John B. Matthews, 1981.

tiger mother: Molly Brodney, Ferris p303.

difficult to be serious: Reitell interview, GTD/RG.

p64 *Borden Stevenson*: the former wife of politician Adlai Stevenson. Borden Stevenson was a generous patron of the arts; *Time* Magazine called her the "deficit sponge" of Chicago's poetic colony: May 24 1954. See Dylan's letters to Oscar Williams of January 5 and June 22 1953 about Stevenson funding him.

Oscar Williams at party: Brinnin's journal, JMB/Delaware, mentions Williams being at the party.

evening of October 25, victims of enchantment, destroyer etc: Brinnin, pp216-19.

Reitell decides not to look after Dylan: Brinnin p218.

p65 *enough to pay his bills*: his airfare from London had been $295 and his bill at the Chelsea would have been some $90 for his 18-night stay in New York. Taken from Brinnin's financial accounts, JMB/Delaware.

drunk and weary etc: Brinnin's journal, JMB/Delaware.

next six speakers: The official programme after Dylan was: October 29 Archibald MacLeish; November 7 Marian Moore; November 12 Katherine Anne Porter; November 19 Edith and Osbert Sitwell; November 22 Robert Frost. Elizabeth Bishop was also due in New York on November 12, as was Osbert Sitwell, who was threatening to pull out unless Brinnin made satisfactory arrangements to look after him – JMB/Delaware, letter and telegram respectively.

packed houses etc: JMB/JHT, November 17 1953.

Reitell's bouts of illness: draft of Brinnin's book, JMB/Delaware.

Brinnin not in this world: Caitlin Thomas 1957, p72. See also pp51-52 of this book.

Algonquin and White Horse: Brinnin pp219-21.

lowest yet, beginning of the last days: Reitell interview, GTD/RG: "marked the beginning of the last days."

p66 *finishes teaching at 2pm etc*: Brinnin's journal, JMB/Delaware.

vitamin injections: draft of Brinnin's book, JMB/Delaware. Brinnin says they were daily.

subway, save money: Ferris, p318.

Stravinsky letter: sent on October 25 to New York. See Craft 1959, pp77-78.

bills paid: Caitlin went to see Dylan's agent, David Higham, a few days after Dylan had left for New York. His publisher, Dent, advanced some money and Higham "got all the bills from all the people – the milkman, the butcher, the pub and so on and we paid them." Higham memoir, CF/Texas.

Reavey: letter to the McAlpines, November 21 1953, QDNT.

p67 *returns to hotel at 4.10am*: private detective notebook entry, copied by FitzGibbon, CF/Texas.

Washington, Boston, McKenna etc: Brinnin's journal, JMB/Delaware.

covers Brinnin's fee: this would have been $362 for Oct 20-Nov 13. The two engagements earned $340. See pp180-81 for details.

wrote himself out of story, MacLeish, Washington etc: Brinnin's journal, JMB/Delaware. Brinnin arrived in New York about 5pm. The event at the Poetry Center started at 8.40 and finished well before 10.30pm. The sleeper left at 1.20am.

p68 *enormously ill, everything more difficult:* Reitell interview, GTD/RG.

Todd warning: memoir, RT/NLS.

houses in the country: Dylan and Caitlin were at McKenna's house for two days in 1952 with Brinnin – see JMB/JHT, January 26 1952 and Brinnin p115ff.

p69 *Becker*: memoir, CF/Texas. After seeing the evening performance of *Under Milk Wood* on October 24, Becker met up with Dylan on a further five occasions.

Al Anderson, beer etc: Todd to Louis MacNeice, November 23 1953, CF/Texas. The other guests, wrote Todd, were Howie Schoenfeld, the poet Alistair Reid and his wife and Herb Hannum. Len and Ann Lye came in after dinner.

photograph in the White Horse: on the back of the photo, Reitell has written "Dylan/White Horse/ about October 30 '53". Brinnin notes (p223) that Dylan and Reitell were in the bar on October 30, with Herb Hannum, after the three of them had been to dinner with Ruthven Todd. It's possible it was taken on October 29 or 31 but it makes no matter. American wall calendars (but not desk ones) always started on a Sunday. In the calendar in the photo, the first column of dates corresponds to Sundays in October 1953. This photo and a variant were auctioned at Christie's in 1997. The catalogue says that Brinnin appears in one of these two photographs but that is incorrect. The man in the white shirt next to Dylan is probably Ernie Wohlleben. The money can be seen in the variant.

p70 *the day with Breit*: see Breit 1954. He wrote that on October 31 he spent "a long day and an evening" with Dylan.

p71 *air pollution*: see the note on p186.

White Horse at 9pm, hopping on benzedrine etc: notes made by a private detective hired by *Time* magazine, copied out by FitzGibbon, DMT/Texas. The *Time* detective's notebook mentions that Slivka and Wagoner were with Dylan. Wagoner, however, has written that "I didn't see him taking any pills of any kind." Email, March 20 2007. It is a puzzle how a detective could identify the nature of pills taken by someone he was observing from across a bar.

ate next to nothing, beer and eggs etc: Brinnin, pp223-24.

Reavey: letter to the McAlpines, November 21 1953, CF/Texas, QDNT.

Moss and drugs: Reitell to Brinnin, November 2 1955, JMB/Delaware: "Howard was also babbling about some improbable potion called Mill House (?) which seems to be the living end so far as drugs are concerned. I get the impression that thousands of down & out peddlers, pushers and smugglers are once again on easy street and living it up from the proceeds!" Moss was taking the tranquilliser and sedative Miltown, as was Brinnin. Todd's letter to MacNeice of November 23 1953 (CF/Texas) mentions Moss as a Feltenstein patient.

p72 *a warm night*: Brinnin, p225. Temperature from the *New York Times*.

Berryman bitter: Haffenden 1982, p122.

Todd at the Chelsea, November 2, beers, working on 'Elegy' etc: memoir RT/NLS.

working on script on November 2: Reitell to Daniel Jones, June 1 1954. Whilst Brinnin writes (p225) that Dylan stayed in bed all day with a painful hangover, Reitell, writing to Jones just seven months after the event, is very clear that on November 2 Dylan worked on *Under Milk Wood*.

air pollution on November 2, threat to those with respiratory problems: see the note on p186.

Dylan recites music hall number: David Wagoner, emails March 4 and 19 2007.

George Reavey at the White Horse: letter to the McAlpines, November 21 1953, CF/Texas, QDNT. The *Time* detective's notebook mentions that Oscar Williams, Ruthven Todd, David Wagoner and Dave Slivka were also present.

p73 *Oscar Williams at the White Horse*: interview, CE/NLW and in DNT 2004, QDNT.

Colony Club, first drinks, etc: Brinnin, pp225-26.

go easy on everything: Todd memoir, RT/NLS.

Todd at the Chelsea November 3, Dylan not feeling well etc, schizoid bar etc: letter to MacNeice, November 23 1953, CF/Texas and unpublished memoir, RT/NLS. Reitell breaks up party: Brinnin p226.

Dylan exhausted etc: Brinnin, p227.

telegram from Caitlin: This version of the telegram is mentioned in a letter from Edith Sitwell to Jane Clark, November 17 1953, quoted in Lycett, p369. The telegram is also mentioned in Murphy's memorandum. After Dylan's death, Liz Reitell met with Dr Gutierrez-Mahoney, who told Murphy that Reitell felt "that she was managing Dylan reasonably well; keeping his drinking within workable limits until he received a telegram – a searing telegram – from Caitlin full of hatred, complaining of impoverishment, saying she and the children would be out on the streets etc. This upset him, particularly as he had sent a hundred and fifty dollars home... It was after the telegram that he went out and returned saying he had drunk fifteen whiskies."

p74 *no longer live together*: According to Brinnin p227, Dylan talked of Caitlin's beauty: "...There is an illumination about her. She shines." In an earlier draft of the book, the following words then followed: "But we can't live together." These words were left out of the published book (JMB/Delaware).

warm night: temperature for 2am taken from the *New York Times*.

just wanted air: Gittins 1986, p145, after interviews and conversations with Reitell in September 1983.

men behind the bar: Todd, memoir RT/NLS.

CuRoi: quoted in N and T, p151. CuRoi's description is in a letter from him of spring 1981 – see p174 of Tremlett, 1993. A highball is a whisky with a mixer, such as ginger ale, and ice.

Wohlleben, Rooney: Todd memoir, RT/NLS.

cigars: CuRoi, as above.

p75 *Lye, the tuxedo and Dylan at the White Horse*: interview with Ann Lye, 1981, by John B. Matthews; also reported in Horrocks 2002, p251.

Todd's research: interview, CE/NLW and in DNT 2004. Todd also checked other bars.

p76 *Brinnin on the eighteen whiskies*: in a letter to FitzGibbon, February 26 1964, CF/Texas.

no money in till etc: Todd, memoir RT/NLS.

Todd's twelve-page letter: to MacNeice, November 23 1953, CF/Texas. Todd describes how he wrote the letter in consultation with Reitell and Rose Slivka; he then gave Reitell a draft to vet, as he put it.

ten years after the death: in a letter to FitzGibbon, March 6 1964, CF/Texas.

thirty years later more precise: Reitell interview, GTD/RG.

p77 *Brinnin's hyperbolic falsehood*: Todd carried out his survey of Dylan's bars "the next day", after being told by Reitell about the eighteen whiskies. It is inconceivable that he did not report to Brinnin and Reitell what he had found.

everyone was somewhere else: Daniel Jones 1977, p54.

Dylan suffocating etc: Brinnin p228.

Todd phoned etc: memoir RT/NLS. In his November 23 1953 letter to MacNeice, Todd wrote that Dylan "did not feel very well." CF/Texas.

feeling dreadful: Reitell interview, GTD/RG.

Breit phoned: Breit 1954.

pneumonia and bronchitis: William Murphy's memorandum, after studying the hospital notes (CF/Texas}. See the appendix.

Lye in the White Horse, tuxedo etc: Todd to MacNeice, November 23 1953, CF/Texas.

too sick to stay for long: Brinnin, p228.

ghastly racking spasms: Ferris, p321.

times of Feltenstein's visits: written in by Reitell on a draft of Brinnin's book, JMB/Delaware. She dates the evening visit to 6pm but Brinnin's journal (at Delaware) written at the time dates it to 4.30pm.

first two injections of morphine: these are noted by Nashold and Tremlett (p152), after interviewing Dr Joseph Lehrman (a pseudonym) in 1996. Lehrman was a neurologist and psychiatrist at Beth Israel hospital in New York. Feltenstein had discussed Dylan's case with him in the spring of 1954.

p78 *very ill*: Brinnin, p228.

prognosis bad: Reitell interview, on the HTV programme, *The Far-Ago*

Land, 1983.

liver failure: Gittins 1986, p163. Gittins reports that Feltenstein later told a colleague of his diagnosis of liver failure.

4.30pm, friend round for dinner: Brinnin's journal, JMB/Delaware.

with considerable alarm: Gittins 1986, p155, after interviewing Brinnin. p45

p79 *private detective*: CF/Texas and in Ferris p322.

speculations about missing hours: George Reavey had heard that during these five hours Reitell and Dylan had left the city – see Kaplan-Williams, *The Life and Death of Oscar Williams*, website. Daniel Jones had an equally implausible theory, that Dylan had drunk spirits all day, passed out and, having ceased to be amusing, was dumped in his room at the Chelsea. When Liz Reitell arrived, argues Jones, Dylan was already on the verge of unconsciousness – see letter to Gittins, December 14 1985.

quarter grain of phenobarbitone to Dylan: Ruthven Todd to Louis MacNeice, November 23 1953, CF/Texas. Todd also mentioned that the phenobarbitone had been given to Reitell by Feltenstein.

those pills: George Reavey to the McAlpines, November 21 1953, CF/Texas – see note below on "the brain episode". Reitell passed the information to Reavey on the evening of November 5 when "Reitell told me a few things at that moment – I didn't speak to her again. Among other things, she said something about giving Dylan pills: 'Those pills…'"

Reitell moaning about pills: Irene Reavey, signed statement to the solicitor Ungoed Thomas, November 18 1953, CF/Texas.

we all take pills: George Reavey notes, GR/Texas.

continued sensitivity about pills: see draft JMB/Delaware.

negative for barbiturates: hospital Medical Summary. And in Murphy's memorandum, which also tells us that Dylan tested negative for other drugs. See appendix for both.

p80 *difficulties with Reitell diagnosis of DTs*: delirium tremens is a disorder caused by abruptly stopping the use of alcohol. It most commonly begins between forty-eight and seventy-two hours after the last drink – but Dylan's last bout of drinking was a mere twelve hours before the "delirium tremens" incident. DTs is also most common in people who have a history of experiencing withdrawal symptoms when alcohol is stopped. But Dylan's own history indicates that he could stop drinking for periods of time without experiencing such symptoms. Brinnin's book gives many examples of Dylan abstaining from alcohol during his American tours. Other examples are provided in DNT 2004 – see the index, p402.

examined Dylan: Reitell interview, GTD/RG.

third injection of morphine: hospital Medical Summary and Murphy's memorandum – see the appendix.

the brain episode: this information, which is in Reavey's November 21 1953 letter to the McAlpines (CF/Texas), could have come only from Reitell since she was the only other person in the room with Feltenstein and Dylan.

warning about coma: Reitell interview, GTD/RG. In his book, Gittins dates the warning about coma to Feltenstein's second visit. But in her interview with Gittins, Reitell clearly dates the warning to the third visit and the injection of morphine and the calling of Heliker.

p81 *Feltenstein leaves hotel*: Todd, after discussion with Reitell, times Feltenstein's departure at 11pm (Todd to MacNeice, November 23 1953, CF/Texas). Jack Heliker's testimony supports the Todd timing: he recalls Reitell telephoning him at about 11pm – Ferris, p322, who interviewed Heliker.

Reitell close to exhaustion: interview, GTD/RG.

sweet calm talks: Ferris notebook, after interviewing Reitell in May 1975.

terrible breathing sounds etc: Ferris notebook; Gittins 1986 p162, both after talking with Reitell. Also in Reitell interview, GTD/RG.

coma at midnight: Jack Heliker, has timed Dylan's fall into unconsciousness at around midnight on November 4/5 (Ferris, p322). Brinnin, drawing upon what Reitell had told him, has also written that when Dylan "passed into a comatose condition" it was "a few minutes after midnight." (letter to John Davenport, November 15 1953, Davenport papers, NLW). Ruthven Todd wrote to Louis MacNeice describing what Reitell had observed: "shortly before midnight, she noticed a sudden change in him. He was blue in the face and she and Jack [Heliker] could find only the faintest tremor of a pulse." (November 23 1953, CF/Texas.)

p82 *timing of phone call for the ambulance*: Ferris p322, and "Dr Turnbull" interviewed by N and T, p154. See below on Turnbull's identity.

Boyce, oxygen in hotel room: Todd to MacNeice, November 23 1953 (CF/Texas) and memoir RT/NLS.

Boyce, oxygen, back of ambulance: Todd memoir, RT/NLS and N and T, p154, after interviewing "Turnbull".

arrival time at hospital: the hospital's Medical Summary. George Reavey gives the timings of Dylan falling into coma at 1am and arrival at hospital at 3am. This is wrong, but the two hour delay in getting Dylan to the hospital is the same (GR/Texas).

admitting doctors: after their interviews with "Turnbull" and other doctors, Nashold and Tremlett name McVeigh and "Turnbull" as the admitting doctors, and McVeigh is also named in Brinnin's account as the "staff physician" put in charge of Dylan. The Medical Summary, written by McVeigh, names the other admitting doctor as F. Gilbertson. This is probably the "Dr Turnbull" interviewed by Nashold and Tremlett, but it's possible that "Turnbull" was Dr Boyce, the emergency doctor who went to the hotel with the ambulance. I have chosen to identify "Turnbull" as Gilbertson but it makes no difference in the story of Dylan's death if "Turnbull" turns out to be Boyce.

Feltenstein withholds information on morphine: this is based on George Reavey's claim "that the hospital wasn't told for more than 24 hours about that 'shot'". (Reavey to Bill Hayter, May 9 1955, GR/Texas). FitzGibbon had also been told that "the hospital authorities were... initially in ignorance of the various injections that had been previously administered." (FitzGibbon, p345.) FitzGibbon had been given Irene Reavey's signed statement, in which she wrote that "The doctor also said that they didn't know if he had been given barbiturates but that the next day they learned a morphine injection had been administered." (statement to the solicitor Ungoed Thomas, November 18 1953, CF/Texas).

questioned in more detail: N and T, p155, after interviewing "Turnbull" (see pp195-96 on his identity), who date Feltenstein's reluctance over the morphine to the early hours of admission.

restoring breathing etc: N and T, pp154-56, after interviewing "Turnbull".

Dilantin, comatose, brain damage, bronchitis etc: Murphy's memorandum, CF/Texas, see the appendix below.

p83 *outside in the corridor, police, hair wet and limp etc*: Brinnin, p231.

five most dreadful days: Brinnin's journal, JMB/Delaware.

5. In on a Thursday, Dead by the Monday

p84 *inferior care*: Dr Cyril Wecht, email February 11 2004: "In the U.S., legally speaking, the standard of care should not have differed because a patient was in a public ward. However, realistically, such a patient most likely would not have received the same quality of care that a paying patient (medical insurance) would have received."

interns and residents: An intern is just out of medical school and usually spends a year rotating through all the services in the hospital. The resident has completed his or her internship and is working in the one area chosen as a specialty.

St Joseph's East: information on St Joseph's East was provided by nurses who had worked on the ward and remembered Dylan's time as a patient – thanks to Sister Rita King, the archivist of the Sisters of Charity, and Priscilla Sassi. St Vincent's had 686 beds, of which half were in general wards, 13% in private rooms and 36% in semi-private rooms. The cost per patient day for the accommodation was: private $20.88; semi-private $16.71; general ward $16.03. (taken by Sandra Opdycke for me from *Financial and Statistical Information Relating to Member Hospitals of the United Hospital Fund of New York*, and *Hospital Statistics for Greater New York*, 1955.)

shortage of nurses: in the early 1950s, there was a national shortage of nurses. The *New York Times* of May 3 1952 ran a front page article called 'Shortage of Nurses Found a Peril to Health of Nation'. The book by P.A. and B.J. Kalisch note that "On a given day from 7.00am to 3-30pm [a patient] would probably see a professional graduate nurse for about six minutes" (1986). In their study (2001) of Ontario hospital admissions, Bell and Redelmeier suggest that not only are hospitals less well staffed on weekends but those who do work are likely to be less experienced; there are also fewer supervisors on duty.

Priscilla Sassi: email, November 3 2004. The ward was divided into sections with eight, six or four beds in each. It had high ceilings and big windows; it was well kept, institutional and sterile-looking.

p85 *paying for nurses*: John Brinnin paid $24 for daytime nursing on Saturday November 7. Rollie McKenna paid $14.50 for eight hours of nursing on November 9, probably from midnight to 8pm. Brinnin's receipts for private nursing care are in his archive at the University of Delaware; McKenna notes her contribution in her Edwards interview (CE/NLW) and there is a photograph of her receipt on page 80 of her book on Dylan.

Todd paying for nurses: interview, CE/NLW. Todd borrowed the money on November 5, according to the interview.

Dr Keating: Todd to Louis MacNeice, November 23 1953, CF/Texas.

discussion with Pappas: according to N and T, pp160-62, after interviewing Pappas and "Turnbull".

Feltenstein's supervision of junior doctors: Brinnin, pp231-37 and N and T, pp158-67, after interviewing Drs "Turnbull", Pappas and Chusid.

p86 *Feltenstein's physical presence, tough talking etc*: Terry Connor and Yvonne Kleinberg, Free Acre friends, emails May 30 and June 1 2007 and phone call May 29 respectively.

Feltenstein's alcohol diagnosis: N and T, pp154-65, after interviewing "Turnbull".

Gutierrez-Mahoney: He had been trained at Harvard Medical School and had co-authored the standard text on neurological nursing (1948).

no brain specialist: Todd has written that Dylan was seen by "Dr Chussett [sic], chief of neurology at St Vincent's Hospital, and Dr Keating, a neurological specialist" on November 5. (Todd to MacNeice, November 23 1953, CF/Texas.) But Nashold and Tremlett, who interviewed Chusid, write that he was not brought in until the afternoon of November 6, when Gutierrez-Mahoney had taken charge of the case (p165). There is no other information available about Keating. Only McVeigh and Feltenstein are mentioned by Brinnin as attending on November 5.

Feltenstein and Davidoff: Brinnin, p232.

p87 *doctors in the dark*: George Reavey to the McAlpines, November 21 1953. George and Irene Reavey talked with the doctors just after midnight on November 6/7.

hospital told about the eighteen whiskies: Gutierrez-Mahoney's letter to Daniel Jones of January 10 1953 refers to "an acute episode which began in the early morning of 4 November 1953." (CF/Texas). This confirms that Reitell and Feltenstein had passed on the eighteen whiskies story to the hospital. Reitell was also telling Dylan's friends about it e.g. she told Todd on November 5 (Todd interview, CE/NLW.)

Sterno, wood alcohol and DTs in the past: Murphy's memorandum, CF/Texas and see the appendix. Kahn and Hirshfeld write about Smoke (2003).

no alcohol test results: none are given in the hospital's Medical Summary, nor in Murphy's review of Dylan's hospital notes. If body fluid tests had been done which revealed significant levels of alcohol, it is inconceivable that the test results would not have been included in the Medical Summary. Since Murphy's principal theory about Dylan's death was that drink was responsible, it is equally inconceivable that he would not have included test results in his memorandum if he had found them in his reading of the hospital notes.

p88 *corroborating Feltenstein*: details on Dylan's appearance etc from N and T, p155, after interviewing hospital doctors.

doctor smelt alcohol: Reavey's notes, GR/Texas.

impression of acute alcoholic encephalopathy: Medical Summary, written by Dr W. McVeigh. See the appendix.

test results: Murphy's memorandum, CF/Texas, and the Medical Summary. See the appendix for both.

not strongly stated: Murphy's memorandum, CF/Texas.

p89 *Feltenstein not concerned about chest disease*: not mentioned by Reitell in correspondence with FitzGibbon and with Bill Read (CF and DMT/Texas), nor in her interview with Ferris, correspondence with Gittins or in the 1983 interview with GTD/RG.

Feltenstein acknowledges failure: in a discussion with Dr Joseph Lehrman (see note above on p193).

morphine and DT's contraindicated: Noyes: "Morphine should never be given." (1953, 4th edition.) The Merck Manual of Diagnosis and Therapy: "Morphine and depressing hypnotics are contraindicated."

p90 *press officer*: Todd memoir, RT/NLS.

Laughlin source of money: Todd to MacNeice, November 23 1953, CF/Texas.

Caitlin not phoned: Brinnin, p232. He had the Boat House number, as his book makes clear. The telegram was sent by David Higham, Dylan's London agent.

Caitlin and the telegram: the producer was Aneirin Talfan Davies who was interviewed by Colin Edwards (CE/NLW).

p91 *raised sugar levels*: Brinnin, p231 and N and T, pp157-165.

Berryman talked to doctors: to Vernon Watkins, November 1953, quoted in Watkins 1983, pp151-52.

Reavey comes to hospital: letters to the MacAlpines, November 18 and 21 1953, CF/Texas, QDNT.

public ward: Oscar Williams interview, CE/NLW and DNT 2004, QDNT. Caitlin has also described her experience of the ward with twenty or thirty people looking in on her as she sat at Dylan's bedside (1986, pp182-83).

p92 *wreck careers*: N and T, pp160-64, after interviewing "Turnbull".

Feltenstein taken off case etc: Brinnin, pp232 and 234 and N and T, pp167-68.

Gutierrez-Mahoney covers up for Feltenstein: see p134 and p92 above.

p93 *Borden Stevenson*: George Reavey to the McAlpines, November 21 1953, CF/Texas. Reavey also reports that as well as Borden Stevenson's offer, "an unknown young man walked into the hospital and said he did not know Dylan Thomas but offered to pay the expenses. He was also refused." Bob MacGregor of New Directions, Dylan's American publisher, has also noted "the various offers the hospital and we had received for financial aid in doing everything to save Dylan's life." MacGregor to David Higham, November 12 1953, ND/Harvard.

phone call from the embassy: Brinnin interview, GTD/RG.

the Grippes: N and T, p176, who interviewed them. QDNT.

how brief the relationship: three weeks in the spring, and three weeks since his arrival on October 20.

Irene Reavey to the Slivkas in waiting-room: signed statement by Irene Reavey sent to the solicitor Ungoed Thomas, November 19 1953,

CF/Texas.

p94 *Lyric theatre etc*: Higham memoir, CF/Texas.

Caitlin in London: Margaret Taylor to the McAlpines, December 9 1953, DMT/Texas.

Todd at hotel, Mr Gross, hotel safe etc: Todd to Louis MacNeice, November 23 1953, CF/Texas and memoir, RT/NLS.

Kevin Rooney: Todd interview, CE/NLW.

Derwood prays: Todd, memoir, RT/NLS.

p95 *Authors' League*: JMB/Delaware.

Dylan still in crisis: Brinnin, p237.

death to be wished for: Brinnin p238.

Marianne Moore: the session was taped and Brinnin begins it with an introduction – Poetry Center archive.

plagued with calls, press reports, rumours etc: Brinnin pp235-36 and 238.

Dylan doomed etc: Brinnin p240.

medical fees beyond means etc: Brinnin p241.

p96 *rent, car loan, Memorial Fund etc*: see extended note on p188 above.

Dr Boyce at the airport: Ruthven Todd to Louis MacNeice, November 23 1953, CF/Texas.

deficit on Caitlin's plane ticket: MacGregor to David Higham, November 12 1953, ND/Harvard.

Dr Boyce with ambulance, sedatives, police escort etc: MacGregor to David Higham, November 12 1953, ND/Harvard. MacGregor notes that the doctor who went to the airport "was the one who had gone to bring Dylan from the hotel the night he was stricken." Ruthven Todd's letter to Louis MacNeice tells us that the doctor who went to the hotel was Dr Boyce. (November 23 1953, CF/Texas).

Slivka on police escort: Todd, memoir, RT/NLS.

Dylan a winded horse: Caitlin Thomas, 1957, p61.

containing Caitlin: Todd, memoir, RT/NLS. Also in George Reavey to the McAlpines, November 21 1953, CF/Texas; and to David Higham, November 18 1953, GR/Texas.

with my own eyes: Reavey to the McAlpines, November 18 and 21 1953, CF/Texas. See also to David Higham, November 18 1953, and to Bill Hayter, May 9 1955, GR/Texas.

p97 *Irene Reavey phones Brinnin*: signed statement by Irene Reavey sent to the solicitor Ungoed Thomas, November 19 1953, CF/Texas.

George Reavey at the Slivkas with Caitlin, met by Brinnin and McKenna: letters to the McAlpines, November 18 and 21 1953, GR/Texas. Todd also tells the same story in his memoir.

threatening to kill Brinnin, moneybags, tears etc: George Reavey notes,

GR/Texas.

go for the jugular: Ferris 1995, p145.

Reavey at the ward: to the McAlpines, November 21 1953, CF/Texas.

p98 *nitwits*: Todd, memoir, RT/NLS.

bigoted doctor: Brinnin p291 Avon American edition, 1966. The passage describing the row between Brinnin and the doctor was left out of the Dent 1965 edition.

butter-brained doctor: Todd memoir, RT/NLS.

Feltenstein consulting Reitell about Caitlin: Brinnin, p242.

menace to herself: Brinnin, p242.

Zeckel at short notice: draft of Brinnin's book, JMB/Delaware.

p99 *River Crest*: Feltenstein paid – see Brinnin, p243. Receipts show that Caitlin was sent to River Crest for a week, costing $137 dollars. The ambulance to take her there cost $25 (JMB/Delaware).

Caitlin pleads with Todd: Todd, memoir, RT/NLS.

Berryman and Kazin at the hospital: Haffenden 1982, pp233 and Mariani 1992, pp273-74.

she saved my life: Dylan to David Wagoner, early November 1953. Email from Wagoner April 28 2007: "I had known Pearl since 1950 when we were at Yaddo together. Her name came up one night (I forget how) when I was alone with Dylan, and he said, "Do you know Pearl? She saved my life." He said nothing else about her and I didn't ask."

Todd, Reitell, Feltenstein at breakfast: Todd to MacNeice, November 23 1953, CF/Texas.

Gutierrez-Mahoney and River Crest, his anger etc: N and T, p174-75, after interviewing Dr Joseph Chusid with whom Gutierrez-Mahoney conferred that morning.

George Reavey: Reavey to the McAlpines, November 21 1953, CF/Texas.

p100 *Tambimutti etc*: Todd interview, CE/NLW. The British doctor was a James Hamilton.

Celtic blood guilt etc: Gittins 1986, p65.

Berrryman on Dylan's last moments: Mariani 1992, pp274, 312. The exact time of Dylan's death is not known for certain. Whilst Berryman puts it at 12-40pm, Brinnin in his book (p245) says a few minutes after 1pm. In a letter written the day after the death, he gives the time as 1-30pm – JMB/JHT, November 10 1953.

see you at the ranch: Reitell interview, GTD/RG.

comforted by Rose: Irene Reavey, signed statement sent to the solicitor Ungoed Thomas, November 19 1953, CF/Texas.

Todd on Berryman: to Louis MacNeice, November 23 1953, CF/Texas.

Laughlin to Higham: November 9 1953, CF/Texas. Brinnin was another early bird with false information on the drink story: on November 10, the day the post-mortem was being carried out, he wrote to John Thompson telling him that "the direct cause of death was an 'insult to the brain', caused by alcoholic poisoning." JMB/Delaware.

p101 *Laughlin and Brinnin toss coin*: see the note on the identification on p204 below.

Stravinsky cries: Craft 1959, pp77-78.

short-shrift from Todd, Feltenstein and Irene: Irene Reavey, signed statement sent to the solicitor Ungoed Thomas, November 19 1953, CF/Texas.

Reavey, Caitlin, Rose at the consulate: Reavey to the McAlpines, 21 1953, GR/Texas.

Becker: memoir, CF/Texas.

Fort Bliss: Shestack 1964.

p102 *Caitlin sends telegram, Moss, Sitwells etc*: Brinnin's journal, JMB/Delaware. Extended version of the Sitwells is in Brinnin 1981, p196.

Brinnin meets Caitlin: Brinnin interview, GTD/RG and his journal.

Caitlin a sick woman: Brinnin to Kimon Friar, January 16 1957, Friar-Brinnin Collection, University of Delaware.

Caitlin a bewildered woman: JMB/JHT, undated, JMB/Delaware.

devil's pawn: letter from Caitlin to Liz Reitell, March 1954, extracts in a Christie's auction catalogue, 1997.

Kolodney, Sitwells, McKenna, Porter, Kazin etc: Brinnin's journal, JMB/Delaware.

Edith on losing a child: Brinnin 1981, p196.

obituaries: Bob MacGregor to David Higham, November 12 1953, ND/Harvard, referring to the *New York Times* and *Herald Tribune*.

p103 *Feltenstein's obituaries*: Sidney Leibowitz, President of the Medical Board, Beth Israel, *New York Times*, September 4 1974; family obituary in the same paper, September 3.

Reitell's suffering: Reitell interview, GTD/RG.

no face-to-face interview, no rigorous examination etc: the only face-to-face interviews were done by Rob Gittins and Geraint Talfan Davies (see p164 above). Bill Read and Constantine FitzGibbon dealt with Reitell through correspondence. Ferris used the phone and letters. Tremlett appears not to have contacted her at all. By the time Tremlett teamed up with Nashold, Reitell was suffering from brain disease. She had died before Lycett started work. Although the interviews with Reitell done by Geraint Talfan Davies and Gittins are valuable, they did not explore in detail the events of November 4/5 e.g. they did not ask about the "get-together" at the hotel noted by the private detective, or about the delay

in getting Dylan to hospital.
Caitlin to Brinnin: December 19 1953, JMB/Delaware

6. The Post-Mortem

p105 *pial oedema*: The pia is one of the meninges, the three layers of thin tissue which are wrapped around the brain. My medical advisors have never heard pial oedema described as a significant finding, nor of it being associated with any specific disease process ("I would not take much notice of the 'pial edema', which is a vague description and one that I have never seen, other than as part of cerebral oedema." Professor Bernard Knight, email, November 16 2003). Pial oedema is certainly not a diagnosis that would be much used by pathologists today, and it is commonly observed at post-mortem examinations. Much more significant is the swelling or congestion of Dylan's brain tissue which is described as cerebral oedema, which is a terminal condition.

fatty liver: Dylan's liver was not only fatty, but its weight of 2,400 grams was very much in excess of normal (about 1500 grams). The mere presence of excessive fat in a liver is not on its own a serious problem and it rarely causes illness. A fatty liver is usually associated with the consumption of alcohol, though it can also be caused by diabetes, obesity and inadequate diet, particularly one deficient in protein. Dylan's fatty liver was probably a result of his drinking, poor diet and obesity. Both the fat and the weight of the liver indicate the possibility of liver damage and malfunction. We cannot be certain of the degree of any liver damage, which can only be assessed during life by liver function tests. In the 1950s, the inclusion of "fatty liver" as a cause of death was a euphemism for "chronic alcoholism" often used by American medical examiners to spare the feelings of grieving relatives. It is likely that today a pathologist would not include Dylan's fatty liver as a cause of death.

p106 *hypoproteinaemia*: puffy face in 1951: interview with Olive Suratgar, CE/NLW. Swollen in February 1952: Anatole Broyard 1997, p123; Sean Treacy also commented on Dylan's puffy face in 1953 and of it being "blown up." – see p47 above. The possibility of hypoproteinaemia is also consistent with descriptions of Dylan as being "bloated" i.e. not fat, but swollen or inflated e.g. Aeronwy Thomas interview, CE/NLW and in DNT 2004; Stravinsky, see above p34; Ruthven Todd, memoir, RT/NLS; CuRoi, above, p74; and Roy Poole, one of the *Milk Wood* actors: "at the time of his last trip... he seemed a little more bloated to me, a little puffier of face." (Poole to Gittins, May 14 1985) Ebie Williams also described

Dylan as being "out like a cask" – see above p118. The bloating is also apparent in the stills pictures of Dylan on television in 1953 – see p43 above. ACTH can produce puffiness but Dylan's course of injections from Feltenstein was too brief to have produced Cushingoid features such as a puffy face. His puffiness was also observed long before he received these injections e.g. by Suratgar in 1951.

p107 *Bernard Knight*: letter and email, December 17 2003 and January 8 2004 respectively.

Sheldon Cohen: see Cohen and Rizzo, 2000.

Bernard Knight looks at evidence: letter, December 17 2003

Dr Cyril Wecht: email, February 11 2004.

p108 *on subjective assessments*: Bernard Knight, email January 12 2004.

a bit woolly: Bernard Knight, email November 16 2003.

p109 *Heliker on drinking*: Ferris, p322, after interviewing Heliker.

Todd on Old Grandad: memoir, RT/NLS.

alcohol on breath: George Reavey notes, GR/Texas.

p110 *Notice of Death*: Office of the Chief Medical Examiner, New York.

James Laughlin at the mortuary: taken from his prose poem "Dylan", which is in Laughlin's Poems New and Selected, New Directions, 1997. Laughlin's prose account is in Epler and Javitch 2006, p297, where he describes the body as puffy and purple.

7. The Verdict

p111 *Gutierrez-Mahoney and William Murphy comments on Feltenstein*: Murphy's memorandum, CF/Texas, also chapter 9 and the appendix.

p112 *the other doctor's comments*: Gittins 1986, p163.

8. The Aftermath

p113 *money problems at the morgue etc*: Todd, memoir RT/NLS.

Welsh Society: Caitlin Thomas 1957, p74.

second-hand clothes: John B. Matthews, 1981 interview with Ann Lye and Rose Slivka.

death mask: Todd interview, CE/NLW and in DNT 2004, QDNT.

p114 *Reitell and Faulkner*: Reitell interview, GTD/RG. Reitell just refers to "William" in the interview but in conversation later with John Hechtel, a friend in Montana, she referred to William Faulkner – email from Hechtel, May 27 2007.

Brinnin not there: Brinnin's journal, JMB/Delaware. He refers to "brief classes" at the university.
Caitlin on the memorial service: Caitlin Thomas 1957, pp73-74.
Caitlin and Berryman: Mariani 1992, p274. Her note about seeing him again is in the Berryman archive at Minnesota.
Welshmen at Todd's door: memoir, RT/NLS.
Memorial Fund details: Dylan Thomas subject file, ND/Harvard. By April 1954, the Fund stood at $22,000 – see Breit 1954a, quoting the Fund's treasurer, Phillip Wittenberg.
easy street: Laughlin to T.S. Eliot, December 8 1953, ND/Harvard.
Lewis Hill on Dylan: Hill to Laughlin, December 15 1953, ND/Harvard.
p115 *Chumley's and the White Horse*: Todd to Stuart Thomas, February 24 1955, CF/Texas.
pocket money for Caitlin, pay Slivkas etc: Dylan Thomas subject file, ND/Harvard.
The undertaker's bill: this is now in DMT/NLW:

Embalming, dressing and casketing	$55
Removal from Bellevue hospital	$15
Hinge panel grey cloth casket with handles and name plate	$100
Zinc lined hermetically sealed outside shipping case with handles	$175
Gentleman's suit and entire clothing	$26.75
Hearse and assistants at chapel 11/13/53	$40
Hearse and assistants at pier 11/16	$45
Use of chapel	$25
Steamship ticket to Southampton	$299
Total	$780.75

helping the children etc: James Laughlin to David Higham, December 3 1953, ND/Harvard.
Laugharne fund: Daniel Jones to the vicar of Laugharne, November 17 1953, Jeff Towns Collection, Dylan Thomas Secondary Manuscripts, NLW.
p116 *Dan Jones telegram*: Gutierrez-Mahoney to Jones, January 10 1953.
Ralph the Books: interview, CE/NLW and in DNT 2004.
p117 *Caitlin's newspaper interview, events on the quayside at Southampton etc*: in the *Evening Post*, November 23 1953.
p118 *Ebie Williams and Leon Atkin*: interviews, CE/NLW.
description of funeral: taken from Margaret Taylor, letter to the McAlpines, December 9 1953; Maureen Colgrove to the McAlpines,

November 26 1953, both at DMT/Texas; Leon Atkin, Leslie Rees, Nellie Jenkins, interviews, CE/NLW.

p120 *feuds put aside*: Paul Potts 1961, p184.

magic again: JMB/JHT, November 17 1953.

new knowledge, inheritance etc: JMB/JHT, November 17, 1953.

resignation, holiday in the Bahamas, lunch with Sitwells, write book etc: Brinnin 1981, pp198-200. The Bahamas is identified on p73.

p121 *congenitally broke*: JMB/JHT, February 27 1954.

phenobarb, analyst etc: JMB/JHT, May 24 and June 17 1954.

manuscript to Sitwells: Brinnin 1981, pp215 and 220. On p227, Brinnin writes that Edith Sitwell had seen the book "in all stages of composition."

benzedrine, cigarettes, streaks of guilt etc: JMB/JHT, February 11 and March 17 1955.

last weeks of Dylan's life: JMB/JHT June 5 and 27 1955.

misery, stupor, drinking, sleeping, bouts of weeping, Miltown etc: JMB/JHT, October 16 and December 4 1955. Also see March 8 1957 to Thompson with a reference to taking Miltown.

p122 *old faith, travel as a solution*: JMB/JHT, February 11 1955.

Brinnin in hospital, costs, self-portrait etc: JMB/JHT, March 12, 17 and 27 1956. Also letter from Frances Brinnin to Thompson, March 16 1956.

new man, new appreciation etc: JMB/JHT, April 21 1956. "I am in many ways 'a new man,' functioning, somatically, with a sort of Swiss precision... and, mentally, with a strange refreshment that has brought a sense of delight in small things, a quiet confidence about work and how to do it, a new appreciation and care for people, a large, easy-mannered sense of myself that allows me to look out and, in the process, forget myself."

London, Edinburgh, Sitwells etc: JMB/JHT, August 28, September 8 and 12 1956.

p123 *a book about Brinnin*: LaFlamme 1956.

Plath, Lameyer, Hughes, Prouty etc: Butscher 1976 p188, Alexander 1991, p114, 189-90.

hearse into band-wagon: John Davenport, 1956.

News Chronicle: November 25 1953.

Mr Oriel: letter from him to Stuart Thomas, 1973, DMT/NLW

p124 *Dylan's bones*: Professor K.W. Dumars MD of the University of California, Irvine, in a letter to Stuart Thomas, July 24, 1978, DMT/NLW

upmarket pilgrimages: *Daily Express* May 26 1978 and *Western Mail* November 4 1978.

Harry Locke's house: see DNT 2004, chapter 2, for history of writing of *Under Milk Wood*.

Texan in the White Horse: Kramer 2005.

p126 *memorial stone*: Cour interview, CE/NLW.

marriage to Hannum etc: uncle's family memoir.

details of Reitell's career in Montana: her CV (see page 184) and an uncle's memoir, as given to Rob Gittins. In Oregon, she worked with the Columbia River Inter-Tribal Fish Commission "to protect salmon resources and the treaty fishing rights of the Nez Perce Tribe of Idaho, the Umatilla and Warm Springs Tribes of Oregon, and the Yakima Nation in the State of Washington."

p127 *Reitell and the video*: Dorothy Bradley, email February 21 2007. For details of the television programme, see p164 above.

p128 *trust fund*: letter and email from Cecil Garland and Dorothy Bradley respectively, February 2007.

mother had brain disease: Marianne Matthews, Reitell's step-daughter, email May 10 2007.

Reitell being read Dylan's poems: see Duncan 2001, pp90-91.

Brinnin in Florida in retirement etc: his obituary, *New York Times*, June 30 1998 and Cifelli 1997, p416.

p129 *Erich Fried etc*: see Lawrie 1995.

lusty play, Controller Wales etc: BBC archives, Caversham.

9. The Cover-Up

p131 *no lawyers after me*: Reitell to Brinnin, JMB/Delaware, quoted in N and T p233.

independent advice: letter to Berryman from a doctor friend, December 3 1953, Minnesota.

Reavey to Davenport: November 1953, John Davenport papers, NLW.

silent fury: Maureen Colgrove to the McAlpines, November 26 1953, DMT/Texas. Those present were Reggie Smith, Maureen Colgrove, John Davenport and someone called Anne.

Reavey to Higham: November 18 1953, GR/Texas.

p132 *Reavey to McAlpines*: November 18, 21 1953, CF/Texas, QDNT.

Irene Reavey to Ungoed Thomas: November 19 1953, CF/Texas.

weekend with Read on letters: Brinnin's journal, JMB/Delaware.

Wynford Vaughan Thomas etc: Brinnin's journal, JMB/Delaware. Besides Vaughan Thomas and the group of Englishmen, those present were Ruthven and Jody Todd, Dave and Rose Slivka and Len and Ann Lye. See also Todd to Louis MacNeice, November 23 1953.

p133 *Brinnin to MacNeice*: referred to in MacNeice's reply of November

30 1953, JMB/Delaware. MacNeice mentions it has been a fortnight since he received Brinnin's letter.

Brinnin to Eliot: Brinnin 1981, p268.

Brinnin to Davenport: November 15 1953, Davenport papers, NLW.

Todd to MacNeice: November 23 1953, CF/Texas. "Yesterday afternoon she came over to see me, to vet this account..." Todd wrote the letter in consultation with Reitell and Rose Slivka.

Todd and Reitell critical of Feltenstein: David Wagoner, letter March 4 2007, describing a meeting with Todd and Reitell a few weeks after Dylan's death.

Daniel Jones on Todd letter: letter to Rob Gittins, December 14 1985.

MacNeice to Stuart Thomas: November 30 1953, DMT/NLW.

p134 *Gutierrez-Mahoney to Dan Jones*: January 10 1954, CF/Texas.

Gutierrez-Mahoney talks to Pappas: N and T, p166, after interviewing Pappas.

p135 *doctors' cover-up*: Caitlin to Brinnin, February 8 1954, JMB/Delaware.

knew to be untrue: see notes on p193.

best face forward: JMB/JHT, March 7 1955.

Todd on Brinnin's cover-up: memoir, RT/NLS.

p136 *Reitell on Brinnin's book*: to Brinnin, Nov 2 1955, JMB/Delaware.

died of conscientiousness: Anon. Review, *Times Literary Supplement*, May 11 1956.

Reavey to FitzGibbon: September 26 1963, CF/Texas.

Reitell to FitzGibbon: March 6 1964, CF/Texas.

ancient nightmare: Reitell to Bill Read, January 20 1965, DMT/Texas.

p137 *Murphy's correspondence with FitzGibbon*: CF/Texas. Murphy's memorandum was written after his visit to St Vincent's on December 3 1964. At first sight, it is puzzling that it contains two references to FitzGibbon's biography, which was not published until late 1965. But Murphy had been sent a draft of the biography in the summer of 1964.

p138 *Murphy and St Vincent's, on Feltenstein, problem to interpret the information*: Murphy's memorandum, CF/Texas.

still revising in January: letter to his publisher, January 8 1965, CF/Texas.

p139 *criticism of Feltenstein removed*: in a typescript draft of the book, FitzGibbon wrote "Again the doctor was summoned. Instead of immediately transferring Dylan to hospital, yet another injection was given..." The phrase "Instead of immediately transferring Dylan to hospital" was removed in the published version, as was an earlier comment that Dylan should have been hospitalised by Feltenstein when he first attended him on November 4 (FitzGibbon's drafts, DMT/Texas).

FitzGibbon and the post-mortem report: there is a reference to FitzGibbon having the post-mortem report in his correspondence with a doctor friend, August 4 1964, CF/Texas. FitzGibbon also refers to the report in his article in the *Spectator* in November 1964, almost a year before his book was published. He later placed the report in his archive in the University of Texas.

FitzGibbon on Reitell and Under Milk Wood: FitzGibbon, pp344-45. He was more pointed in earlier drafts of the account – see CF/Texas.

no libel difficulties: report on FitzGibbon's draft by Oswald Hickson, Collier & Co., 8 and 9 December 1964, CF/Texas.

Murphy to FitzGibbon: January 4 and February 5 1965, DMT/NLW.

p140 *Murphy to a friend*: letter to Colin Edwards, September 29 1965, CE/NLW.

10. Biographer's Droop

p142 *eating Dylan*: FitzGibbon, *Spectator*, November 27 1964.

p144 *not catching on, Ferris*: letter to the *Guardian*, December 1 2004.

Ferris knows about inhaler: see Ferris, p325.

Ackerman: see his *Welsh Dylan*, 1998, pp135-36.

p145 *necrography*: a term coined by FitzGibbon in his 1964 *Spectator* article. A necrography deals with a person's death, and the events that happened before and after.

N and T not given access: phone conversation with Tremlett, December 2003.

p146 *sky high*: N and T, p159.

no sugar found: see the appendix for the hospital data.

laboratory findings: Murphy to FitzGibbon, December 16 1964, CF/Texas.

diabetes sanitised: N and T, p179.

three separate points: N and T, pp152, 162 and 168.

p147 *hospital information published*: see chapter 2 of DNT 2004 and Thomas 2005.

doctors were clear: Lycett, p370.

immediate cause of death: pneumonia is described as the primary cause which brought about the oedema, the immediate cause. Death certificate, DMT/NLW.

admission to hospital: Lycett, p370. Lycett seems to be at sixes and sevens on this matter– on the one hand, he writes that Dylan fell into a coma about midnight and reached hospital "within minutes". On the other, he also writes, in the same paragraph, that Dylan arrived at the hospital at 1.58am, two hours later.

p148 *nothing in Reitell's diary*: Lycett, who now has the diary, kindly provided this information. He also described the diary as petering-out around October 26 and ending on November 3 (emails, November 2003 and 2006).

Lycett persuaded by Gutierrez-Mahoney: Lycett, p374.

brain disease: Lycett, pp368, 374.

Books and Articles

J. Ackerman (1998) *Welsh Dylan*, Seren

P. Alexander (1991) *Rough Magic: A Biography of Sylvia Plath*, Viking

Anon. (1940) "John Malcolm Brinnin", *The Gargoyle*, November 1940, Univ. of Michigan

Anon. (1953) "Welsh Poet Thomas to Give Reading", *The Bennington Biweekly*, April 24

Anon. (1953) "Welsh Lyric Poet, Dylan Thomas, to Read", *Amherst Student*, May 18

J. Augustine (1950) "Modern Poets: Orderly Auden Contrasts with Moody Thomas", *The College News*, Bryn Mawr, March 15

H. Breit (1954) "Letter from New York", *London Magazine*, February

(1954a) "Dylan Report", *New York Times Book Review*, April 18

(1957) *The Writer Observed*, Redman

J. Berryman (1988) *We Dream of Honour: Letters to his Mother*, Norton

S.N. Bogorad (1956) "I Remember Dylan Thomas", *Centaur*, Univ. of Vermont, Spring

J. M. Brinnin (1955, 1965) *Dylan Thomas in America*, Avon and Dent respectively

(1960) *A Casebook on Dylan Thomas*, Crowell

(1981) *Sextet*, Delacorte Press

(1982) *Beau Voyage: Life Aboard the Last Great Ships*, Thames and Hudson

(1986) *The Sway of the Grand Saloon: A Social History of the North Atlantic*, Arlington

(n.d.) *A Passing of Papers*, an unpublished memoir, Delaware

A. Broyard (1997) *Kafka was the Rage: A Greenwich Village Memoir*, Vintage

E. Butscher (1976) *Sylvia Plath: Method and Madness*, Seabury

(1979) *Sylvia Plath: The Woman and the Work*, Owen

E. M. Cifelli (1997) *John Ciardi: A Biography*, Univ. of Arkansas

E. Coleman (1958) "Samuel Barber and Vanessa", *Theatre Arts*, January

R. Craft (1959) *Conversations with Stravinsky*, Faber

(1972) *A Chronicle of a Friendship 1948-71*, Gollancz

A. Curnow (1982) "Images of Dylan", *NZ Listener*, December 18

D. Daiches (1954) untitled, in Tedlock 1960.

T. Dardis (1955) *Firebrand: The Life of Horace Liveright*, Random House

J. Davenport (1956) A review of *Dylan Thomas in America, Twentieth Century*, June

G.T. Davies (2008) *At Arm's Length*, Seren

J.A. Davies (1998) *A Reference Companion to Dylan Thomas*, Greenwood

D. Davin (1985) *Closing Times*, OUP

E. Divine (1953) "Peerless Reading", *The Duke Chronicle*, May 15

D.J. Duncan (2001) *My Story as Told by Water,* Sierra Club Books

C. Edwards (1968) *Dylan Remembered, an unfinished biography*, National Library of Wales

B. Epler & D. Javitch eds.(2006) *James Laughlin: the Way it Wasn't*, New Directions

P. Ferris (1977, 1999 and 2006) *Dylan Thomas*, Dent and Y Lolfa
   (1995) *Caitlin: The Life of Caitlin Thomas*, Pimlico
   (2000) *Dylan Thomas: The Collected Letters*, Dent

C. FitzGibbon (1964) "The Posthumous Life of Dylan Thomas", the *Spectator*, November 27
   (1965) *The Life of Dylan Thomas*, Little, Brown

H. Foote (2004) *Genesis of an American Playwright*, Baylor

J. Fuller (1957) "Trade Winds", *Saturday Review*, November 16

J. Fryer (1993) *The Nine Lives of Dylan Thomas*, Kyle Cathie

R. Garlick (1995) "Dylan Thomas in Tenby", *Planet*, February/March.

D. van Ghent (1956) "A Poet's Corpse: or Me and Dylan", *Centaur*, Univ. of Vermont, Spring

O. Ghiselin (1967) "Dylan", *Utah Alumnus*, Fall

R. Gittins (1986) *The Last Days of Dylan Thomas*, Macdonald

J. Gordon (2003) "Being Sylvia Being Ted Being Dylan: Plath's 'The Snowman on the Moor'", *Journal of Modern Literature,* Fall

L. Griffiths (2004) "Dylan Thomas: Poet of his People", *Trans. Hon. Soc. Cymrodorion*, 11

R. Eberhart (1954) untitled, in Tedlock 1960

D. Hall 1992) *Their Ancient Glittering Eyes: Remembering Poets*, Ticknor and Fields

L. Hammer (2001) "Plath's Lives", *Representations*, Summer

E. Hardwick (1960) "America and Dylan Thomas" in J.M. Brinnin 1960

J. Haffenden (1983) *A Life of John Berryman*, Routledge

B.B. Heyman (1992) *Samuel Barber: The Composer and his Music*, OUP

R. Horrocks (2002) *Len Lye*, Auckland Univ. Press

D. Jones (1977) *My Friend Dylan Thomas*, Dent

G. Kahn & A. Hirschfeld (2003) *The Speakeasies of 1932*, Glenn Young Books.

A. Kazin (1957) "The Posthumous Life of Dylan Thomas", *The Atlantic*, October

C.A. Kirk (2004) *Sylvia Plath: A Biography*, Greenwood

K. Kramer (2005) "Eddie Brennan on Waterfront, White Horse, Dylan Thomas", *The Villager*, Dec-Jan.

S. Krim (1956) "Hipster Digs Dylan Thomas in Semi-Hip Downtown Bar", *Village Voice*, November 7

G. LaFlamme (1956) "With More Triumphant Faith" in *Centaur*, Univ. of Vermont, Spring

S. W. Lawrie (1995) "Crossing Borders through the Ether: Erich Fried and *Under Milk Wood*", *Austrian Exodus* ed. E. Timms and R. Robertson, EUP.

J. Lindsay (1968) *Meeting with Poets*, Muller

A. Livi (1949) "Sugli Scogli Di Rio", *Inventario*, II, 3, Autumno

E. Lutyens (1972) *A Goldfish Bowl*, Cassell

A. Lycett (2003) *Dylan Thomas: A New Life*, Weidenfeld and Nicolson

G. McGowan (1953) "Poet Renders Varied Selections", *Williams Record*, May 2.

R. McKenna (1982) *Portrait of Dylan*, Dent

P. Mariani (1992) *Dream Song: the Life of John Berryman*, Paragon House

A. Miller (1987) *Timebends: a Life*, Methuen

H. Miller (1989) *Auden: An American Friendship*, Paragon

E. Milton (1993) "Dylan Thomas at Mount Holyoke", *Antioch Review*, Spring

H. Moss (1969) "A Thin, Curly Little Person", *Writing Against Time*, Morrow

J. Nashold & G. Tremlett (1997) *The Death of Dylan Thomas*, Mainstream Publishing

J. Oppenheimer (1989) *Private Demons: The Life of Shirley Jackson*, Ballantine

P. Osborn (1953) "Unique Reading of Poetry", *Syracuse Daily Orange*, April 29

P. Potts (1961) *Dante Called You Beatrice*, Readers Union/Eyre & Spottiswode

G. Plimpton (1998) *Truman Capote*, Picador

M. Powell (1992) *Million-Dollar Movie*, Heinemann

C. Reitell (1931) *Let's Go Fishing*, McGraw-Hill
(1937) *How to be a Good Foreman*, Ronald Press Co
(1948) *Cost Accounting*, International Textbooks, 3rd edition (with G.L. Harris)

J. Reitell (1936) "The Rise of the Professoriat", *The Saturday Evening*

Post, April 25

(1936) "Meet the Convention Wife", *The Saturday Evening Post*, December 26

(1937) "There's No Accounting for Wives", *The Saturday Evening Post*, September 25

(1938) "104 Degrees", *The Saturday Evening Post*, February 26

(1941) "Guest Room Door", *The Saturday Evening Post*, April 5 1941

(1941) "Song for Commencement", *The New Yorker*, June 14

J. Reitell & A. Lowe (1927) *Pennsylvania*, Badger

E. Reitell/Rytell (1941) *Hanya Holm and Dance Company*, Mansfield Theater

(1965) "Scientific Writing for the General Public", Montana Academy of Sciences

(1966) "The Forest Products Industry in Montana" Bulletin 31, Montana Forest and Conservation

(1966) "Montana's Recreation Challenge", *Montana Business Quarterly*, Fall

S. Roussillat (1954) untitled, in Tedlock, 1960.

R. Sanders (1987) *The Downtown Jews*, Dover

M. B. Shavelson (2003) "Against the Dying of the Light", *Bostonia*, Fall

M. Shestack (1964) "The Day Dylan Died", *The Village Voice*, September 24

A. Sinclair (1975) *Dylan Thomas: Poet of his People*, Joseph
(1999) *Dylan the Bard*, Constable

E. Sitwell (1970) *Selected Letters*, ed J. Lehmann and D. Parker, Macmillan.

H. Smith (1954) "Whose is this Guilt?", *Saturday Review*, March 13

E.W. Tedlock (1960) *Dylan Thomas: the Legend and the Poet*, Heinemann

C. Thomas (1957) *Leftover Life to Kill*, Putnam
(1986) *Caitlin: Life with Dylan Thomas*, Secker and Warburg (with G. Tremlett)
(1999) *Double Drink Story: My Life with Dylan Thomas*, Virago

D.N. Thomas (2000) *Dylan Thomas: A Farm, Two Mansions and a Bungalow*, Seren
(2001) "Under Milk Wood's Birth-in-Exile", *New Welsh Review*, Spring
(2002a) *The Dylan Thomas Trail*, Y Lolfa
(2002b) "Dylan's New Quay: More Bombay Potato than

Boiled Cabbage", *New Welsh Review*, Summer

(2003) *Dylan Remembered 1914-1935*, vol one, Seren

(2004) *Dylan Remembered 1935-1953*, vol two, Seren

(2005) "Escaping the Vacuum – the death of Dylan Thomas", *Planet*, February/March

R. Todd (n.d.) Dylan Thomas, an unpublished memoir, National Library of Scotland

G. Tremlett (1993) *Dylan Thomas: In the Mercy of his Means*, Constable

M. Wainwright (2007) "The Great Floods of 1947", the *Guardian*, July 25

A.M. Wald(2002) *Exiles from a Future Time: the Forging of the Mid-Twentieth-Century Literary Left*, Univ. of North Carolina Press

G. Watkins (1983) *Portrait of a Friend*, Gomer

V. Watkins (1956) "Dylan Thomas in America: A Comment", *Encounter*, June

N. Wenborn (2000) *Stravinsky*, Omnibus Press

R.B. West (1972) "Dylan Thomas in Iowa 1951", *The San Francisco Fault*, October (the date is an error; Dylan was in Iowa in 1950)

R. Wilbur (1977) An interview, *The Paris Review*, 72

Health and medical

C.M. Bell and D.A. Redelmeier (2001) "Mortality among Patients Admitted to Hospitals on Weekends as Compared with Weekdays", *New England Journal of Medicine*, August

M. Bell et al (2004) "A Retrospective Assessment of Mortality from the London Smog Episode of 1952: The Role of Influenza and Pollution", *Environmental Health Perspectives*, January

S. Cohen and P.L. Rizzo (2000) "Asthma Among the Famous: Dylan Thomas", *Allergy and Asthma Proceedings*, May-June

L. Greenburg et al. (1962) "Report of an air pollution incident in New York City November 1953", *Public Health Rep.* January

C.G. Gutierrez-Mahoney and E. Carini (1948) *Neurological and Neurosurgical Nursing*, Mosby

M. Helpern with B. Knight (1979) *Autopsy: Memoirs of Milton Helpern*, Harrap

M. Houts (1968) *Where Death Delights: The Story of Dr Milton Helpern and Forensic Medicine*, Gollancz

A. Hunt et al (2003) "Toxicologic and Epidemiologic Clues from the

Characterisation of the 1952 London Smog Fine Particulate Matter in Archival Lung Tissues", *Environmental Health Perspectives*, July

K. Johnson (2002) "You should have seen the air in 1953", *New York Times*, September 29

P.A. & B.J. Kalisch (1986) *The Advance of American Nursing*, Little, Brown

W.P.D. Logan (1949) "Fog and Mortality", *The Lancet*, 256:78

B. McCauley (2005) *Who Shall Take Care of our Sick? Roman Catholic Sisters and the Development of Catholic Hospitals in New York City*, John Hopkins

B.W. Murphy (1968) "Creation and Destruction: Notes on Dylan Thomas", *British Journal of Medical Psychology*, 41, 149

M. Noyes (1953) *Modern Clinical Psychiatry*, Saunders, 4th edition

S. Opdycke (1999) *No One Was Turned Away: The Role of Public Hospitals in New York City Since 1900*, OUP

H.H. Salter (1864) *On Asthma: Its Pathology and Treatment*, Blanchard and Lea

D.A. Seehusen et. Al. (2003) "Cerebrospinal Fluid Analysis", the *Journal of the American Academy of Family Physicians*, September 15

G.R. Stuart (1938) *A History of St Vincent's Hospital in New York City 1849-1938*, Stuart

M. Walsh (1965) *With a great heart: the story of St Vincent's Hospital and Medical Center of New York, 1849-1964*

Acknowledgements

My greatest debt is to Dr Simon Barton. He co-authored the chapter in *Dylan Remembered* vol 2, that dealt with Dylan's death. He has continued to be a generous source of advice and guidance.

I am grateful to Professor Bernard Knight for his unstinting help and encouragement, and to Professor Sandra Opdycke for letting me draw on her knowledge of New York hospitals, and her research notes. And she was always mavenly when I needed it. Likewise, I am indebted to Professor Bernadette McCauley, who drew on her research into St Vincent's hospital, and made available her experience and contacts, including Denis in Otto's bar on Fifth Avenue. Thanks to Sister Rita King, archivist for the Sisters of Charity, New York, who provided information about St Joseph's East and contacted former nurses; and to Priscilla Sassi, who was a student nurse at St Vincent's, 1951 and 1954. Brenda Maurer kept us all in touch, and Mary Edwards helped in many different ways and occasions with an essential supply of information.

Dr Robert Pitcher and Dr John F. Pickup, consultant histopathologist and principal pharmacist respectively at the Royal Cornwall Hospital, helped with the original chapter in *Dylan Remembered*, vol 2. Dr Cyril Wecht, coroner and chief forensic pathologist to Allegheny County, Pittsburgh, advised on a number of points relating to the post-mortem and drug therapies. Thanks, too, to Dr Sheldon Cohen, Dr Stephen Rowlands and to a sterling trio of chemists – Skyrme May in New Quay, Vic Rishko in Aberaeron and Laugharne's Susan Siggery.

Many thanks to Rob Gittins. He provided transcripts of interviews with Liz Reitell and John Brinnin, letters from Reitell, her curriculum vitae and an uncle's family memoir, as well as letters from Daniel Jones and Roy Poole. This in turn led to help from Reitell's family, Lois Gridley and Megan Gridley Conley. Several of Reitell's Montana friends helped: Dorothy Bradley, Cecil Garland, John Hechtel and Harriet Marble. Thanks also to Marianne Matthews, daughter of Reitell's fourth husband, Eldon Smith. Karole Lee, of the Montana Wilderness Association, helped us make contact.

John B. Matthews, chair of the Len Lye Foundation, provided a transcript of his 1981 interview with Ann Lye and Rose Slivka. Paul Ferris shared material from his files, Andrew Lycett, George Tremlett and David Wagoner kindly answered queries and Aeronwy Thomas persevered. Thanks also to Kasey Clark, Tony Doyle, Mary Edwards and Victoria Gold who carried out research for me in America.

Many others also helped and encouraged, including Jane Augustine, John Barnie, Charles Burroughs, Geraint Talfan Davies, Ron McFarland, Steven W. Lawrie, Joan Miller, Jack Rothman, Barbara Todd, Christopher Todd and Jeff Towns. David Griffith Rees, Senior Advisor to the President, and Kathy Posey, Registrar, at Bennington College, Vermont, were extremely helpful in facilitating research there.

Anne de Furia of Berkeley Heights Public Library and Laurel Hessing, a Free Acres historian, provided invaluable help in unearthing information about Milton Feltenstein and his residence at Free Acres. Anne also helped track down information on Jane Reitell.

Several present and former residents of Free Acres helped to illuminate Dr Feltenstein's interests, personality and character, including Terry Connor, Yvonne Kleinberg, Daryl Maslow Hafter, Joseph Romano, Linus Yamane and Tetsuo Yamane. Thanks, too, to JoAnn Schawb of the Union County Surrogate Office, Elizabeth, New Jersey.

I am particularly grateful to Dick Tague, a volunteer searcher at the USGenWeb Census Project, who provided the census information on Feltenstein's parents, and also helped me access other data in America, including that on John Brinnin.

Every researcher needs a good home library and mine has been the National Library of Wales in Aberystwyth. Many thanks to Simon Evans, Iestyn Hughes, Maredudd ap Huw, Richard E. Huws, Ceridwen Lloyd-Morgan, Rhiannon Michaelson-Yeates, Dafydd Pritchard and Scott Waby. As usual, staff in the north and south reading rooms provided excellent advice and help.

My two virtual homes-from-home were the Harry Ransom Humanities Research Center at the University of Texas at Austin – thanks to Richard Workman, Nicholas Bacuez, Hollie Jenkins, Lisa Richter and Kristin Walker, Docx, University of Texas

Libraries. And the Special Collections Library at the University of
Delaware – with special thanks to Iris Snyder, Shaun Mullen and
Rebecca Johnson Melvin. Many other libraries and archives also
provided valuable assistance:
Robin Smith, National Library of Scotland
Lee Sands, Records and Archives, BMA House, London
John Winrow, National Museums Liverpool
Terry Wells, Carmarthen Archive office
Rachel Hassall, University of Bristol Theatre Collection
Anne de Furia, Berkeley Heights Public Library
Rebecca Cape, Special Collections, Lilly Library, University of
Indiana
Barbara Bezant, Special Collections, the University of Minnesota
Jennie Rathbun, Houghton Library, Harvard
Heidi Fetzer, Special Collections, University of Georgetown
Meg Rich, Special Collections, Princeton University Library
James Thull and Teresa Hamann, Montana State University Library
Terry Caddy and Jill Kinyon, College of Forestry and
Conservation, Montana
Linder Schlang, Mansfield Library, University of Montana
Beth Alvarez, University of Maryland Libraries
Steven Siegel, Library and Archive, the Poetry Center, New York.
Stephen Novak and Bob Vietrogoski, Columbia University
Medical Center
Richard Iannacone and Sidney van Nort, The City College of
New York
Fernanda Perrone, Special Collections, Rutgers University Libraries
Steele Memorial Library, Elmira, NY
June Houghtaling, Towanda Public Library
Bridget Arthur Clancy, Presbyterian Historical Society,
Philadelphia
Ashley Koebel, Burton Historical Collection, Detroit Public Library
Shannon Wait, Bentley Historical Library, University of Michigan
Steve Sturgeon, Special Collections, Utah State University
Emma Kruger, Special Collections, University of Utah
Barbara Lamonda and Prudence J. Doherty, University of Vermont
Tony Doyle, Hunter College Library
Mary O'Brien, Syracuse University Archives
Lori Dubois, Williams College Libraries

Margaret Brill and Tom Harkins, Duke University Library and Archives
Oceana Wilson and Melissa Tacke, Crossett Library, Bennington College
Diana Peterson, Haverford College Library
Marion Walker, Amherst College Library
Jacques Roethler, Special Collections, University of Iowa Libraries, Iowa City
Linda Stahnke, University of Illinois Library
Wook-Jin Cheun, Reference Department, Indiana University Library
Corrine Robinson Slouber, Doe/Moffitt Libraries, University of California, Berkeley
Marianne Hansen, Special Collections, Bryn Mawr

I am grateful to Muriel Keyes of the *Antioch Review* for providing a copy of Edith Milton's article. Permissions granted came from Peggy Fox of New Directions, Mrs Kate Donahue, Aeronwy Thomas and the Office of the Chief Medical Examiner, New York. I acknowledge the copyright of the estate of Paul Potts in the extract taken from his book, *Dante Called You Beatrice*.

Many thanks to Dylan Iorwerth and Dyfan Williams at *Golwg*, and Ann and the late John Jones of Llun a Gair bookshop, Aberaeron, for help with production. Peter Jones and Hywel Raw-Rees provided helpful information. Paul Boland and his staff at Llanerchaeron let me roam and wander at will. Very special thanks to Angela, Caroline, Dai, Joy, Mair and Mari, who also kept Pashka in chocolate biscuits. Nick and the two Janets kept me in tea, and Jim and Gwen Bowles at Teifi Computers kept me afloat.

Finishing touches were made in Le Vrétot, Normandy – thanks to Sue and Ian Williams at La Baillyerie who kept us all in veg. Mick Felton and his colleagues at Seren kept calm and, up in Ilkley, Paul Henderson kept reading. Ben, Cai and Jac kept the cat happy, Keri Nicholas and Margaret Barton kept faith in the Pontarddulais Paraffin Gang, and Llinos kept cutting.

Everything I write – everything I do – is all the better for Stevie Krayer. She did the index, too. Finally, to Siân and Danny, simply the best.

Picture Acknowledgements

Dylan as a young man, Dylan in his coffin: Douglas Glass, with thanks to Chris Glass

Dylan in *The Outing* and Dylan in the White Horse: Jeff Towns/Dylan's Bookstore Collection

Dylan in Vermont: Special Collections, University of Vermont

Dylan's earnings, final accounts: University of Delaware

Dylan's earnings, June 1 accounts: Harry Ransom Center, University of Texas

Milton Feltenstein: Graeme Blaikie, Mainstream Publishing. We were unable to trace the photographer but acknowledge his/her copyright

Milton Feltenstein, self-portrait in wood: Joe Romano

Liz Reitell, 1937: Bennington College, Vermont

The young Liz Reitell: Paul Ferris

The older Liz Reitell: Andrew Lycett

Liz Reitell, 1983: Geraint Talfan Davies

Dylan's funeral: the *Evening Post*

Ron Cour: Glenys Cour

John Brinnin on tour, 1947: Henri Cartier-Bresson, with thanks to his estate and Magnum

John Brinnin in Italy: not known

Majoda: David Evans, with thanks to Eunice Thomas and Peter Chetcuti

William and Vera Killick: Rachel Willans

Index